HANDBOOK OF
ARCHITECTURAL
AND CIVIL DRAFTING

HANDBOOK OF ARCHITECTURAL AND CIVIL DRAFTING

JOHN A. NELSON

 VAN NOSTRAND REINHOLD COMPANY

NEW YORK   CINCINNATI   TORONTO   LONDON   MELBOURNE

To my daughter, Jennifer

Copyright © 1983 by Van Nostrand Reinhold Company Inc.
Library of Congress Catalog Card Number 82-50875
ISBN 0-442-26865-3 (cloth)
ISBN 0-442-26864-5 (paper)

Printed in the United States of America

Published by Van Nostrand Reinhold Company Inc.
135 West 50th Street
New York, New York 10020

Van Nostrand Reinhold
480 Latrobe Street
Melbourne, Victoria 3000, Australia

Van Nostrand Reinhold Company Limited
Molly Millars Lane
Wokingham, Berkshire, RG11 2PY England

16 15 14 13 12 11 10 9 8 7 6 5 4 3 2 1

Library of Congress Cataloging in Publication Data

Nelson, John A., 1935-
   Handbook of architectural and civil drafting.

   Includes index.
   1. Architectural drawing. 2. Mechanical drawing. 3. Structural
drawing. 4. Topographical drawing.
I. Title.
NA2700.N44   1983   720′.28′4   82-50875
ISBN 0-442-26865-3
ISBN 0-442-26864-5 (pbk.)

ACKNOWLEDGMENTS

The author wishes to thank the following for reviewing the manuscript and providing critical input:

Clarence T. O'Brien, Land Surveyor
New York State Department of Environmental Conservation

Robert Franciose, Chairman
ANSI Drafting Standards (Y14) Committee

R. Michael Holcombe, Chairman
Drafting & Design Department
Asheville-Buncombe Technical Institute
Asheville, North Carolina

Richard B. Landry
Architectural Designer/Drafter

Hubert T. Stratton, A.I.A.
Winchester, VA

David A. Madsen, Chairman
Drafting Technology Department
Clackamas Community College
Oregon City, OR

Special thanks to Dr. Donald H. Delay of Antioch/New England Graduate School

Delmar Staff

Industrial Education Editor — Mark W. Huth
Associate Editor — Kathleen E. Beiswenger
Technical Editor — Harry A. Sturges

Illustrations

Alvin Company
Berol USA
Home Planners, Inc.
Keuffel & Esser Company
Teledyne Post
U.S. Geological Survey
U.S. Department of the Interior
Vemco Corporation
Wild-Heerbrugg

Classroom Testing

The instructional material in this text was classroom tested in the vocational drafting department at Conval Vocational High School — Peterborough, New Hampshire 03458.

PREFACE

Drafting is a communication skill that enables a designer, engineer, or architect to convey his or her ideas through the draftsperson to the skilled craftspersons who will ultimately do the building. From major calculations, general specifications and preliminary sketches of a project, the draftsperson must prepare an exact, detailed drawing. The job may include making computations from information in engineering handbooks and tables and, in some cases, actually describing the materials and processes to be used. Every facet of a project must be detailed with precision and clarity through the graphic language which is the essence of drafting.

Draftspersons are vital to virtually every phase of life in the United States. They make the drawings from which our homes, factories, and skyscrapers are built. Our roads and bridges, our refrigerators and washing machines start with their work. They make the drawings for our new automobiles—over 27,000 drawings for each new model!

The demand for draftspersons has been growing steadily. According to the U.S. Department of Labor, 250,000 draftspersons were employed in American industry on January 1, 1970. During 1975, the figure had risen to 290,000, and it is estimated that 385,000 will be needed in the 1980s. The term "draftsperson" includes women; nearly 12 percent of all draftspersons in the United States are women.

Those who intend to make drafting their career should include as much algebra, geometry, trigonometry and science as possible in their high school programs. The standards which must be met are high, but the rewards are great.

There are various fields of drafting: mechanical, electro-mechanical, architectural, electronic, civil and technical illustration are some of the major ones. The draftsperson usually specializes in one field in order to become truly competent. A skilled draftsperson in any field, however, must know and fully understand how the craftsperson will make whatever is drawn. In this way, and only in this way, can the draftsperson create a drawing that is both functional and feasible.

What are the chances for advancement in the field? For a good draftsperson, the opportunities are excellent. The draftsperson can move up the ladder from a junior to a senior position, to group leader, or to drafting supervisor. Related jobs in technical sales, purchasing, planning, marketing, and inspection are other possibilities for combining interests and skills. It is not unusual for a draftsperson to find success in this challenging and stimulating field which continues to expand, influencing so many aspects of our lives.

INTRODUCTION

This drafting handbook has been written to provide a nontechnical approach to the world of drafting. A special effort has been made to present all principles in illustrations and in concise descriptions which use words and phrases of the trade in a manner that will be understandable to all interested readers. Although technical principles are presented in varying degrees of complexity, the primary emphasis is placed on points of major importance.

This book has a three-fold purpose: to serve as a text for anyone wishing to gain an insight into the profession of drafting; to serve as a practical guide for the architectural drafting student; and to function as a ready reference handbook for professional draftspersons, technical illustrators, technical writers, and architects.

It is hoped that by reading and studying this text, the beginning student will also be able to read and understand the many kinds of blueprints used in industry today.

Personal thanks are extended to my wife, Joyce, for her moral support and untiring efforts in typing this material.

John A. Nelson

CONTENTS

EQUIPMENT

SUGGESTED EQUIPMENT

Drafting equipment is very delicate and expensive. Extreme care must be used in adjusting, cleaning, using, and storing all instruments. Proper care of equipment is the responsibility of each student. In order to function in a professional manner, each student should have the following equipment.

Drafting table or drafting board
Drafting stool
Drafting machine or a T square
45° triangle
30°–60° triangle
Center wheel compass
Drop bow compass
Dividers
Mechanical, architectural, civil, and metric scales
Template assortment
French curves
Drafting brush
Dry cleaning pad
Protractor
Eraser
Erasing shield
Sandpaper paddle
Drafting tape
Pencils or lead holders

Drafting Machines

A drafting machine is a device which attaches to the drafting table and replaces the T square and triangles. The two types of drafting machines are the arm type and the track type, figure 1-1. On both types a round head holds two straightedges at right angles to one another. The head can be rotated to set the straightedges at any angle. Most machines are available with interchangeable straightedges marked with different scales along their edges.

A drafting machine is a precision instrument and should be checked for accuracy once a week. The instructions for checking and adjusting a drafting machine are included with the manufacturer's information.

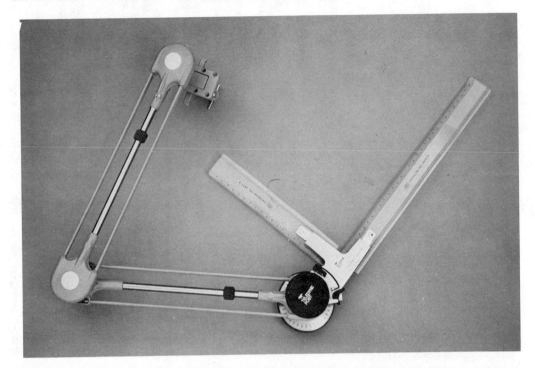

Fig. 1-1 (A) Arm-type drafting machine

Fig. 1-1 (B) Track-type drafting machine

T Square

The T square is used to draw horizontal lines, figure 1-2. Draw these lines only against the upper edge of the blade. Make sure the head is held securely against the left edge of the drawing board to guarantee parallel lines. This rule is followed as most drawing boards are not perfectly square. The left-handed drafter would reverse this procedure and place the head of the T square against the right edge of the board.

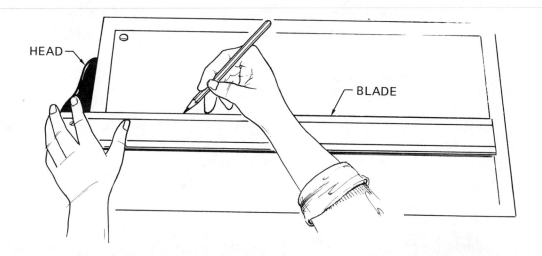

Fig. 1-2 Hold the T square head firmly against the drawing board edge with one hand. Draw horizontal lines with the other hand

Parallel Straightedge

A parallel straightedge is sometimes used in place of a T square, figure 1-3. It is attached horizontally across the drawing board by a vertical wire threaded through both ends. This allows the straightedge to be moved up and down the drawing board and still remain parallel to the surface.

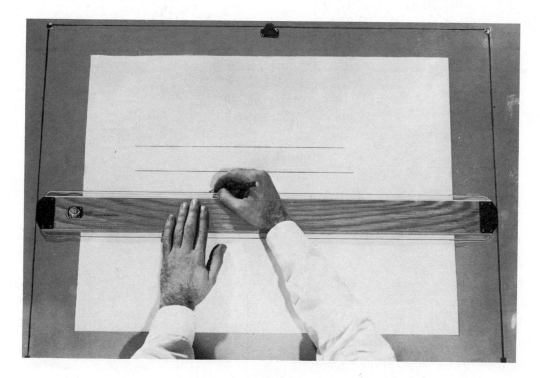

Fig. 1-3 Parallel straightedge

Triangles

There are two triangles used by drafters. One is called the 30–60-degree triangle, figure 1-4, usually written as 30°–60°. The other is a 45-degree triangle, figure 1-5, written as 45°. The 30°–60° contains a 30-degree, 60-degree, and 90-degree angle. The 45° consists of two 45-degree angles and one 90-degree angle.

Triangles are made of plastic and come in various sizes. When laying out lines, triangles are placed firmly against the upper edge of the T square. Pencils are placed against the left edge of the triangle and lines drawn upwards, away from the T square. Parallel angular lines are made by moving the triangle to the right after each new line has been drawn. Any angle divisible by 15 can be made by combining the 30°–60° and 45° triangles, figure 1-6.

Fig. 1-4 30°-60° triangle

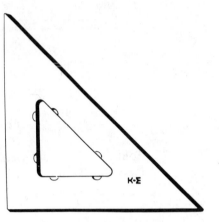

Fig. 1-5 45° triangle

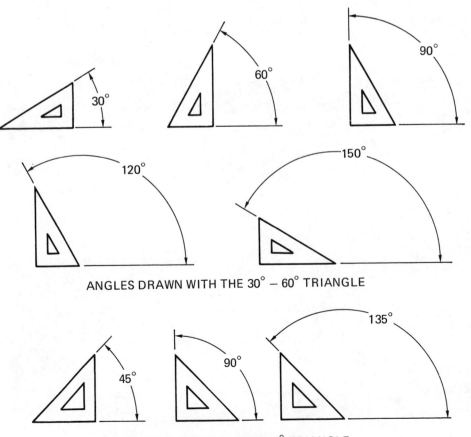

ANGLES DRAWN WITH THE 30° – 60° TRIANGLE

ANGLES DRAWN WITH THE 45° TRIANGLE

Fig. 1-6 Triangles

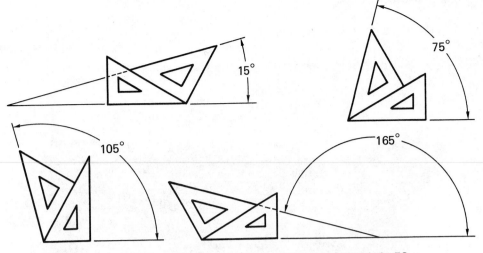

ANGLES DRAWN WITH THE COMBINED TRIANGLES

Adjustable Triangle

An adjustable triangle may take the place of both the 30°–60° and 45° triangles, figure 1-7. It is recommended, however, that this tool be used for drawing angles that cannot be made with the two standard triangles. The adjustable triangle is set by eye and is, therefore, not as accurate as the solid triangle.

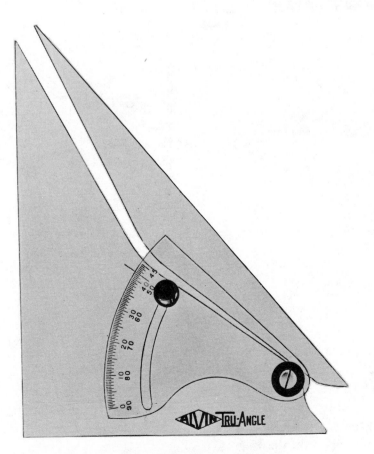

Fig. 1-7 Adjustable triangle

Drawing Instrument Sets

Typical drawing sets include compasses, dividers, and ruling pen, figure 1-8. Many sets include a variety of tools not normally used by a drafting student. It is recommended that only those tools actually needed be purchased.

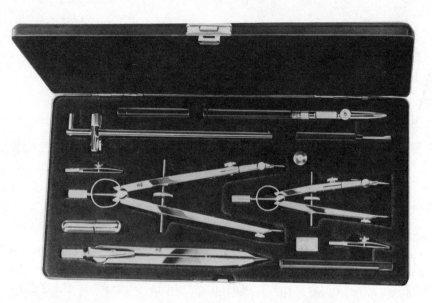

Fig. 1-8 Drawing instrument set

Divider

A divider is like a compass except it has a metal point on each leg, figure 1-9. It is used to lay off distances and to transfer measurements.

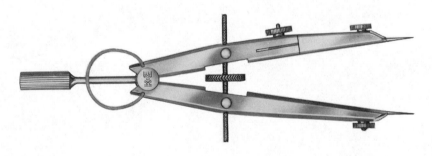

Fig. 1-9 Divider

Templates

A template is a thin, flat piece of plastic with various shapes cut in it, figure 1-10. It is designed to speed the work of the drafter and to make the finished drawing more accurate. There are templates to draw circles, ellipses, plumbing fixtures, nuts and bolts, screw threads, electronic symbols, springs, gears, and structural metals, to name just a few. Templates come in many sizes to fit the scale being used on the drawing.

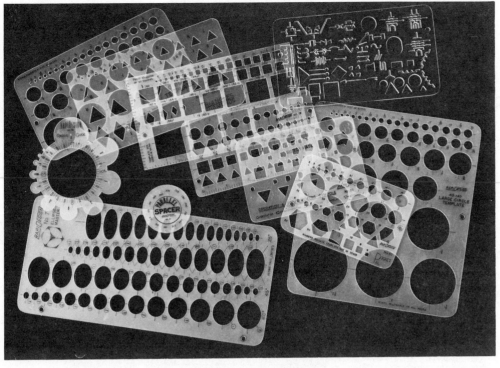

Fig. 1-10 Templates

French Curves

French curves are thin, plastic tools which come in an assortment of curved surfaces, figure 1-11. They are used to produce curved lines that cannot be made with a compass. Such lines are referred to as *irregular curves.*

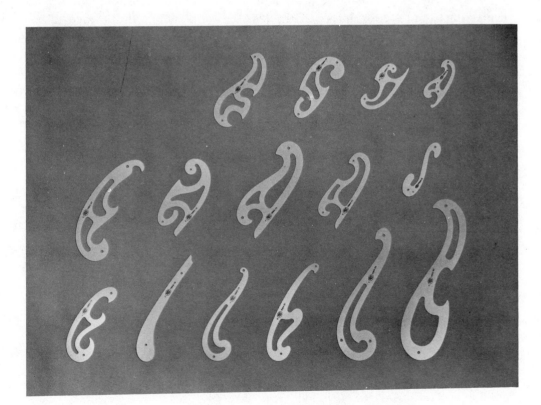

Fig. 1-11 French curves

Protractor

A protractor is used to measure and lay out angles, figure 1-12.

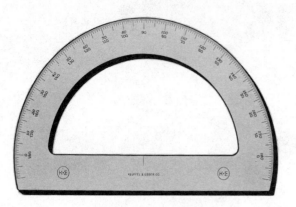

Fig. 1-12 Protractor

Pencils

Pencils come in 18 degrees of hardness ranging from 9H, which is very hard, to 7B, which is very soft, figure 1-13. The scale of hardness is as follows:

9H 8H 7H 6H 5H 4H   3H 2H H F HB B   2B 3B 4B 5B 6B 7B

Hard   Medium   Soft
accuracy   general purpose   art work

4H lead is recommended for layout work, extension lines, dimension lines, center lines, and section lines. 2H lead is used for object or visible edge lines and hidden lines. One should experiment with various leads to determine which lead gives the best line thickness. This varies depending on the pressure applied to the point while drawing lines.

Pencils are sharpened with a pencil sharpener. The important thing is that enough wood is removed to ensure that the lead, not the wood, of the pencil comes in contact with the T square or triangle edge.

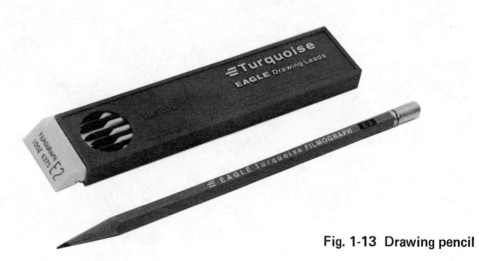

Fig. 1-13 Drawing pencil

Lead Holders and Leads

Lead holders hold sticks of lead, figure 1-14. The leads designed for lead holders come in the same range of hardness and are used for the same purposes as regular mechanical pencils. The main advantage is that they are more convenient to use. Leads are usually sharpened in a lead pointer, figure 1-15, or on a sandpaper paddle.

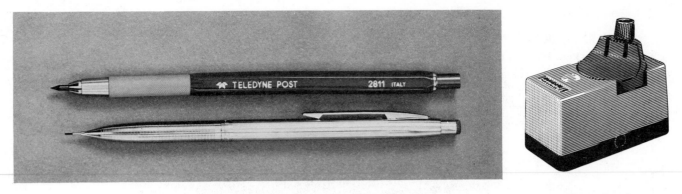

Fig. 1-14 Lead holders   **Fig. 1-15 Lead pointer**

Erasing Shield

An erasing shield restricts the erasing area, figure 1-16. In this way correctly drawn lines will not be disturbed during the erasing procedure. It is made from a thin, flat piece of metal with various size holes cut in it. To use, place the shield over the line to be erased and erase through the shield.

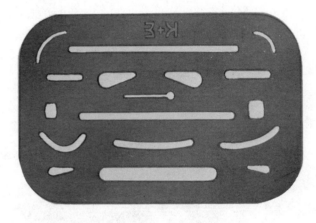

Fig. 1-16 Erasing shield

Drafting Brush

The drafting brush is used to remove loose graphite and eraser crumbs from the drawing surface, figure 1-17. Do not brush off a drawing surface by hand as it tends to smudge the drawing.

Fig. 1-17 Drafting brushes

Dry Cleaning Pad

A dry cleaning pad is used to erase minor smudges from the drawing surface, figure 1-18. Extreme care should be used as improper use of the dry cleaning pad will dull the lines of the drawing.

Fig. 1-18 Dry cleaning pad

Erasers

There are various kinds of erasers available to a drafter. One of the most commonly used is a soft, white eraser. If good drawing habits are developed, erasing can be kept to a minimum.

An electric eraser saves time, but care must be taken not to rub through the drawing paper, figure 1-19. This can be avoided by placing a thick sheet of paper beneath the drawing to cushion it.

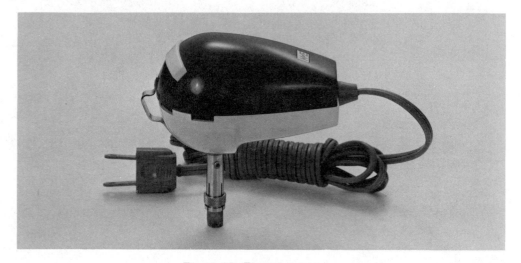

Fig. 1-19 Electric eraser

Proportional Dividers

Proportional dividers are used to enlarge or reduce an object in scale, figure 1-20. This tool has a sliding, adjustable pivot which varies the proportions of the tips of each leg.

Fig. 1-20 Proportional dividers

Sandpaper Paddle

A sandpaper paddle consists of several layers of sandpaper attached to a small wooden holder, figure 1-21. The sandpaper is used to sharpen pencil and lead points. Do not sharpen leads over a drawing as the graphite will smear the drawing surface.

Fig. 1-21 Sandpaper paddle

Compasses

There are two main types of compasses, figure 1-22. One is the friction-joint type and the other is the spring-bow type. The *friction-joint type* is still widely used for lightly laying out pencil drawings which will be inked. The disadvantage of this type compass is that the setting may slip when strong pressure is applied to the lead.

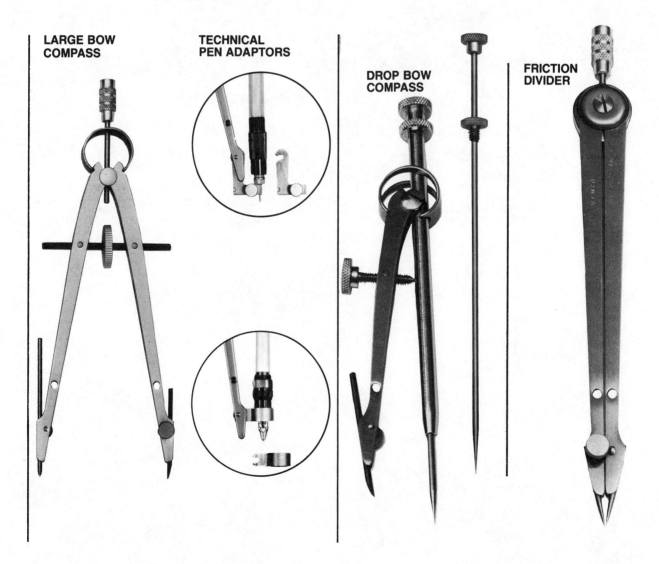

Fig. 1-22 Compasses

The *spring-bow type* is best for pencil drawings and tracings as it retains its setting even when strong pressure is applied to obtain dark lines. The spring, located at the top of the compass, holds the legs securely against the adjusting screw. The adjusting screw is used to make fine adjustments.

Compass leads should extend approximately 3/8 inch (9). The metal point of the compass is extended slightly more than the lead to compensate for the distance it enters the paper. The lead is sharpened with a sandpaper paddle to produce clean, sharp lines. The flat side of the lead faces outward in order to produce very small diameter circles, figures 1-23 and 1-24.

The compass is revolved between the thumb and the index finger. Pressure is applied downward on the metal point to prevent the compass from jumping out of the center hole, figure 1-25.

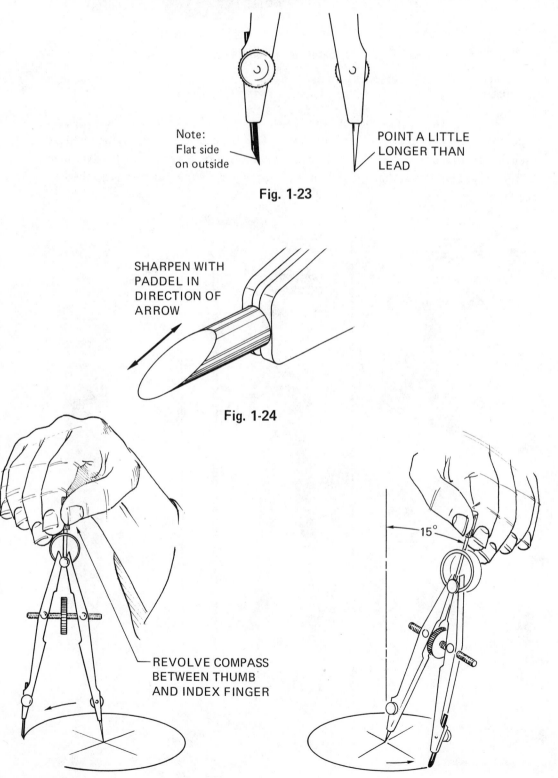

Note:
Flat side
on outside

POINT A LITTLE
LONGER THAN
LEAD

Fig. 1-23

SHARPEN WITH
PADDEL IN
DIRECTION OF
ARROW

Fig. 1-24

REVOLVE COMPASS
BETWEEN THUMB
AND INDEX FINGER

15°

Fig. 1-25

Paper Sizes

Paper sizes come in two standard increments in inches. All sizes fold up to the basic A size paper of 8 1/2 x 11 inches or 9 x 12 inches. Paper also comes in standard metric sizes and folds up to the basic A-4 size of 210 x 297 millimetres, figures 1-26 and 1-27.

INCHES			MILLIMETRES	
SIZE	DIMENSIONS		SIZE	DIMENSIONS
A	8 1/2 x 11	9 x 12	A-4	210 x 297
B	11 x 17	12 x 18	A-3	297 x 420
C	17 x 22	18 x 24	A-2	420 x 594
D	22 x 34	24 x 36	A-1	594 x 841
E	34 x 44	36 x 48	A-0	841 x 1189

Fig. 1-26

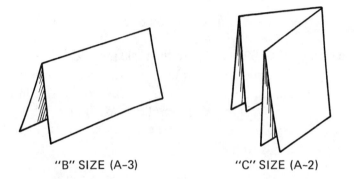

"B" SIZE (A-3)   "C" SIZE (A-2)

Fig. 1-27 All sizes fold up to "A" size (A-4)

Scales

There are various kinds of scales used by drafters, figure 1-28. A number of different scales are included on each instrument. They save the drafter the work of computing new measurements every time a drawing is made larger or smaller than the original.

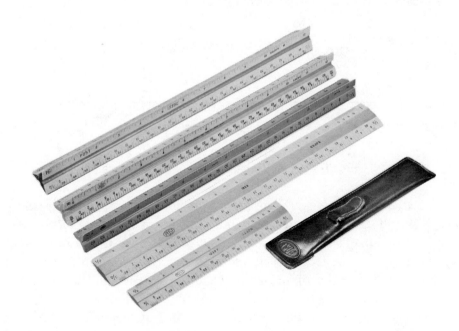

Fig. 1-28 Scales

Scales come open divided and full divided. A *full-divided scale* is one in which the units of measurement are subdivided throughout the length of the scale. An *open-divided scale* has its first unit of measurement subdivided, but the remaining units are open or free from subdivision.

Mechanical engineer's scales are divided into inches and parts of an inch. To lay out a full-size measurement, use the scale marked 16. This scale has each inch divided into 16 equal parts, or divisions of 1/16 inch. To use, place 0 on the point where measurement begins and step off the desired length, figure 1-29.

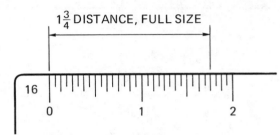

Fig. 1-29 1 3/4″ measured out at full scale

To reduce a drawing 50 percent, use the scale marked 1/2. The large 0 at the end of the first subdivided measurement lines up with the other unit measurements that are part of the same scale. The large numbers crossed out in figure 1-30 go with the 1/4 scale starting at the other end. These numbers are ignored while using the 1/2 scale. To lay out 1 3/4 inches at the 1/2 scale, read full inches to the right of 0 and fractions to the left of 0.

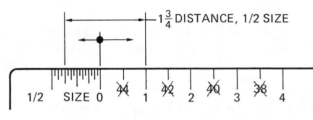

Fig. 1-30 1 3/4″ measured out at 1/2 scale

The 1/4 scale is used in the same manner as the 1/2 scale. Measurements of full inches are made to the left of 0, however, and fractions to the right because the 1/4 scale is located at the opposite end of the 1/2 scale, figure 1-31.

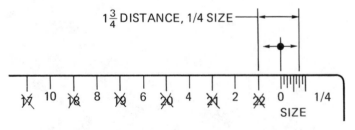

Fig. 1-31 1 3/4″ measured out at 1/4 scale

The *architect's scale* is used primarily for drawing large buildings and structures. The full-size scale is used frequently for drawing smaller objects. Because of this, the architect's scale is generally used for all types of measurements. It is designed to measure in feet, inches, and fractions. Measure full feet to the right of 0, inches and fractions of an inch to the left of 0. The numbers crossed out in figure 1-32 correspond to the 1/2 scale. They can be used, however, as 6 inches as each falls halfway between full-foot divisions. Measurements from 0 are made in the opposite direction of the full scale because the 1/2 scale is located at the opposite end of the scale, figure 1-33.

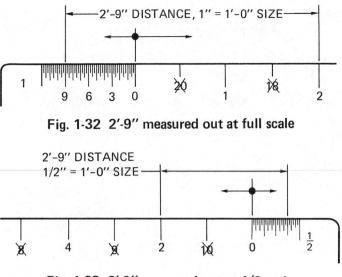

Fig. 1-32 2'-9" measured out at full scale

Fig. 1-33 2'-9" measured out at 1/2 scale

A *civil engineer's scale* is also called a *decimal inch scale*. The number 10, located in the corner of the scale in figure 1-34, indicates that each graduation is equal to 1/10 of an inch or .1". Measurements are read directly from the scale. The number 20, located in the corner of the scale shown in figure 1-35, indicates that it is 1/2 scale. To read 1/4 scale, the #40 scale (not shown) would be used.

A metric scale is used if the millimetre is the unit of linear measurement. It is read the same as the decimal scale except it is in millimetres, figure 1-38.

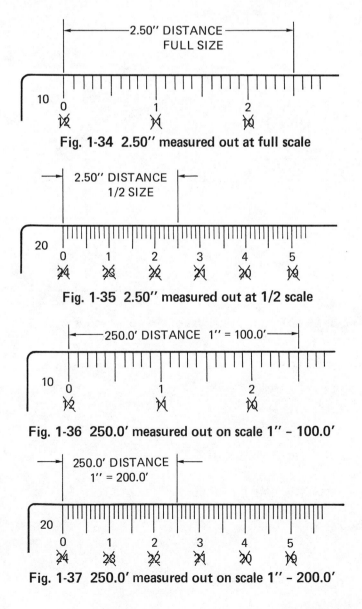

Fig. 1-34 2.50" measured out at full scale

Fig. 1-35 2.50" measured out at 1/2 scale

Fig. 1-36 250.0' measured out on scale 1" – 100.0'

Fig. 1-37 250.0' measured out on scale 1" – 200.0'

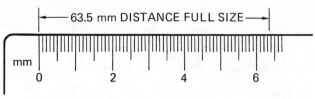

Fig. 1-38 63.5 mm measured out at full scale

WHITEPRINTERS

There are many types of whiteprinters available for use in drafting rooms. These machines reproduce a drawing through a chemical process. Most work on basically the same principle. A bright light passes through the translucent original drawing and onto a coated whiteprint paper. The light breaks down the coating on the whiteprint paper, but wherever lines have been drawn on the original drawing, no light strikes the coated sheet. Then the whiteprint paper is passed through ammonia vapor for developing. This chemical developing causes the unexposed areas — those which were shaded by lines on the original — to turn blue or black, figure 1-39.

On most whiteprinters there are controls to regulate the speed and the flow of the developing chemical. Each type of machine requires different settings and has different controls. Before operating any whiteprinter, read all of the manufacturer's instructions.

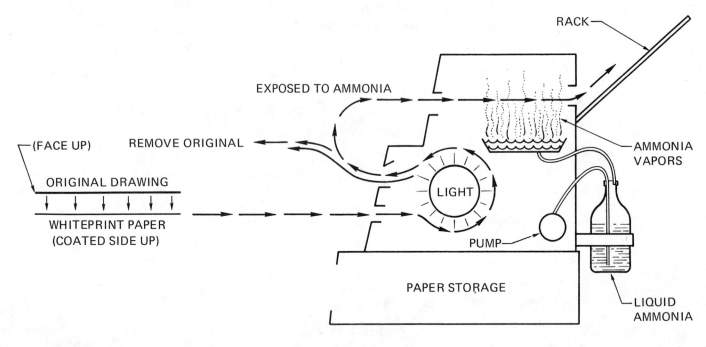

Fig. 1-39 Basic operating principles of ammonia-vapor whiteprinter

UNIT 2

LETTERING

LETTERING

Lettering is a skill that every drafter must perfect. Lettering on a drawing must be easy to read and understand. With practice and a knowledge of the proper order of strokes, anyone can learn to make uniform, legible letters.

The single stroke, uppercase Gothic letter is the most frequently used style of lettering on drawings. These letters are drawn either on a slant or vertically straight. Only one style is used on a drawing, however.

Whichever style is chosen, all letters should appear to have the same height, proportion, inclination, weight, and spacing between letters and words. Drawing guidelines is one way to help control lettering.

In Architectural Drafting there exists no standard alphabet as there is in the Mechanical Drafting field. Most Architectural Draftspersons take pride in developing their own style. Whatever your own style, it is important that it is uniform and consistent on all drawings. All lettering must be legible, neat and straightforward. This chapter illustrates how to construct the standard uppercase, single-stroke, Gothic letters and numbers. From this style and order of strokes you will be able to develop your own personal style.

Guidelines

Guidelines help keep the height and inclination of letters uniform. They are drawn very lightly with a hard (4H or 6H) pencil, so lightly that they need not be erased. The light horizontal lines are drawn 1/8 inch (3) apart. Vertical or inclined lines are added to help space the letters, figure 2-1.

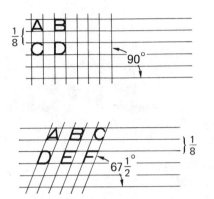

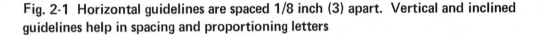

Fig. 2-1 Horizontal guidelines are spaced 1/8 inch (3) apart. Vertical and inclined guidelines help in spacing and proportioning letters

Order of Strokes

Knowing the proper order of strokes makes it easier to draw each letter. When lettering, there are no upward strokes. Every stroke is downward, with the exception of horizontal lines which are drawn to the right, figure 2-2.

The order of strokes and proportion of inclined letters are the same as those for vertical letters. With inclined letters, the curved lines are more elliptical than circular, and straight lines lean to the right.

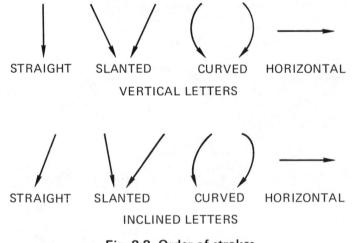

Fig. 2-2 Order of strokes

Study how letters are drawn in figure 2-3, both vertical and inclined styles. Notice how each is well-balanced and in proportion to the other letters. Numbers are drawn in the same proportion as letters. Fractions are drawn 3/8 inch (9) high. Use a sharp 2H lead pencil for lettering.

Left-handers may find that the order of strokes recommended do not work for them. These students should consult with their instructor and experiment with the order of strokes until each letter can be drawn smoothly, legibly, and in proper proportion.

Vertical style

Inclined style

Fig. 2-3 How to form uppercase Gothic letters and numerals

Spacing of Letters

Although the space between letters of a word is not actually equal, it must appear to be, figure 2-4. Improperly spaced letters make the text very difficult to read. It requires a great deal of practice to learn proper spacing, but the finished work will make the effort worthwhile.

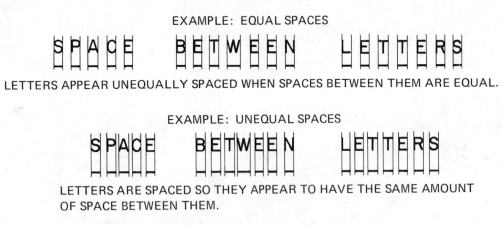

EXAMPLE: EQUAL SPACES

LETTERS APPEAR UNEQUALLY SPACED WHEN SPACES BETWEEN THEM ARE EQUAL.

EXAMPLE: UNEQUAL SPACES

LETTERS ARE SPACED SO THEY APPEAR TO HAVE THE SAME AMOUNT OF SPACE BETWEEN THEM.

Fig. 2-4 Spacing of letters

Word and Sentence Spacing

- The area between *words* = the height of the letters
- The area between *sentences* = twice the height of the letters
- The area between *lines* = from 1/2 to 1 1/2 times the height of the letters

BORDERS

A drawing must have a frame around it to give it a good appearance. This frame is referred to as a *border*, figure 2-5. Borders should have the following measurements:

PAPER SIZE	LEFT	TOP, BOTTOM, AND RIGHT
A & B	1 1/4"	1/4"
C	1 1/4"	3/8"
D	1 1/4"	1/2"
A4 & A3	30 mm	6 mm
A2	30 mm	9 mm
A1	30 mm	12 mm

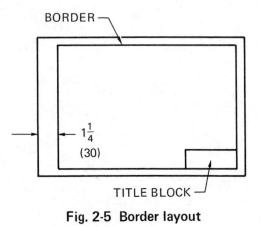

Fig. 2-5 Border layout

UNIT 3

DRAWING TECHNIQUES

WORK HABITS

To become an efficient drafter, the beginning student should have average or above average talent in mechanical reasoning, finger dexterity, and artistic ability. The student's competency in each area must be continually improved by repetition of exercises. In order to gain speed, neatness, and accuracy, it is important to develop good work habits. Many habits, such as keeping equipment neatly stored, clean, and ready for immediate use, are very basic work habits. Other, more involved habits to develop include using the correct steps in centering, laying out, and darkening drawings.

Correct work habits and procedures are emphasized throughout this text. Practice each so that drawings will be made quickly, neatly, and accurately. Do not take shortcuts or the finished drawing will suffer as a result.

ALPHABET OF LINES

Each line used to make a mechanical drawing has its own meaning. These lines of various shapes and weights (thicknesses) are called an *alphabet of lines.* As drawings become more complicated, it is most important that lines follow the suggested shape and weight illustrated in figure 3-1. Alphabet of lines should all be the same blackness. They differ only in line thickness.

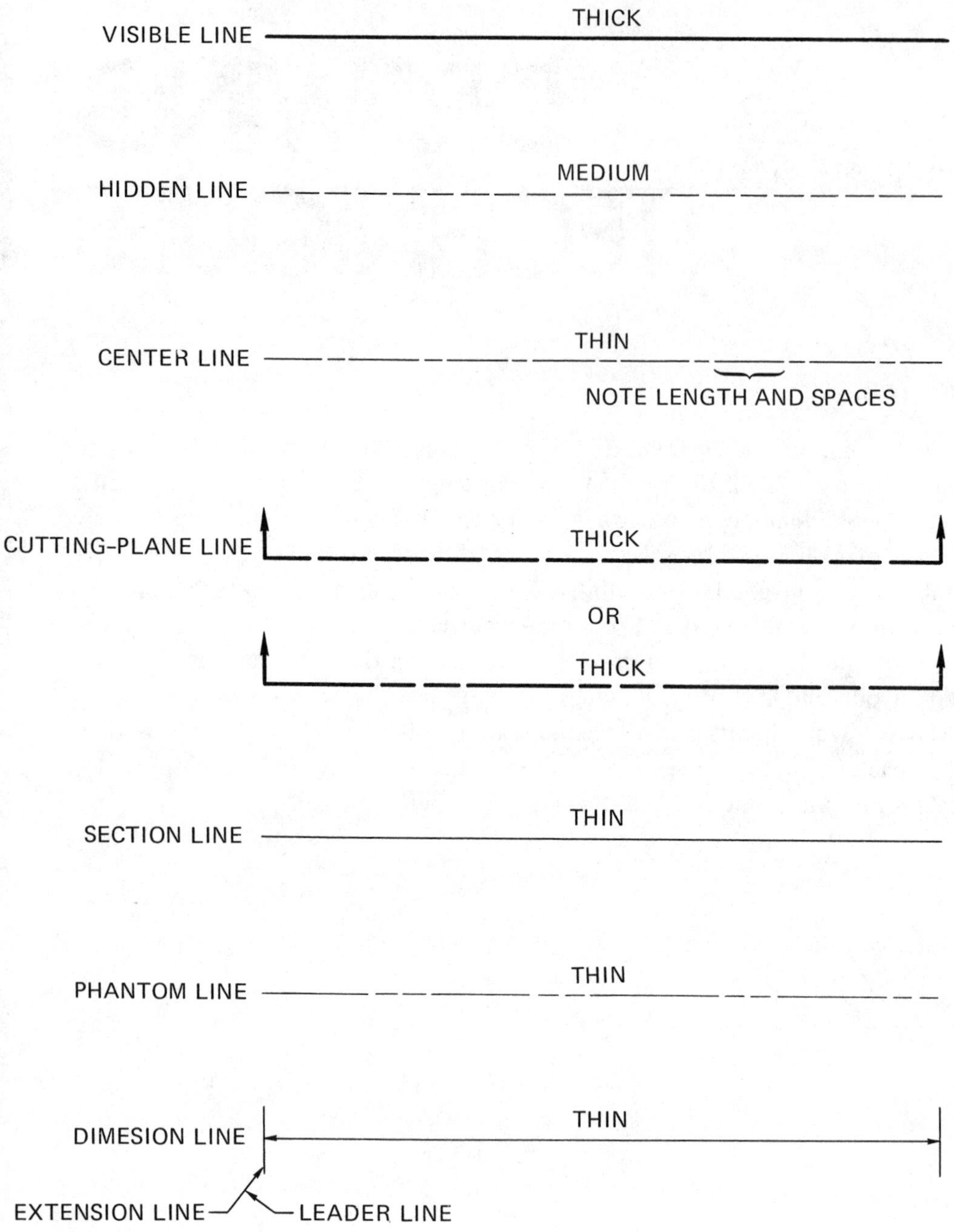

VISIBLE LINE ———————————— THICK ————————————

HIDDEN LINE — — — — — — MEDIUM — — — — — — —

CENTER LINE —— — —— — —— THIN —— — —— — ——
NOTE LENGTH AND SPACES

CUTTING-PLANE LINE — — — — THICK — — — —

OR

— — — — THICK — — — —

SECTION LINE ———————— THIN ————————

PHANTOM LINE ——— — —— — THIN —— — ——— — ——

DIMESION LINE |←——————— THIN ———————→|

EXTENSION LINE — — LEADER LINE

Fig. 3-1 Alphabet of lines. Note length of lines, dashes, and spaces

Steps Used to Design and Lay Out a Floor Plan

Step 1.   Complete a program form paying strict attention to such things as the traffic pattern and keeping the various areas (sleeping/living/eating) isolated from each other. Now make three or four sketches of each floor plan including all the required features needed. Pick the best sketch for each floor

Step 2.   With a sharp 4H pencil, lightly make a layout, in scale, of the selected sketch. Draw the outside wall first using width and length dimensions of even 2'-0'' units (4'-0'' units are even better). Using the correct outside wall thickness, usually approximately 5 1/2 inches thick, draw the permitted outer wall.

Step 3.   Lightly block in the inside walls, usually approximately 4 1/2 inches thick, as close to the sketch as possible. Many times, when laying out to scale, minor changes from the original sketch must be made.

Step 4.   Locate and draw in the doors, windows, and chimney and fireplace, figure 3-2.

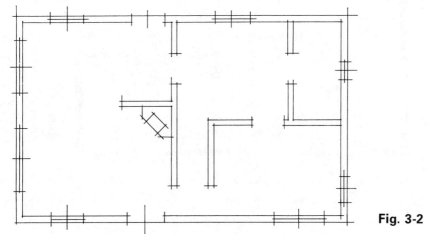

Fig. 3-2

Step 5.   On another sheet of paper lay out the stairs. It is important to know the exact stair opening before going further. Add this stair opening to your layout.

Step 6.   Take the time to review your layout. Check for the following:

- Are the three major areas adequately separated?
- Is the traffic pattern the best it can be?
- Are there any poor features such as a long hallway or basement stairs in a poor location? Is each room adequately lighted? Does each bedroom have a closet? Etc.?
- Are all rooms standard size?
- Is the general layout as functional as possible?
- Check all dimensions.

Step 7.   Add door swings, figure 3-3.

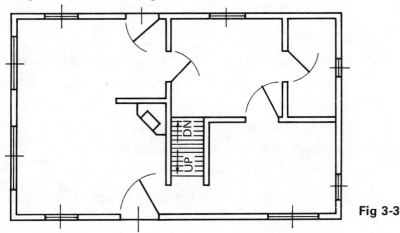

Fig 3-3

Step 8.   Lightly add all counters, cabinets, shelves, sink(s), water closet(s), and any other minor details such as the stove and refrigerator.

Step 9.   Using light guidelines, neatly letter, dimension, and add all notes and callouts to your layout.

Step 10.   Stop and recheck all work.

Step 11.   Have this *light* layout plan approved by the instructor.

Step 12.   After approval, carefully darken in all work using sharp, black lines, like figure 3-4.

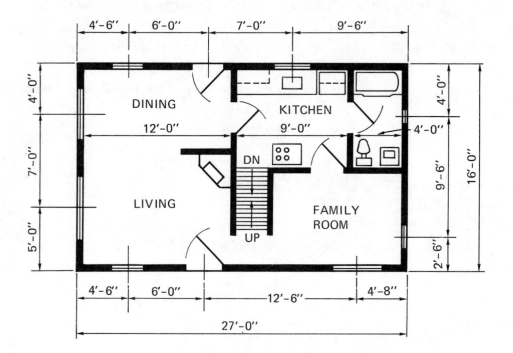

Fig. 3-4

THINGS TO AVOID

Much will be said about developing good drafting habits. The following are considered *poor* drafting practice:

- Do not use a scale as a straightedge for drawing lines.

- Do not draw horizontal lines with the lower edge of the straightedge.

- Do not cut paper with a knife using the edge of a straightedge or triangle as a guide.

- Do not work with an unsharpened pencil.

- Do not sharpen a compass lead over the drawing board.

- Do not jab the dividers or compass points into the drawing board.

- Do not draw a circle or radius with a compass unless the point is sharp and extends 3/8 inch (9) from the edge of the compass.

- Do not use dividers as pincers or picks.

- Do not start any drawing unless all equipment is clean.

- Do not fill a drawing pen over a drawing.

- Do not put a compass away without opening it to relieve the spring tension.

GEOMETRIC CONSTRUCTION

GEOMETRIC CONSTRUCTION

Knowing how to construct geometric shapes helps a drafter to make accurate drawings. This unit explains the terms and principles of geometry through simple geometric constructions.

When laying out a geometric construction, use very light lines made with a 4H pencil lead. When the construction is completed, use a 2H lead to darken the shape with thin, black lines.

Figure 4-1 illustrates some common geometric shapes.

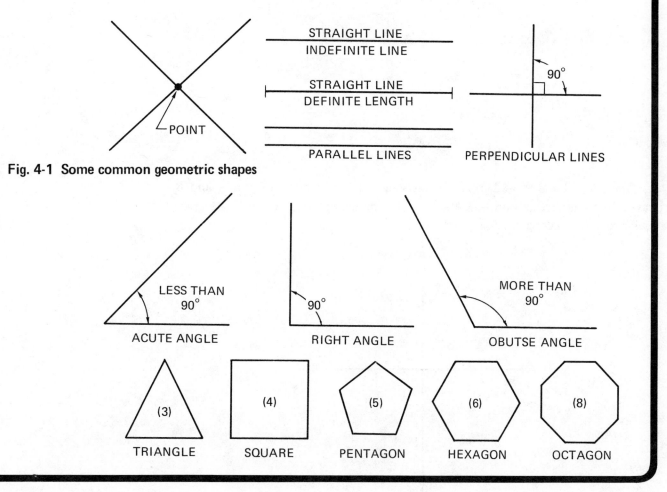

Fig. 4-1 Some common geometric shapes

HOW TO BISECT A LINE

- *Bisect* means to cut in half.
- Where two lines cross is their point of *intersection*.
- *Perpendicular* means at right angle (90°).

Given:

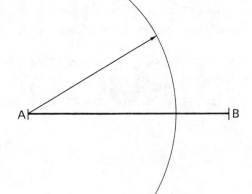

LINE AB

Step 1. Set the compass point at approximately two-thirds the length of line AB and swing an arc from point A.

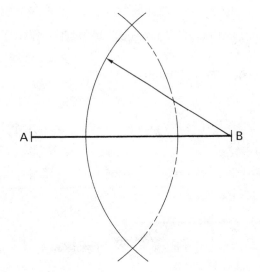

Step 2. Using the same compass setting, swing an arc from point B.

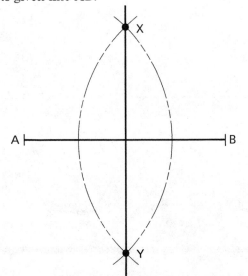

Step 3. Points X and Y are formed by the intersection of arcs A and B. Draw a line connecting points X and Y. The line connecting X and Y is perpendicular to and bisects given line AB.

HOW TO BISECT AN ANGLE

Given:

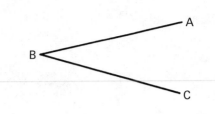

ANGLE ABC

Step 1. Set the compass point at any convenient radius and swing an arc from point B.

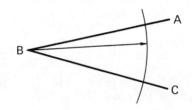

Step 2. Points X and Y are formed where the arc crosses lines A and C. Swing two identical arcs from points X and Y.

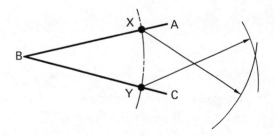

Step 3. Point Z is formed where the arcs from X and Y cross. Draw a line from B to Z. Line BZ bisects angle ABC.

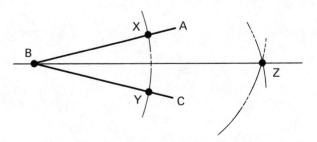

HOW TO SWING AN ARC OR CIRCLE THROUGH THREE GIVEN POINTS

Given:

B +

+ C

A +

POINTS A, B, C

Step 1. Connect points B and C with a straight line. Connect points A and B with a straight line.

Step 2. Using the method outlined for bisecting a line, bisect lines AB and BC.

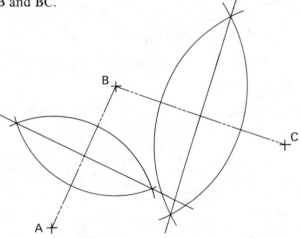

Step 3. Point X is formed where the two extended bisectors meet. Point X is the center of arc or circle ABC which is drawn using radius XA.

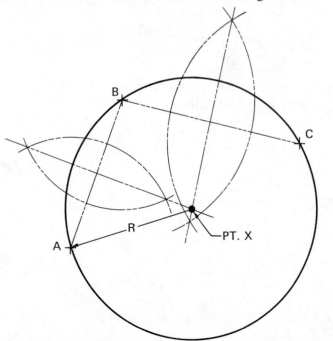

HOW TO LOCATE THE CENTER OF A CIRCLE

Given:

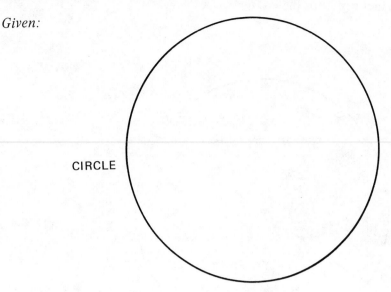

CIRCLE

Step 1. Using a drafting machine or T square, draw a horizontal line across the circle at a place approximately halfway from the top to the center of the circle. Where this line passes through the circle forms points A and B.

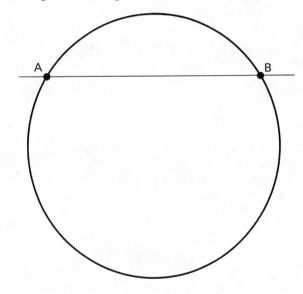

Step 2. Draw perpendicular lines downward from points A and B. Where these lines cross the circle forms points C and D.

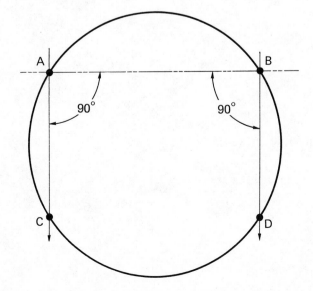

Step 3. Carefully draw a line from C to B and from A to D. Where these lines cross is the exact center of the given circle.

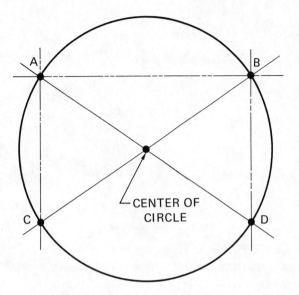

HOW TO DRAW A HEXAGON

Given:

Distance across the flats, or surface, of the desired hexagon

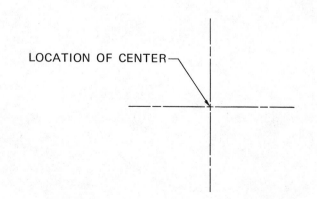

Step 1. Draw a circle with a diameter equal to the distance across the flats of the desired hexagon.

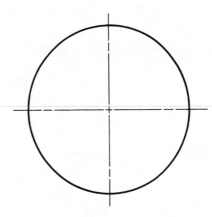

Step 2. Draw two horizontal lines (or two vertical lines if the hexagon is to be illustrated in another position) tangent to the circle.

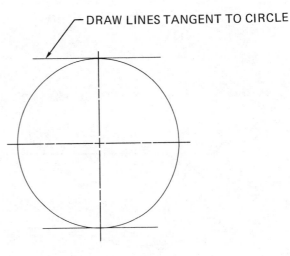

Step 3. Using a 30°–60° triangle, complete the hexagon as shown. Use the correct line weight. Darken the hexagon.

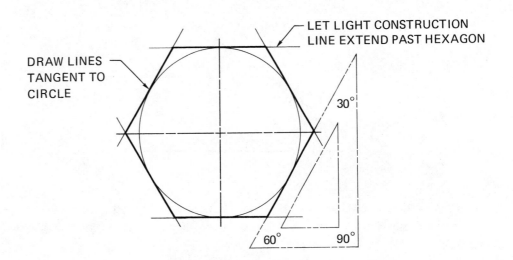

HOW TO DIVIDE A LINE INTO EQUAL PARTS

Given:

A |————————————————| B
LINE AB

Problem: To divide line AB into three equal parts:

Step 1. Draw a line 90 degrees from either end of the given line.

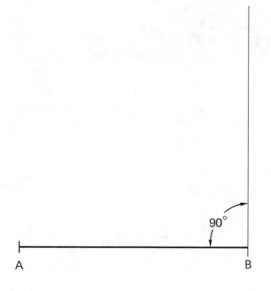

Step 2. Place the scale with its 0 on point A of the given line. Pivot the scale until the 3-inch measurement, or any multiple of 3 units of measure, is on the perpendicular line drawn in Step 1.

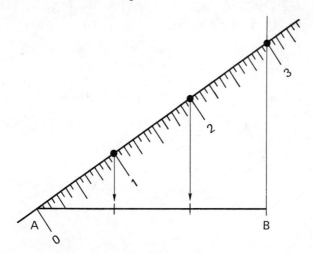

Step 3. Place dots at points 1 and 2 as shown. Project lines 90 degrees downward from these points. Add hash marks where projected lines cross given line AB.

HOW TO TRANSFER ODD SHAPES

Method I

> *Given:* TRIANGLE ABC

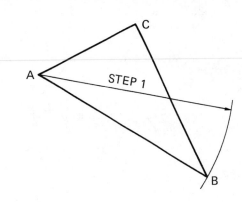

Step 1. Place the compass point at letter A, extend lead to letter B. Draw a light arc at the desired location. Letter the point A. Fix letter B at any convenient place on arc. (Letter each point as you proceed.)

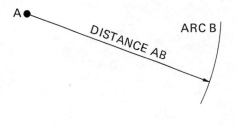

Step 2. Place the compass point at letter B of the original drawing and extend compass lead to letter C. Transfer distance BC as illustrated.

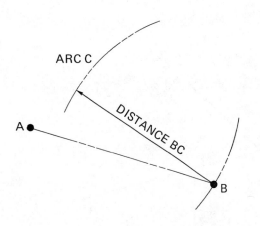

Step 3. Place compass point at letter A of the original drawing and extend compass lead to letter C. Transfer distance AC as illustrated.

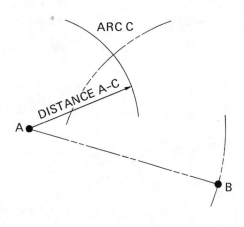

Step 4. Locate and letter each point.

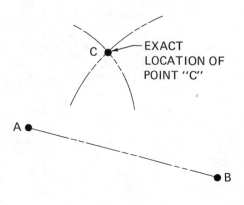

Step 5. Connect points A, B, and C. Original shape has been transferred.

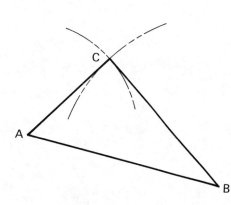

HOW TO TRANSFER ODD SHAPES

Method II

Given:

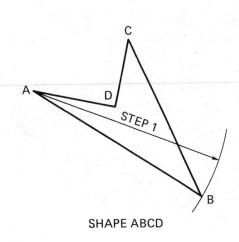

SHAPE ABCD

Step 1. Using the same procedure as used to transfer a three-sided, odd-shaped figure, locate and transfer distance AB.

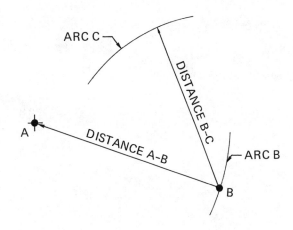

Step 2. Fix point B at any convenient place on arc B. Measure and transfer distance BC.

Step 3. Measure and transfer distance AC. Locate point C where distances AB and BC cross. Letter point C.

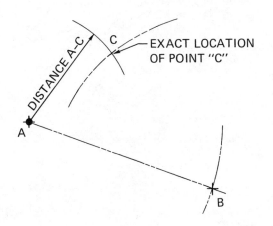

Step 4. Measure and transfer distances AD and CD. Point D is where arcs AD and CD cross. Letter point D.

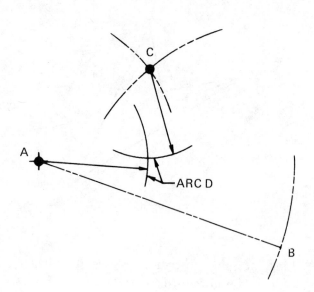

Step 5. Connect points AB, BC, CD, and DA. The shape has been transferred.

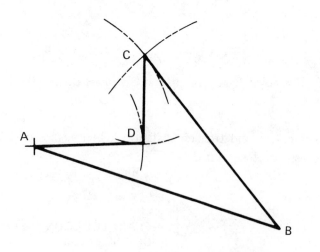

HOW TO TRANSFER COMPLEX ODD SHAPES

Given:

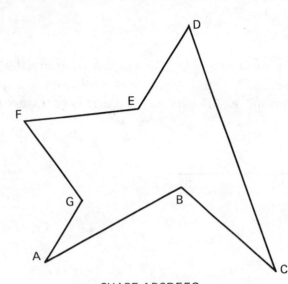

SHAPE ABCDEFG

The transferring of more complex shapes is easier if the basic shape is seen a a series of triangles.

The first step is to lay out the longest triangle contained within the basi shape, in this case ADC. Once the longest triangle is transferred, continue tran ferring all other points using the same procedure as in previous exercises. It wi ease the transfer problem even more if letters or numbers are placed around th object in a systematic order.

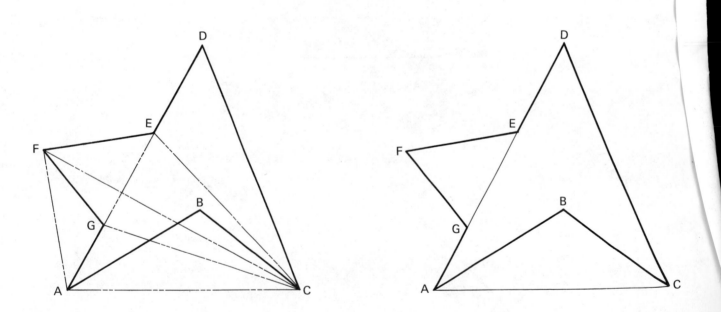

HOW TO LOCATE TANGENT POINTS

A *tangent point* is the exact point where one line stops and another line starts. *Tangent* means to touch. As an example, a tangent point is the exact point where a **straight** line stops being a straight line, and a curved line starts.

Tangent points are projected from the compass swing point at 90 degrees to the straight line next to it. Place a hash mark at each tangent point on the basic layout of each drawing, A, B, C, and D. This light layout work is done with a sharp 4H pencil lead.

Drawing A

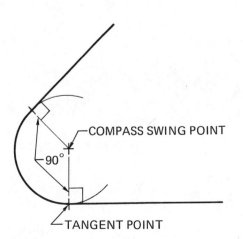

Drawing B

Drawing C

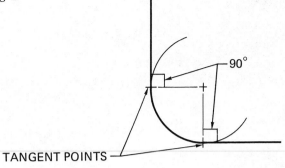

90°

TANGENT POINTS

Drawing D

TANGENT
POINTS

When one arc blends into another arc, the tangent point is found by drawing a light line from one swing point to the next swing point. The tangent point is where this line crosses the arc. Add a hash mark at each point.

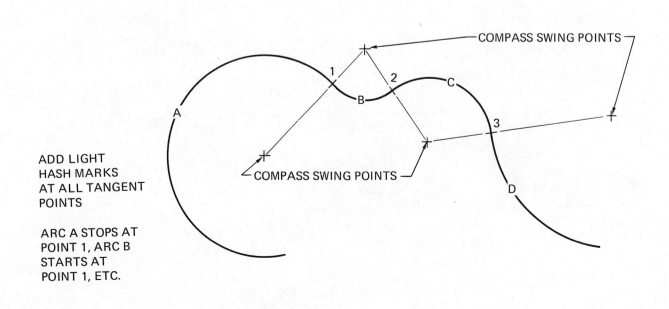

COMPASS SWING POINTS

1
2
B
C
A
3
D
COMPASS SWING POINTS

ADD LIGHT
HASH MARKS
AT ALL TANGENT
POINTS

ARC A STOPS AT
POINT 1, ARC B
STARTS AT
POINT 1, ETC.

HOW TO DRAW AN ELLIPSE

Given:

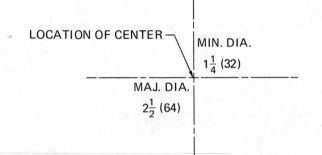

Step 1. Lightly draw a circle the size of the major diameter given. Using the same center, lightly draw a circle the size of the minor diameter. Number points 3, 6, 9, and 12.

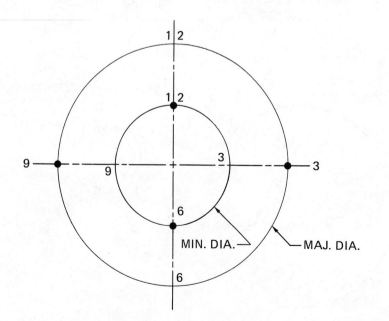

Step 2. Divide the given circles into 12 equal parts. Use a 30°–60° triangle as 12 x 30° = 360°, which is the total number of degrees in a circle. Number each point in order, clockwise around the circle.

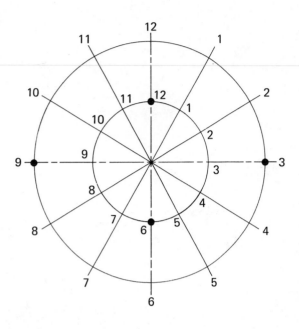

Step 3. Project at 90 degrees downwards from points, 10, 11, 1, and 2 located on the major diameter above the center line. Project at 90 degrees upwards from points 8, 7, 5, and 4 located on the major diameter below the centerline.

Project horizontal lines from points located on the minor diameter. These lines are projected until they meet the corresponding numbered lines projected from major diameter. The points of the ellipse are formed by the intersections.

Form the ellipse by connecting all newly formed points with french curves.

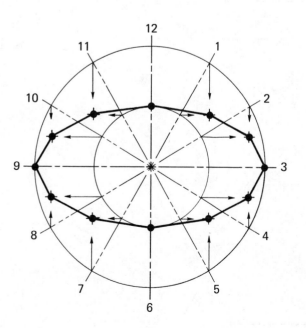

HOW TO DRAW AN OGEE CURVE

Method I. Both Parts of Curve Have Same Radius

Given:

LINES AB AND CD

Step 1. Draw a line from B to C. Bisect line BC to find point X.

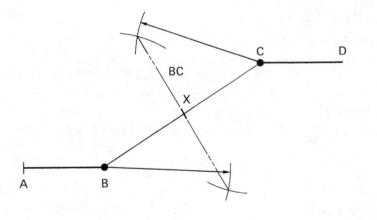

Step 2. Bisect line BX.

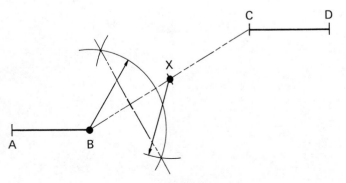

Step 3. Bisect line XC.

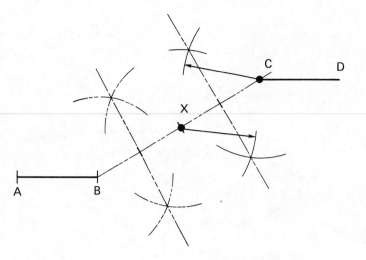

Step 4. Project 90 degrees upwards from point B and 90 degrees downwards from point C to bisect line and locate swing points.

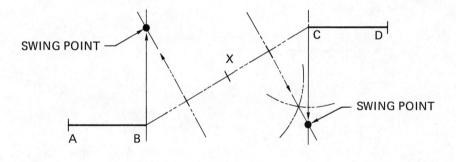

Step 5. Swing arcs BX and XC from swing points. Use hash marks to indicate tangent points.

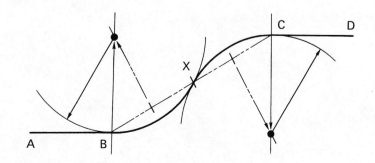

HOW TO DRAW AN OGEE CURVE

Method II. Parts of Curve Unequal

Given:

LINES AB AND CD

Problem: To place point X two-thirds the distance *from* B on line BC.

    Step 1. Draw line BC. Divide line BC into three equal parts. Place point X on second division from point B.

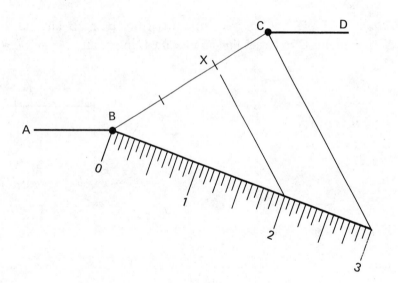

    Step 2. Bisect line BX.

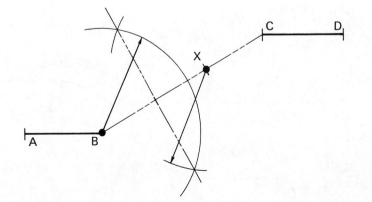

Step 3. Bisect line XC.

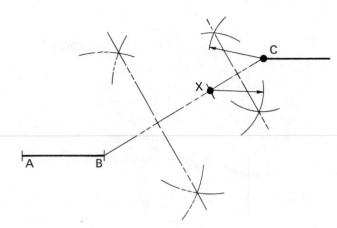

Step 4. Project 90 degrees upwards from point B and 90 degrees downwards from point C until they meet the bisectors of lines BX and XC. Swing points are located where these lines meet.

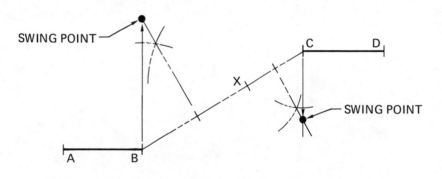

Step 5. Swing arcs BX and XC from swing points to complete drawing. Use hash marks to indicate tangent points.

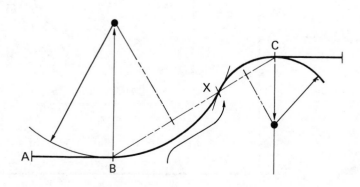

HOW TO CONSTRUCT AN ARC TANGENT TO TWO LINES
AT RIGHT ANGLES (90°)

Given:

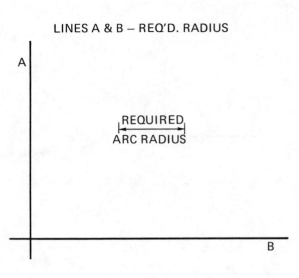

LINES A & B – REQ'D. RADIUS

Step 1. Out of the way, swing an arc from line A and another arc from line B that are both equal to the radius required.

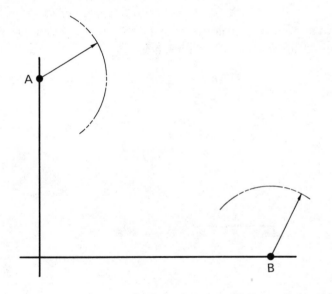

Step 2. Draw lines tangent to arcs A and B and parallel to lines A and B.

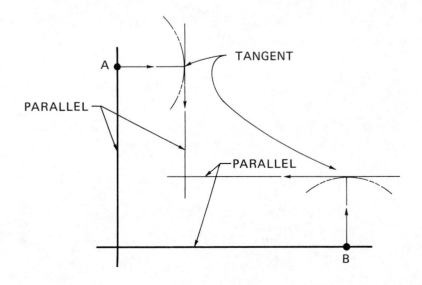

Step 3. Where these lines cross is the center for the required radius. Swing the required radius. Add tangent points and thicken to correct line weight.

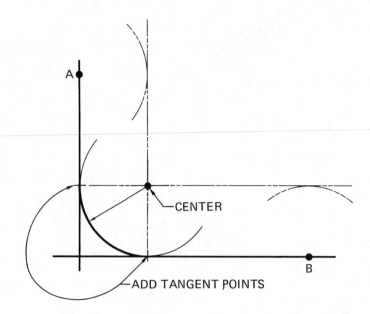

HOW TO CONSTRUCT AN ARC TANGENT TO AN OBTUSE ANGLE (MORE THAN 90°)

Given:

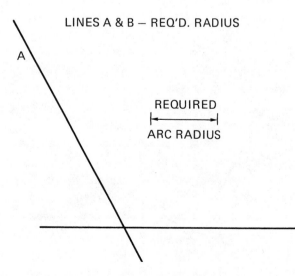

Step 1. Out of the way, swing an arc from line A and another arc from line B that are both equal to the radius required.

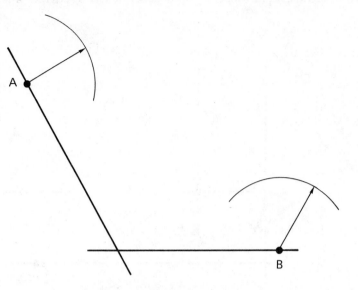

Step 2. Draw lines tangent to arcs A and B and parallel to lines A and B.

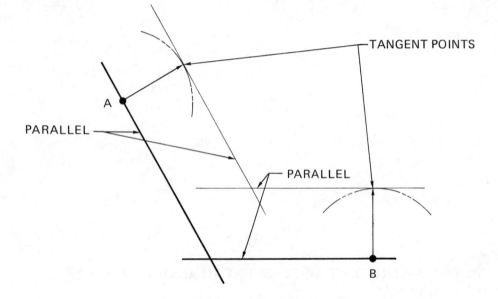

Step 3. Where these lines cross is the center for the required radius. Swing the required radius. Add tangent points and thicken to correct line weight.

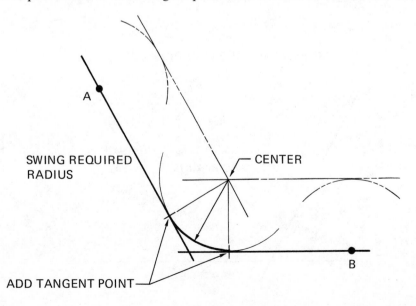

HOW TO CONSTRUCT AN ARC TANGENT TO
AN ACUTE ANGLE (LESS THAN 90°)

Given: LINES A & B — REQUIRED RADIUS

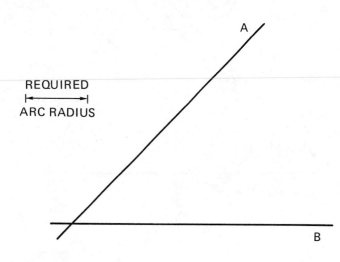

Step 1. Out of the way, swing an arc from lines A and B that are both equal to the radius required.

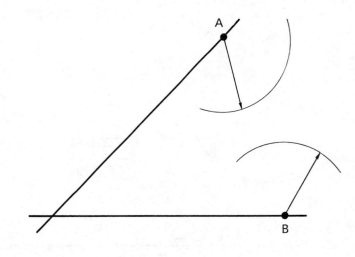

Step 2. Draw lines tangent to arcs A and B and parallel to lines A and B.

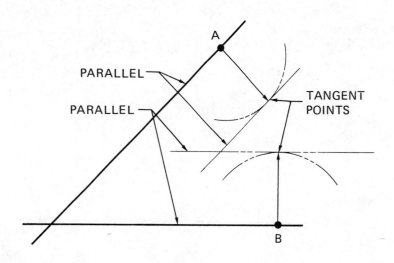

Step 3. Where these lines cross is the center for the required radius. Swing the required radius. Add tangent points and thicken to correct line weight.

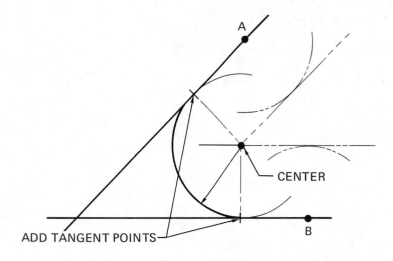

HOW TO CONSTRUCT AN ARC TANGENT TO A STRAIGHT AND A CURVED LINE

Given: LINES A AND B — REQUIRED RADIUS

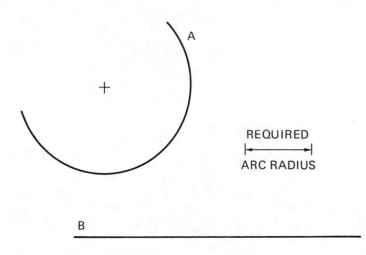

Step 1. Out of the way, swing an arc from line A and another arc from line B that are both equal to the radius required.

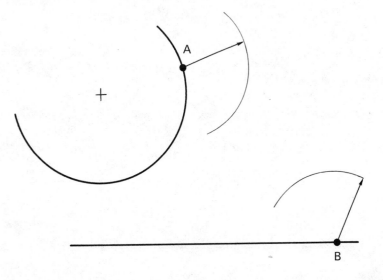

Step 2. Draw lines tangent and parallel to lines A and B.

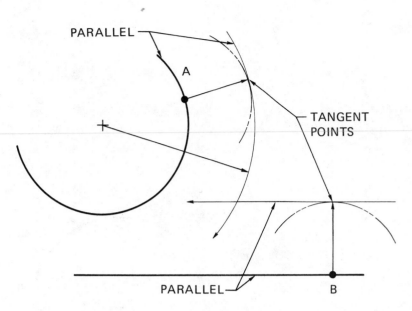

Step 3. Where these lines cross is the center for the required radius. Swing the required radius. Add tangent points and thicken to correct line weight.

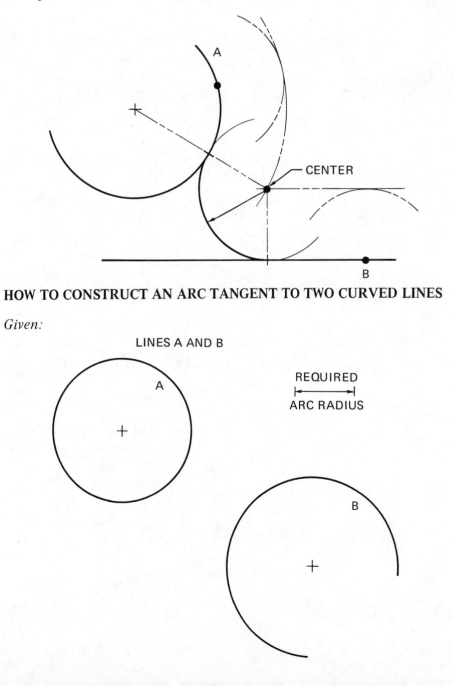

HOW TO CONSTRUCT AN ARC TANGENT TO TWO CURVED LINES

Given:

Step 1. Out of the way, swing an arc from line A and another from line B that are both equal to the radius required.

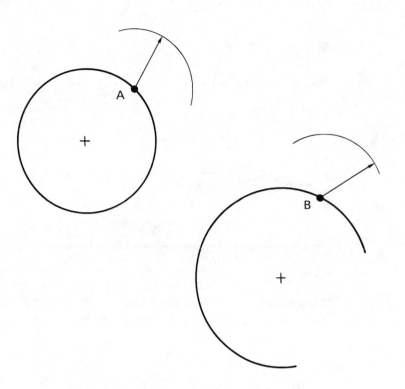

Step 2. Draw a line tangent and parallel to line A.

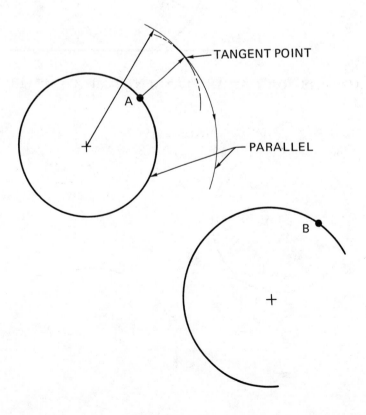

Step 3. Draw a line tangent and parallel to line B.

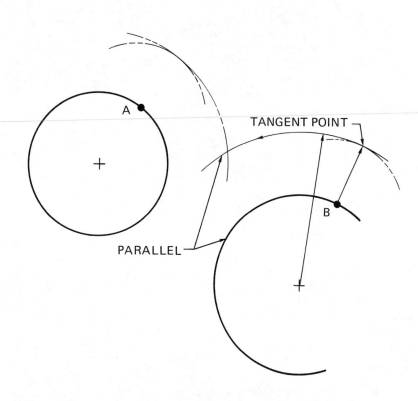

Step 4. Where these lines cross is the center for the required radius. Swing the required radius. Add tangent points and thicken to correct weight.

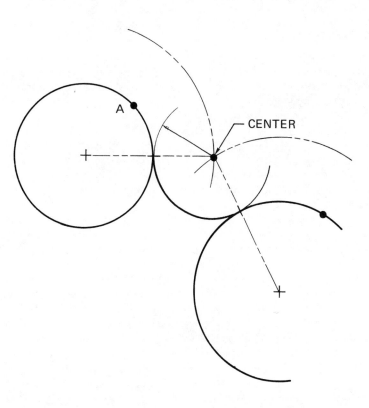

UNIT 5

MULTIVIEW DRAWINGS

MULTIVIEW DRAWING SYSTEM

A *multiview drawing* views an object from more than one place. The top view, for instance, shows how the object appears when looking directly down on it; the front view drawing shows how the object appears when looking directly at the front of it, and so on. A standard method of layout is followed so that all drawings are made in basically the same manner. Each view is in direct relationship to the next, but each view illustrates the object from a different viewpoint.

Figure 5-1 shows a pictorial view of a die to help explain the relationship between views. A *pictorial view* shows the object as it appears to the eye. Figure 5-2 shows how the die appears if viewed downward from above the die. Figure 5-3 shows how it appears looking at it directly from the front. Figure 5-4 shows the die viewed from the right side.

In Architectural Drafting each view is usually presented on a separate sheet of paper. It is important to know and understand the standard multiview system so the Architectural Drafter can apply these same multiview principles even though each view will probably appear on separate sheets. In order to simplify the multiview system, simple objects are used for illustrations. In actual practice, the *Floor Plan (s)* is the top view; the other views are projected from the Floor Plan (s). In Architectural Drafting, a left side view is always provided along with the standard right side view.

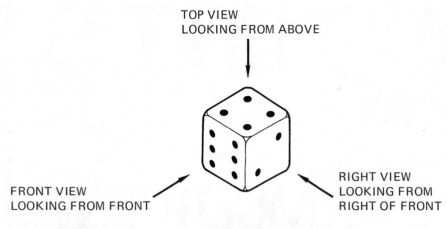

TOP VIEW
LOOKING FROM ABOVE

FRONT VIEW
LOOKING FROM FRONT

RIGHT VIEW
LOOKING FROM
RIGHT OF FRONT

Fig. 5-1 Pictorial view of die

TOP VIEW

FRONT VIEW

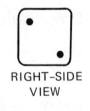

RIGHT–SIDE
VIEW

Fig. 5-2 Top view   **Fig. 5-3 Front view**   **Fig. 5-4 Right-side view**

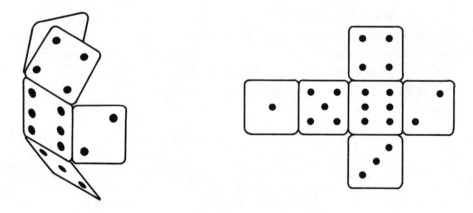

Fig. 5-5 Die opened up and flattened out

If the die is opened up and flattened out, figure 5-5, a better understanding of the multiviews can be gained.

Figure 5-6 shows the six sides of the die unattached to each other and illustrates the three most frequently used views in the circle: the top, front, and side views. Nearly all multiview drawings made of three views use those circled in figure 5-6.

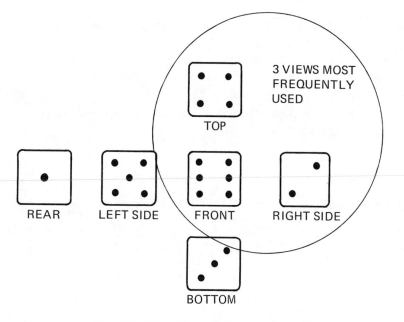

Fig. 5-6 Six sides of die, unattached

PLACEMENT OF VIEWS

Referring to the die, the side with six dots has the most detail. Use this side for the front view, figure 5-7. Directly to the right of the front view is the right-side view. It is projected from the front view as shown in figure 5-8. Directly above the front view is the top view. It, too, is projected from the front view as shown in figure 5-9.

These are the usual three views. If a left-side view is needed, it is projected from the front view to the left. The front, top, and right-side views are the views most often used.

Fig. 5-7 Front view

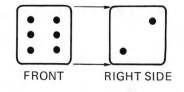

Fig. 5-8 Project the right-side view from front view without measuring height

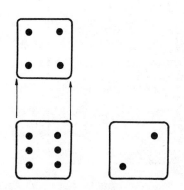

Fig. 5-9 Project the top view upwards from the front view without measuring the width

ADDING 45-DEGREE ANGLE PROJECTION LINES (MITER LINES)

From surface A in the top view, project horizontally as shown in figure 5-10. From surface A in the right-side view, project vertically. Where projections cross, construct a 45-degree angle. Project all points up to the 45-degree line, called a *miter line,* and over to check work and save drawing time. This is done lightly with a 4H lead.

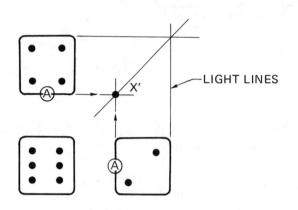

Fig. 5-10 45-degree projection lines

REQUIRED VIEWS

A drawing must be clean and simple so that there are no questions concerning what the drawing means.

The round cannon ball in figure 5-11 needs only one view to describe its size and shape. If the top and side views were added, it would be repetitious of the front view without providing any additional information.

An object such as the flat gasket in figure 5-12 needs only one view and a callout stating required thickness.

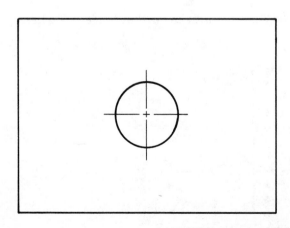

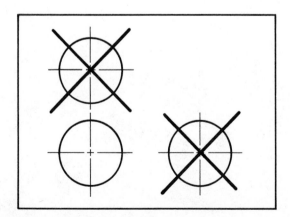

Fig. 5-11 One-view drawing

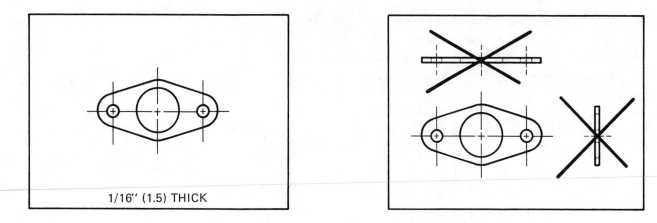

1/16" (1.5) THICK

Fig. 5-12 One-view drawing

Many objects can be illustrated with only two views. A third only duplicates the same information. Figure 5-13 shows an example of a drawing requiring only two views. Do not use more views than needed to illustrate an object.

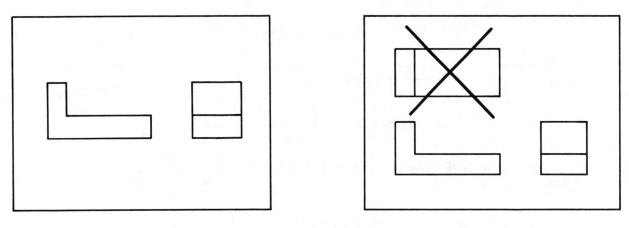

Fig. 5-13 Two-view drawing

In the simple system of multiview drawing, the front view is the starting view from which other views are made. The front view is first selected according to these rules:

- The front view is the most important view.
- The front view should show the basic shape in profile.
- The front view should be drawn so that it appears stable. To accomplish this, the heavy part is placed at the bottom of the view.
- The front view should be placed so that the other views have as few hidden edges as possible.
- The front view should show the most detail.

Before beginning a three-view drawing of any object, make some isometric sketches, such as the one illustrated in figure 5-14. Isometric drawing is discussed in Unit 6. This eliminates possible errors in the finished drawing and is helpful in selecting the proper view as discussed in rules for selecting a front view on pages 112 and 113.

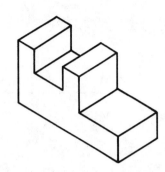

Fig. 5-14 Isometric of object

Follow these basic steps before beginning a three-view drawing:

1. Visualize the object.
2. Decide which view to use as the front view by sketching it in various positions, figure 5-15. Choose the one that most closely follows the rules for selecting the front views discussed on pages 112 and 113.

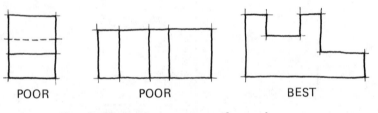

POOR   POOR   BEST

Fig. 5-15 Selecting proper front view

3. Decide how many views are needed to completely illustrate the object.
4. Decide in which position the front view will be placed. Figure 5-16 illustrates poor and good positioning.
5. Sketch all views. Use 1 inch (25) between views regardless of the scale being used. Make sketches freehand. Do not measure distances nor use a straightedge while sketching. Make sure views are neat and centered on the page, figure 5-17.

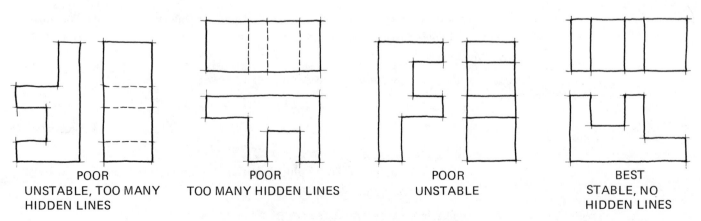

POOR
UNSTABLE, TOO MANY
HIDDEN LINES

POOR
TOO MANY HIDDEN LINES

POOR
UNSTABLE

BEST
STABLE, NO
HIDDEN LINES

Fig. 5-16 Front view positioning

The example shown on the left of figure 5-17 is poorly centered. It has wasted space on both sides of the top and front views, and both views are too close to the top and bottom of the paper. Objects should never be drawn within 1/2 inch (12) of the border lines. The example shown on the right of figure 5-17 is better than the first example because it appears balanced and well centered.

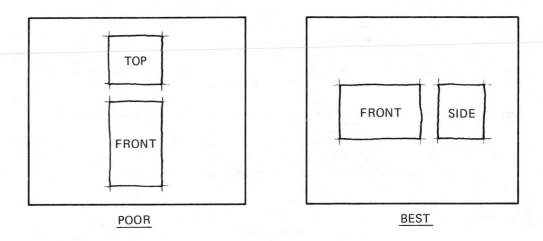

POOR

BEST

Fig. 5-17 Centering sketches

PRECEDENCE OF LINES

Sometimes lines coincide, figure 5-18. When this happens the drafter must choose which line to show. The order of precedence, or importance, of lines is:

1. Visible edge or object lines
2. Hidden lines
3. Center lines

Object lines, therefore, are more important than hidden lines. Hidden lines are more important than center lines. If a center line coincides with a cutting-plane line, the cutting-plane line is shown.

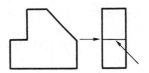

THE OBJECT LINE COINCIDES WITH THE HIDDEN LINE

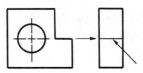

THE OBJECT LINE COINCIDES WITH THE CENTER LINE

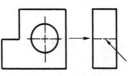

THE HIDDEN LINE COINCIDES WITH THE CENTER LINE

Fig. 5-18 Precedence of lines

CENTERING

The drawing must be centered within the work area of the paper or the border, if one is provided. A full 1 inch (25), regardless of the scale being used, should be placed between all views drawn in this text.

Figure 5-19 shows the procedure used to center a drawing within a specified work area.

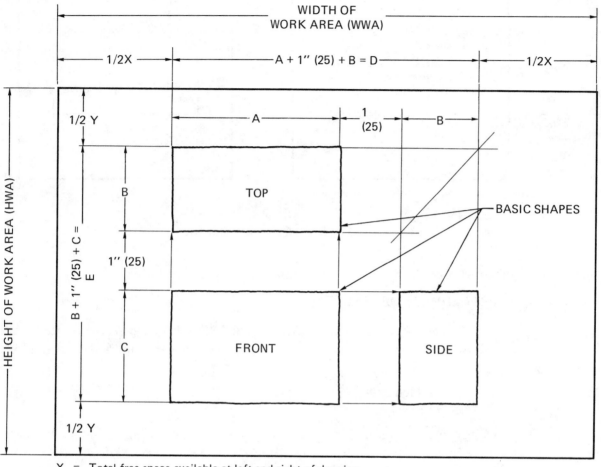

X = Total free space available at left and right of drawing
Y = Total free space available at top and bottom of drawing
D = Width of entire drawing, including 1" (25) between views
E = Height of entire drawing, including 1" (25) between views

Fig. 5-19 Centering sketch

The total width (D) of the drawing is determined by adding measurement A to measurement B and then adding 1 inch (25) for the distance between views. The total height (E) of the drawing is determined by adding B to C and then adding 1 inch (25) for the distance between views. The total height and width of the work area is found by measuring it directly from the paper.

To center the drawing horizontally, subtract D from the width of the work area. The answer represents the available free space. This free space (X) is divided by two. One half of X is placed to the right of the views, and one half of X is placed to the left of the views.

To center the drawing vertically, the same basic procedure is followed. Subtract E from the height of the work area, divide the answer (Y) by two, and place half of Y to the top of the drawing and half of Y to the bottom.

This centers the drawing within the work area. Regardless of the drawing size or available work area, the same process is followed each time a drawing is to be centered.

INTERSECTIONS

Figure 5-20 illustrates the basic methods of showing intersections on a drawing. When two lines intersect, the drawing must show if they touch or pass by each other. Note how these lines are drawn in the figure.

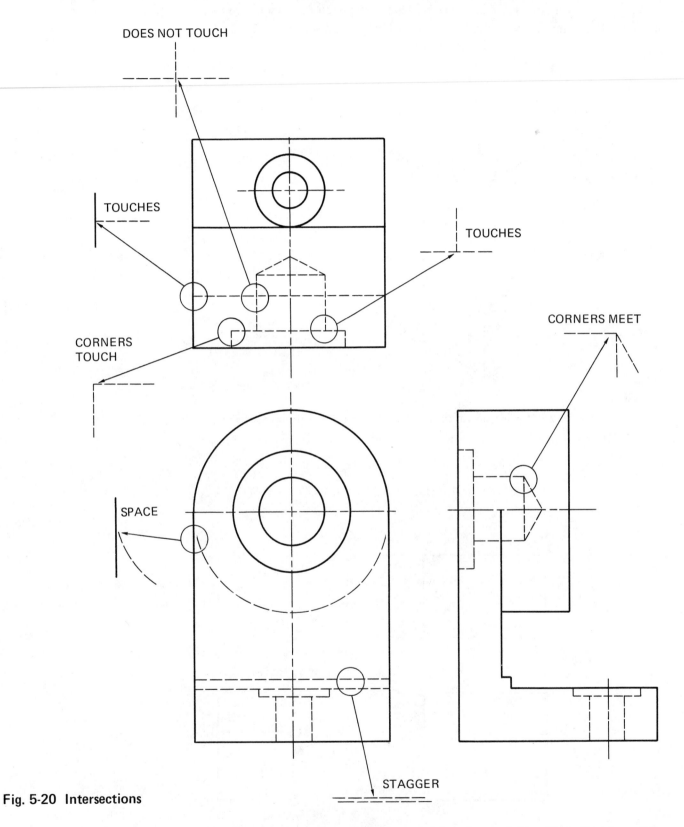

Fig. 5-20 Intersections

Hidden lines are drawn medium weight, figure 5-21. Note the size of the dash and space in the illustration.

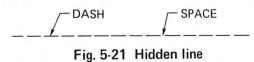

Fig. 5-21 Hidden line

NUMBERING DRAWINGS

Numbering each corner of the more difficult drawings makes them easier to visualize and draw. Think of a drawing as a group of points joined together by lines. If the ends of the lines can be found, all that has to be done to complete a drawing is to connect the ends. Once the ends have been found and numbered in one view, the same can be done in other views by projection, figure 5-22.

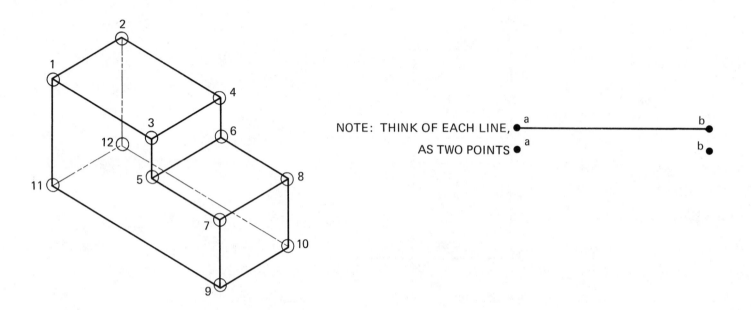

NOTE: THINK OF EACH LINE, AS TWO POINTS

Fig. 5-22 An isometric drawing with each corner numbered and ends connected.

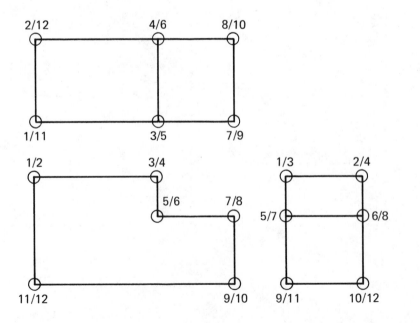

A three-view drawing of the isometric drawing above (Fig. 5-22) with each corner numbered and ends connected.

PROJECTING NUMBERS

Given:

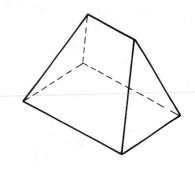

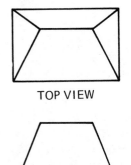

TOP VIEW

FRONT VIEW

Fig. 5-23

Step 1. Assign a number to each corner of the top view of figure 5-24. Project those points down to the front view. Number the points in the front view.

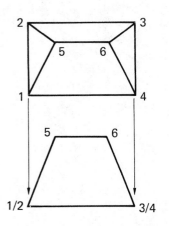

Fig. 5-24

Step 2. Project the points across from the front view, and the same points from the top view, over to the 45-degree line. Where the lines meet the 45-degree line, project down to the side view. The points are located where these lines cross. Number all points.

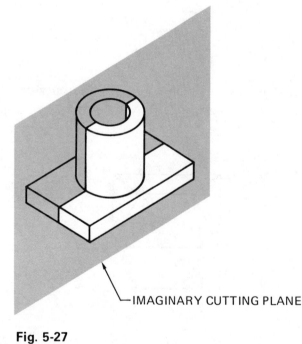

ISOMETRIC VIEW

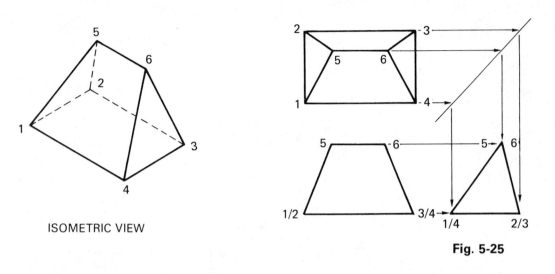

Fig. 5-25

Cutting-Plane Line

Cutting-plane lines are imaginary cuts through the object. Think of a saw cutting through an object. The cutting-plane line is represented by a thick, dark line, figure 5-26.

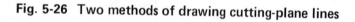

EITHER ——————————— OR ——————————————

NOTE LENGTH OF LINES, SIZE OF SPACE, AND THICKNESS

Fig. 5-26 Two methods of drawing cutting-plane lines

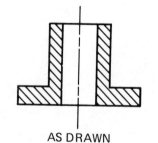

DIRECTION OF SIGHT
Fig. 5-28

IMAGINARY CUTTING PLANE

Fig. 5-27

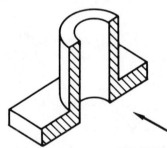

AS DRAWN
Fig. 5-29

To better visualize this, figure 5-27 shows an imaginary cutting plane passing through an object. In figure 5-28, the object has been cut in half. The arrow shows the surface which will be drawn as a cut section drawing. The completed cut section drawing is shown in figure 5-29.

Figure 5-30(a) illustrates the object with an imaginary cutting plane passing through it. Figure 5-30(b) shows that the cutting-plane line is drawn through the object. In this case, the plane cuts downward from the top view so the cutting-plane line is shown in the top view. Arrows are placed at the ends of the cutting line and are faces in the direction of sight. What remains after the object has been cut is projected into the front view and shown sectioned, as illustrated in figure 5-30(c).

In figure 5-30 (c), the cutting plane is passed through from front to back. The bottom piece remains. The cut section line, therefore, is located in the front view, the direction of sight is downward, and the top view is shown as the sectioned view.

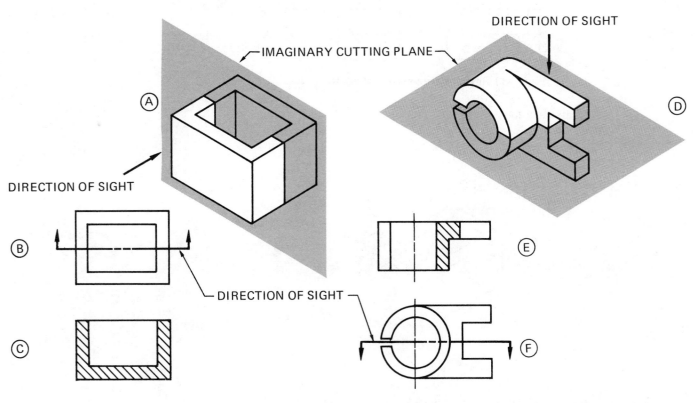

Fig. 5-30 Cut-section drawing examples

Section Lining

Section lining shows where the cutting plane passes, revealing the material used to make the object. Section lines are dark, thin lines drawn at a 45-degree angle and uniformly spaced by eye, figure 5-31. Though there are various symbols to represent specific kinds of materials, they are seldom used. Specific materials are identified by name on the detail drawing or parts list for the object.

If the cut object is made up of two pieces, both cut sections are drawn at a 45-degree angle, but in opposite directions, as shown in figure 5-32.

If the cut object is made up of three pieces, the cut section lines are drawn at 45-degree angles as shown in figure 5-33.

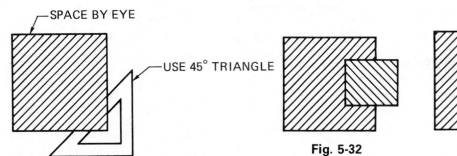

Fig. 5-31 Section lining

Fig. 5-32

Fig. 5-33

KINDS OF SECTION VIEWS

Full Section

A *full section* is simply a regular view that has been cut all the way through. All hidden lines can now be seen so they become visible lines. In figure 5-34, the hidden lines in the front view are not easy to visualize. A full section is therefore made of the object.

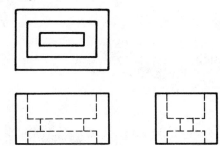

Fig. 5-34 Regular three-view drawing

Step 1. Add an imaginary cutting plane.

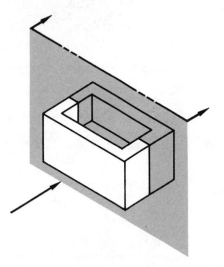

Step 2. Think of the front view as it would appear cut.

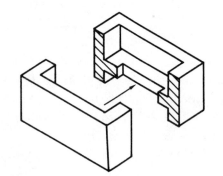

Step 3. Draw the views.

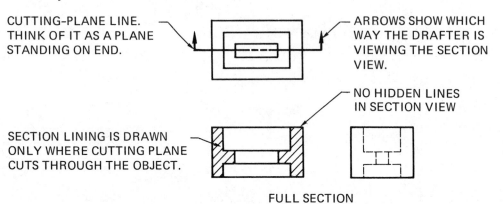

CUTTING-PLANE LINE. THINK OF IT AS A PLANE STANDING ON END.

ARROWS SHOW WHICH WAY THE DRAFTER IS VIEWING THE SECTION VIEW.

NO HIDDEN LINES IN SECTION VIEW

SECTION LINING IS DRAWN ONLY WHERE CUTTING PLANE CUTS THROUGH THE OBJECT.

FULL SECTION

Half Section

In a *half-section drawing,* the object is cut only halfway through and a quarter is removed. A half section shows the inside of the object as well as the outside in the same view. This type of section is best used when the object is *symmetrical;* that is, the same shape and size on both sides of the center line. To make a half section drawing of figure 5-35:

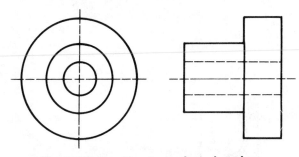

Fig. 5-35 Regular two-view drawing

Step 1. Add an imaginary cutting-plane line.

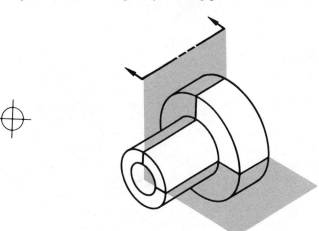

Step 2. Think of the right-side view as it would appear cut.

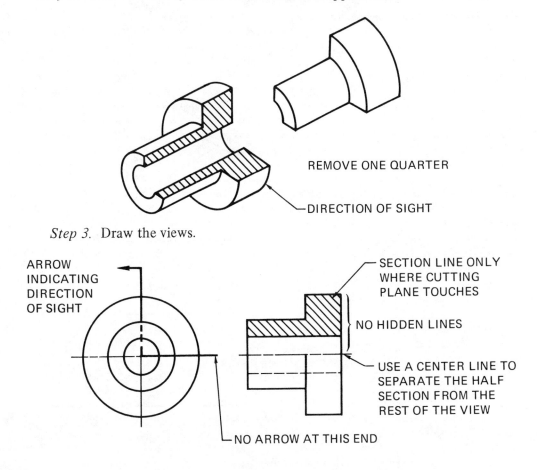

REMOVE ONE QUARTER

DIRECTION OF SIGHT

Step 3. Draw the views.

ARROW INDICATING DIRECTION OF SIGHT

SECTION LINE ONLY WHERE CUTTING PLANE TOUCHES

NO HIDDEN LINES

USE A CENTER LINE TO SEPARATE THE HALF SECTION FROM THE REST OF THE VIEW

NO ARROW AT THIS END

Broken-Out Section

Sometimes only a small area needs to be sectioned in order to make the interior of an object easy to understand. In this case a *broken-out section* is used. The broken line is put in freehand and is made visible-line thickness. The cutting-plane line can be omitted because it coincides with the center line. Figure 5-36 illustrates the procedure used to make a broken-out section drawing.

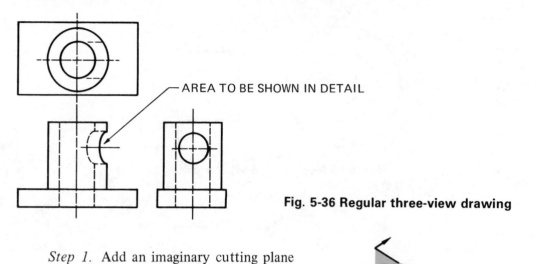

AREA TO BE SHOWN IN DETAIL

Fig. 5-36 Regular three-view drawing

Step 1. Add an imaginary cutting plane through the area to be broken out.

Step 2. Think of that area as it would appear broken out.

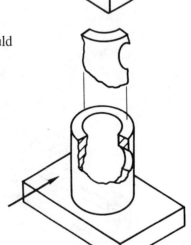

Step 3. Draw the views. No cutting lines are required.

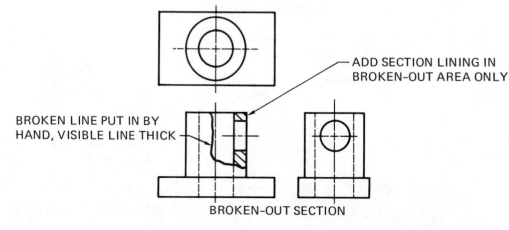

ADD SECTION LINING IN BROKEN-OUT AREA ONLY

BROKEN LINE PUT IN BY HAND, VISIBLE LINE THICK

BROKEN-OUT SECTION

Offset Section

An *offset section* is done as a full section and shows details that do not appear in a true full-section drawing. The cutting line is bent at 90 degrees to pick up important details. The bends of the cutting lines are not projected to or shown in other views. To make an offset section of figure 5-37:

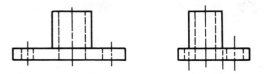

Fig. 5-37 Regular three-view drawing

Step 1. Add an imaginary cutting-plane line. Have it bend at 90-degree turns so it passes through the important features that must be described.

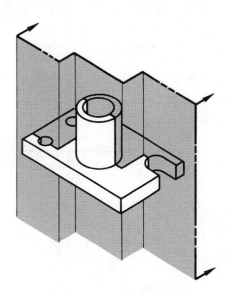

Step 2. Think of the view as it would appear cut.

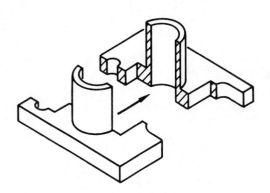

Step 3. Draw the views. The right side is not needed. Section only where the cutting-plane line cuts through the object.

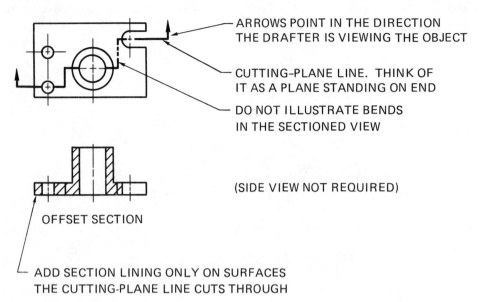

ARROWS POINT IN THE DIRECTION
THE DRAFTER IS VIEWING THE OBJECT

CUTTING-PLANE LINE. THINK OF
IT AS A PLANE STANDING ON END

DO NOT ILLUSTRATE BENDS
IN THE SECTIONED VIEW

(SIDE VIEW NOT REQUIRED)

OFFSET SECTION

ADD SECTION LINING ONLY ON SURFACES
THE CUTTING-PLANE LINE CUTS THROUGH

Removed Section

A *removed section* is the same as a revolved section except, as the name implies, the section is "removed" and drawn away from the object. Study the examples in figure 5-38. Note how they are called out; i.e., section A-A.

REMOVED SECTION

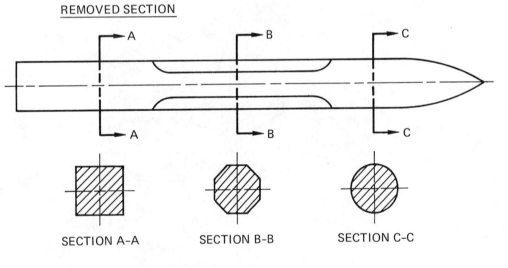

SECTION A-A   SECTION B-B   SECTION C-C

Fig. 5-38

Removed Section

Figure 5-39 is a sample of a removed section of a typical stair layout. This illustrates details and dimensions that would be impossible to illustrate in the usual multiviews.

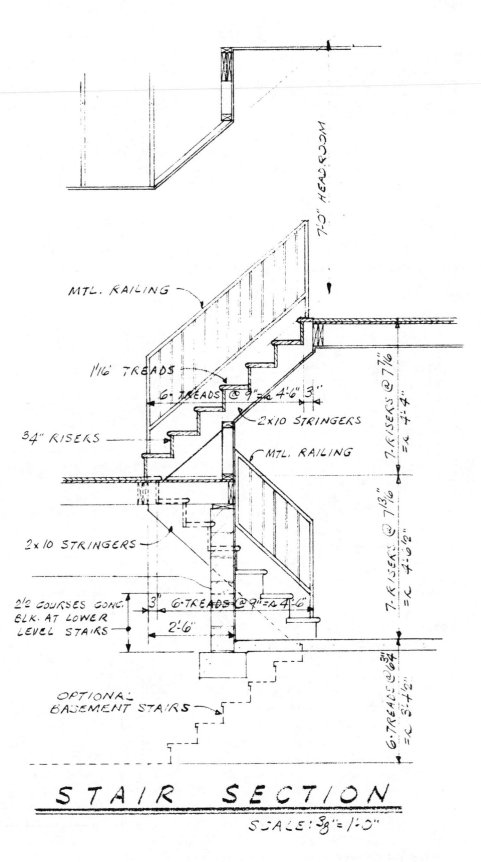

STAIR SECTION

SCALE: 3/8" = 1'-0"

Fig. 5-39

CONVENTIONAL BREAKS

Long objects, such as the pipe illustrated in figure 5-40, would appear very long if the entire length is drawn. Usually such objects are drawn to scale and shortened by using a *conventional break*.

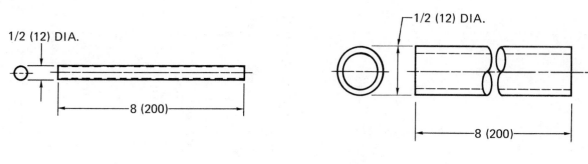

1/2 (12) DIA.

8 (200)

1/4 SIZE

NOTE HOW SMALL THE PIPE APPEARS.

1/2 (12) DIA.

8 (200)

FULL SIZE

NOTE HOW IT IS EASY TO UNDERSTAND

Fig. 5-40 Use of conventional breaks

Other Breaks

Study figure 5-41. It illustrates other methods of drawing breaks.

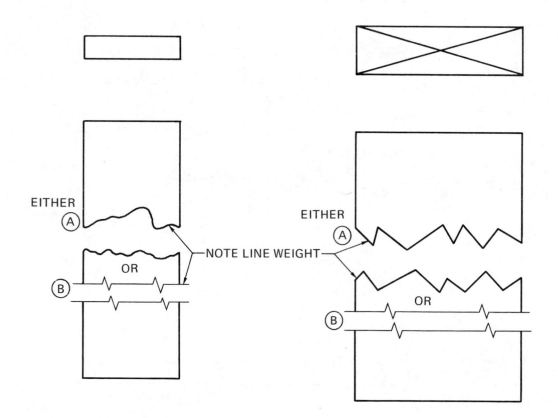

EITHER
Ⓐ

OR
Ⓑ

NOTE LINE WEIGHT

EITHER
Ⓐ

OR
Ⓑ

Fig. 5-41 Other types of break lines

Many objects have inclined surfaces that are not parallel to the regular planes of projection. To show its true shape, an auxiliary view must be drawn.

An *auxiliary view* has a line of sight that is perpendicular to the inclined surface. Auxiliary views are always projected from the inclined surface at an angle of 90 degrees with the fold line. Auxiliary views give:

- True size

- True shape (or true angle)

- Points in order to draw other views

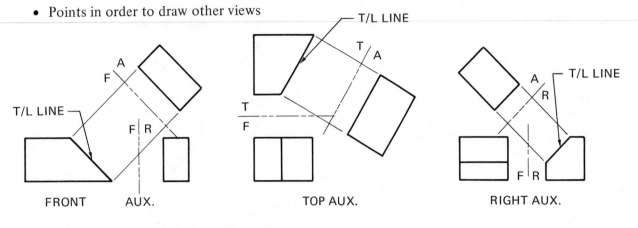

Fig. 5-42 Examples of auxiliary views

Projecting Auxiliary Views

In the front view of figure 5-43, line a/d is true length. Using descriptive geometry to find the true length line, draw a fold line parallel to the true length line. In the next view it will be the true shape and size. Do not forget to skip a view. In this case, the front view is skipped.

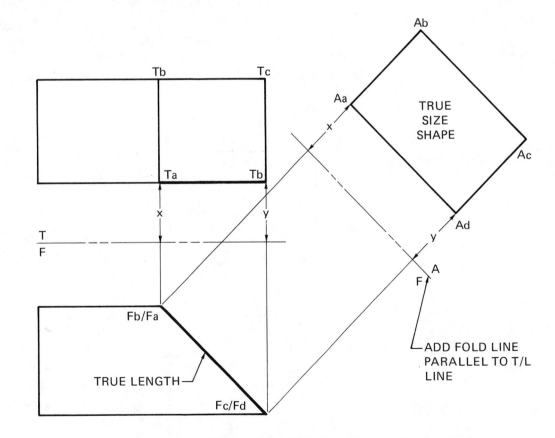

Fig. 5-43 Projecting an auxiliary view from the front view

AUXILIARY VIEW USED TO DRAW OTHER VIEWS

Auxiliary views are sometimes used to complete other views. Study the problem in figure 5-44. Follow steps one through four to complete the front view, figure 5-45.

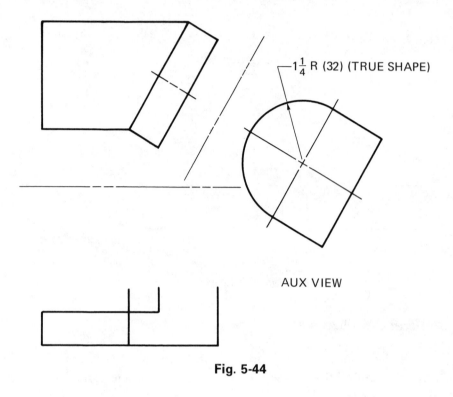

Fig. 5-44

Step 1. In the auxiliary view, divide the arc into equal segments of 30 degrees from the center.

Step 2. Project these points to the top view.

Step 3. From the top view, project these points downward.

Step 4. Using descriptive geometry methods, locate each point in the front view.

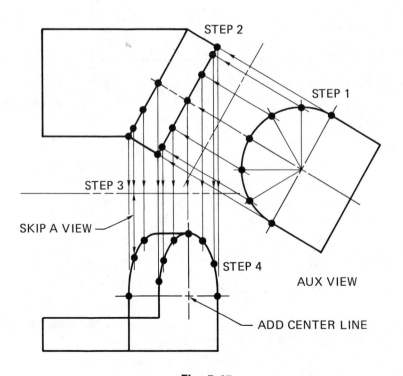

Fig. 5-45

UNIT 6

DESCRIPTIVE GEOMETRY

Descriptive geometry is a strict step-by-step procedure used to layout true shape, true size, true angle(s), true distances and many other engineering functions.

NOTATIONS

- Every view and point is labeled on a drawing by *notations*.

- All points in space are called out in lowercase letters.
  Examples: a, b, c, d, e, etc.

- Each view is called out in uppercase letters..
  Example: F = Front view   L = Left side view
  T = Top view   A = Auxiliary views
  R = Right side view   B-Z = Any other views

FOLD LINES

A *fold line* indicates a 90-degree change in direction. Fold lines are illustrated by a thin, black line, figure 6-1. Figure 6-2 illustrates a regular three-view drawing without fold lines. Figure 6-3 shows a regular three-view drawing with fold lines.

- Combine uppercase letters with lowercase letters to pinpoint a point on a particular view.
  Example: "aT" = This means point "a" in the top view.

- Combine two or more points to locate a line.
  Example: Line "aT/bT" means line "a-b" in the top view.

Note when using descriptive geometry, the 45-degree projection line is not used.

Make notations at every fold line to identify the view, figure 6-4.

Line a-b is called out in each and every view, figure 6-5. Note that lower case letters are used.

FOLD LINE

Fig. 6-1

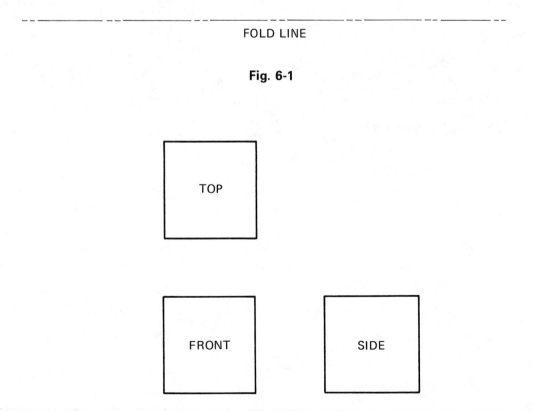

TOP

FRONT   SIDE

Fig. 6-2

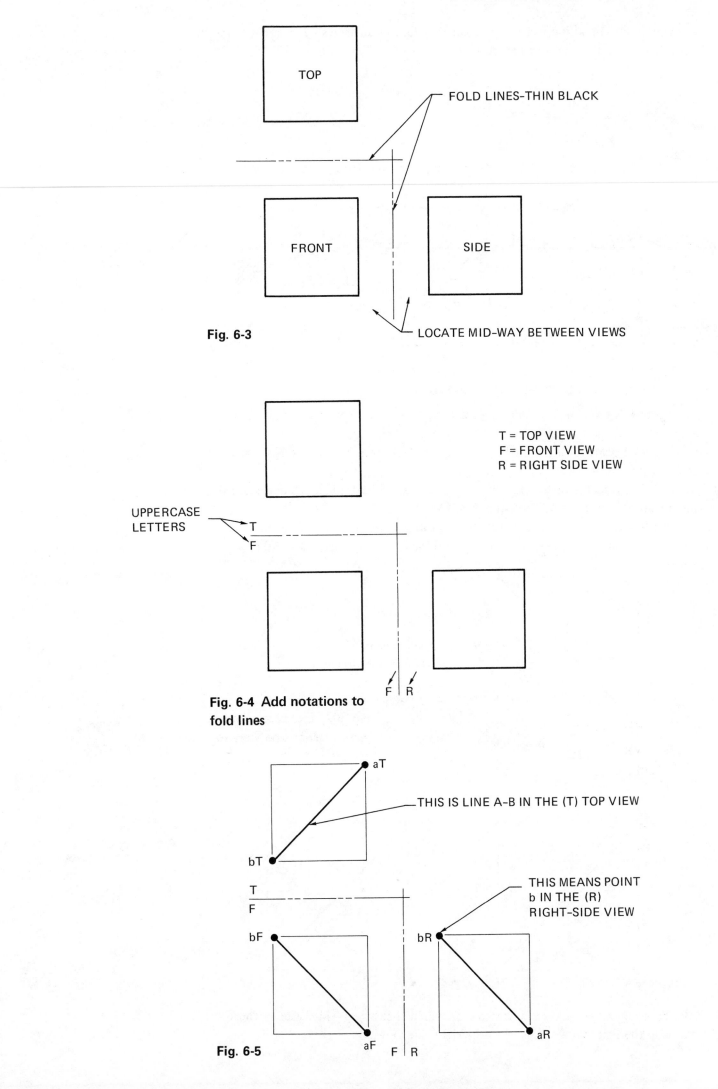

Fig. 6-3

FOLD LINES–THIN BLACK

LOCATE MID-WAY BETWEEN VIEWS

T = TOP VIEW
F = FRONT VIEW
R = RIGHT SIDE VIEW

UPPERCASE LETTERS

Fig. 6-4 Add notations to fold lines

THIS IS LINE A–B IN THE (T) TOP VIEW

THIS MEANS POINT b IN THE (R) RIGHT-SIDE VIEW

Fig. 6-5

Any point on a line must appear on that line in all views. Do not use 45-degree projection lines. Project 90 degrees from all fold lines, figure 6-6.

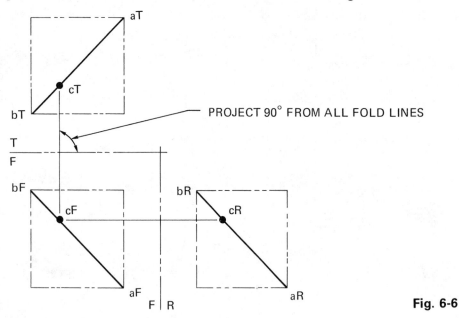

PROJECT 90° FROM ALL FOLD LINES

Fig. 6-6

PROJECTING FROM ONE VIEW TO ANOTHER

Figure 6-7 gives an example of projecting from one view to another. In this case, a right-side view is projected.

Step 1. Locate point a in the top view and measure how far it is from the fold line (dimension "x").

Step 2. Project a to the front view and across the fold line at 90 degrees, the same distance from the fold line (dimension "x").

Step 3. Do the same with point b in the top view. Project to the front and project across the same distance from the fold line. Always project at 90 degrees from the fold lines.

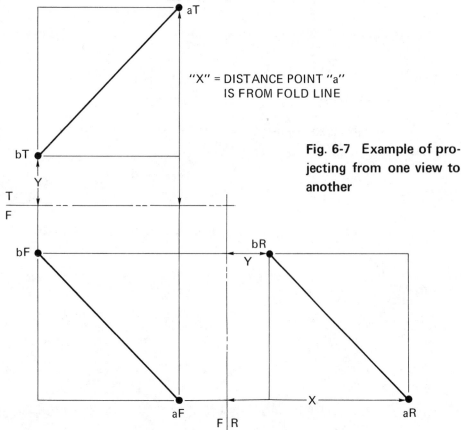

"X" = DISTANCE POINT "a"
IS FROM FOLD LINE

Fig. 6-7 Example of projecting from one view to another

Rule To Remember: Always skip a view when measuring. Measure in the top view, skip the front view, transfer to the right-side view.

PROJECTING TRUE LENGTH

To find true length (T/L), an *auxiliary view* must be added. An auxiliary view is drawn from the front, top, or right view, figure 6-8.

To draw an auxiliary view:

1. Start with the regular views.
2. Add fold lines between views.
3. Label each point and each view on the fold line.
4. Draw another fold line parallel to any one of the lines in any view.
5. In the next view, it will appear as true length.
6. Remember to label all points.

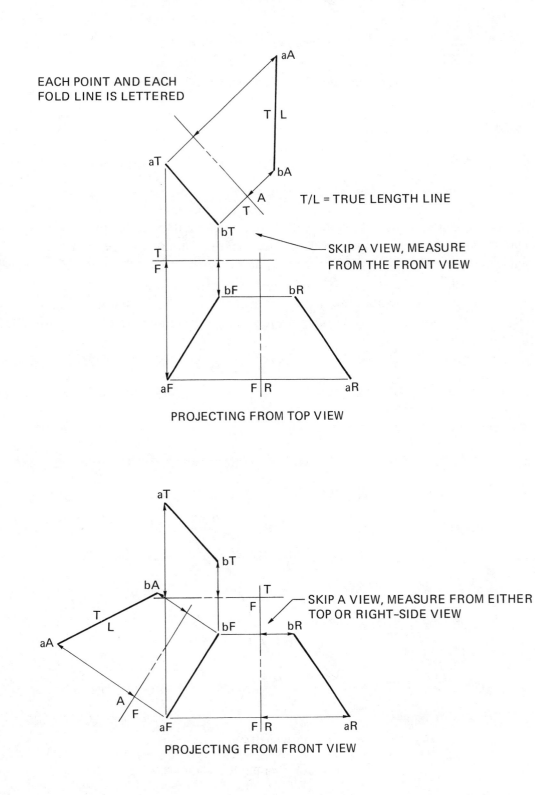

EACH POINT AND EACH
FOLD LINE IS LETTERED

T/L = TRUE LENGTH LINE

SKIP A VIEW, MEASURE
FROM THE FRONT VIEW

PROJECTING FROM TOP VIEW

SKIP A VIEW, MEASURE FROM EITHER
TOP OR RIGHT-SIDE VIEW

PROJECTING FROM FRONT VIEW

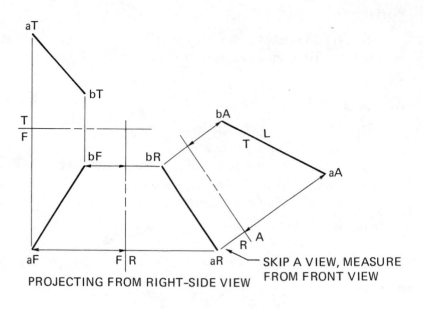

PROJECTING FROM RIGHT-SIDE VIEW — SKIP A VIEW, MEASURE FROM FRONT VIEW

Fig. 6-8 Explanation for projecting true length lines

POINT VIEW

Lay a pencil on the desk and look directly down at it. You are looking at its true length. Now pick up the pencil, close one eye, and look directly at the lead end of the pencil. Notice that the pencil is no longer a line. It is now a point. This is the *point view* of the pencil. Notice also that the pencil was turned exactly 90 degrees from its true length to the point view.

Many times the point view of a line must be drawn. To draw the point view, figure 6-9, find true length, draw a fold line perpendicular (⊥) to the true length line, and draw the point view in the next view. Label each point. Skip a view to find the X length.

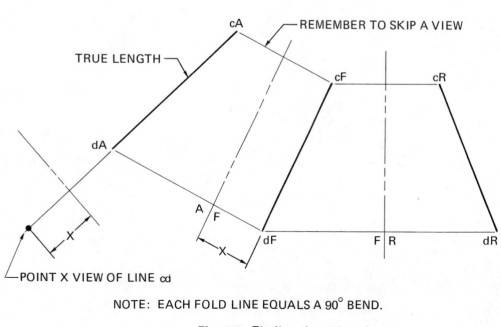

NOTE: EACH FOLD LINE EQUALS A 90° BEND.

Fig. 6-9 Finding the point view

PLANE SURFACES

A *plane surface* is a boundary which is connected by three or more points. The same steps are used to find a surface as were used to locate points in various views.

For example, given figure 6-10, draw triangle abc (△ abc) in the right-side view.

Figure 6-11 shows how to construct the right-side view. Remember to always skip a view; in this case, the front view.

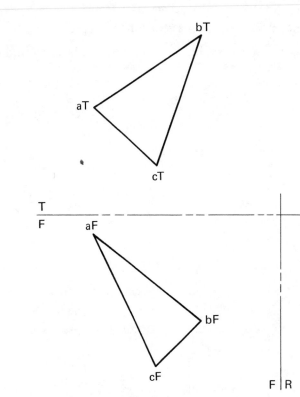

Fig. 6-10

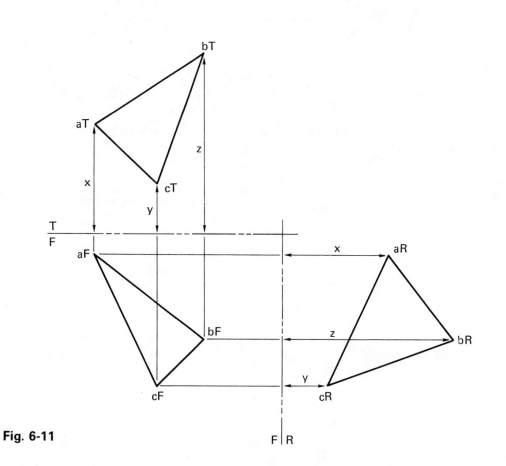

Fig. 6-11

EDGE VIEW

An *edge view* of a surface is the view one would see if the plane surface was turned on end and looked at in that position. To find an edge view, figure 6-12:

1. On any view, draw a line parallel to the fold line between views and through a point. In figure 6-12, a line is drawn in the front view, through point c, and parallel to the fold line.
2. Find the same line in the next view. It will be true length in this view.
3. Add a fold line perpendicularly to the true length line. The point view will be found in the next view as shown.
4. Add the other points to form a straight line representing the edge view.

NOTE: The surface now appears as a line and will be used later to find true shape.

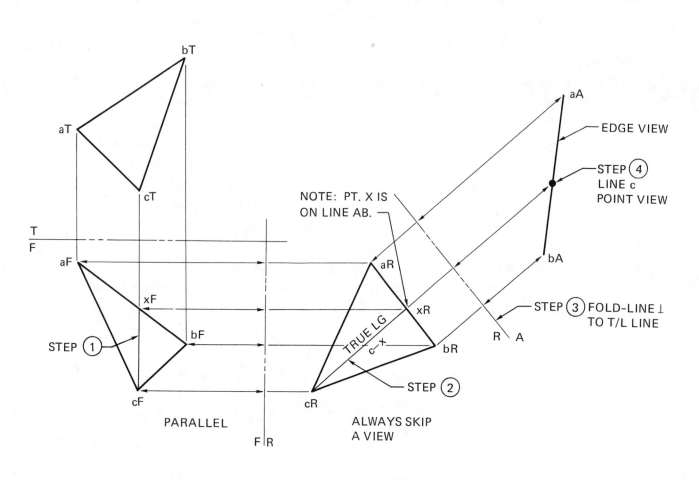

Fig. 6-12 Locating an edge view

TRUE SHAPE

The edge view must be found before drawing the *true shape*, figure 6-13. Use the same steps as those to find the edge view on page 84 and add:

5. Add fold lines parallel to the edge view.

6. In the next view the true shape will be 90 degrees from edge view. Do not forget to skip a view to get the distance.

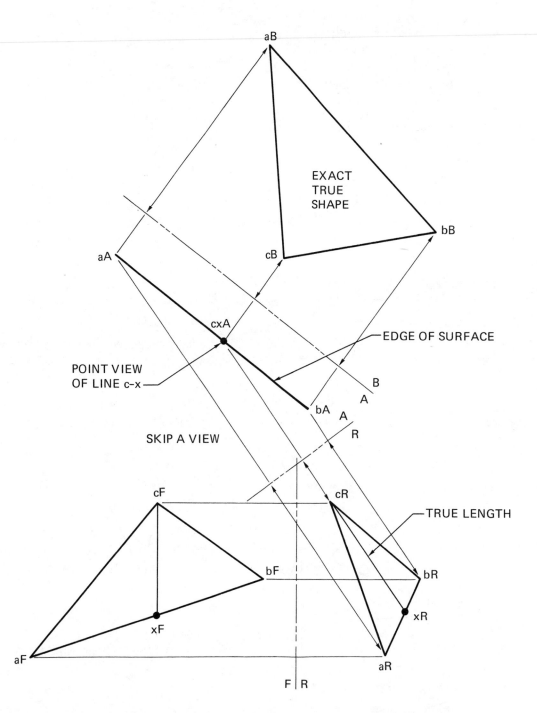

TAKE A SHEET OF PAPER AND HOLD IT UP SO ONLY THE EDGE OF IT CAN BE SEEN. ROTATE IT 90 DEGREES TO GET THE TRUE SHAPE.

Fig. 6-13 Projecting true shape

ANGLES BETWEEN TWO SURFACES

Descriptive geometry has other uses besides illustrating true shape and size. These are shown on the next few pages. Most of the same steps are used; i.e., find true length, point view, and so on. The exact angle between these surfaces must be known.

Follow these steps in order to find the angles between two surfaces, figure 6-14:

1. Add fold lines parallel to the fold.
2. Draw true length of the fold.
3. Find the point view of the fold.
4. Bring the other points along (c and d) and measure the angle between the edge view.

Always work accurately and add all notations.

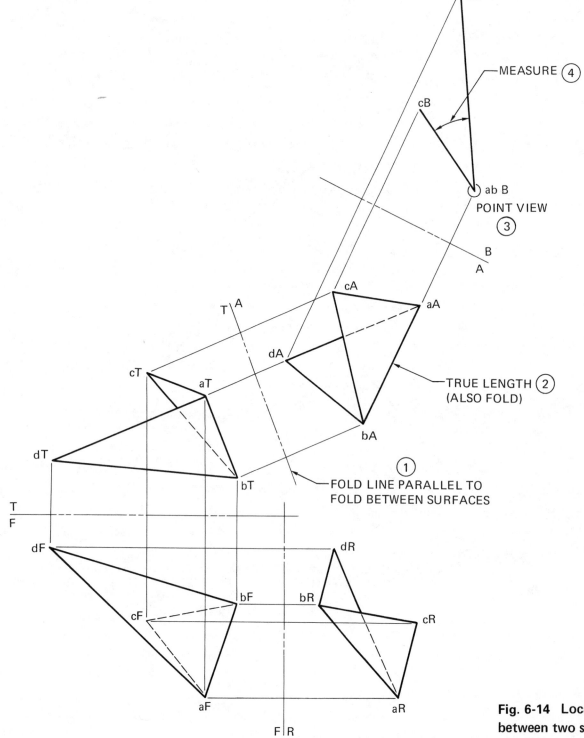

Fig. 6-14 Locating angles between two surfaces

VISIBILITY OF LINES

Visibility of lines is done by inspection and reasoning. Line aT-dT (looking into the top view, arrows 1) is closest to the fold line and appears solid in the front view. Line dT/cT is also solid. Line xT/dT is visible. Line xT/aT is between xT/bT. Therefore, in the front view, bT/xT is a hidden line. Look in one view and reason what line is closest to the fold line. In the next view it will be solid. Study figure 6-15 and apply the same reasoning to figure 6-16.

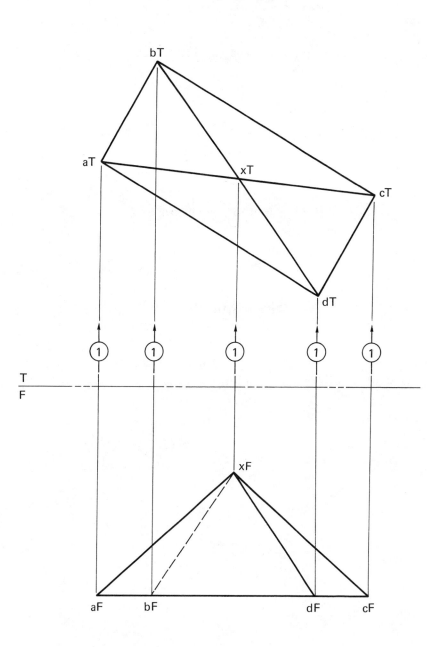

Fig. 6-15 Explanation for visibility of lines

Figure 6-16 shows two pipes: a-b and c-d. In the top view, which pipe is in front of the other? In the front view, which pipe is in front of the other?

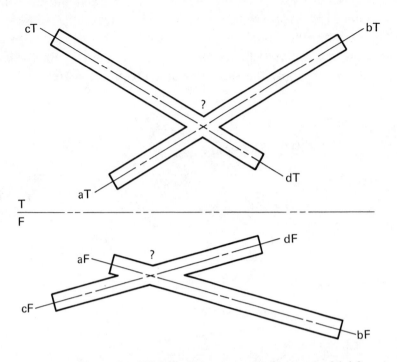

Fig. 6-16 Which pipe crosses in front of which?

Step 1. Starting from the front view where the pipes cross, draw a light line up to the top view, figure 6-17(A). Where pipe a-b crosses pipe c-d in the top view, line a-b is closer to the fold line than line c-d. Line a-b is closer to the fold line than c-d, therefore, and is a solid line in the front view.

Step 2. Use the same method for the other crossover. From the top view draw a light line down to the front view, figure 6-17(B). Where pipe a-b crosses c-d in the front view, pipe c-d is closer to the fold line than a-b. Line c-d, therefore, is in front of a-b and is a solid line in the top view.

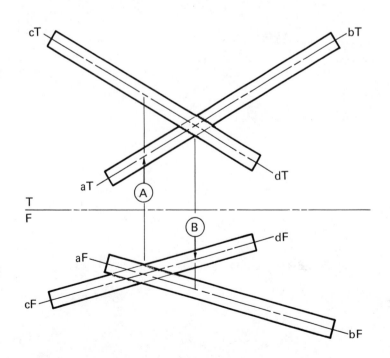

Fig. 6-17 (1) Line a-b is in front of line c-d in the front view.
(2) Line c-d is in front of line a-b in the top view.

UNIT 7

HOUSE CONSIDERATIONS

FACTORS INFLUENCING THE STYLE OF A HOUSE

A house is usually the largest single purchase an individual makes. The house will influence the living and working habits of everyone residing in it. Many factors determine the style of a house:

1. Surrounding architecture is an important consideration. To build a contemporary style house in a quaint village, where early American style is prevalent, could be awkward.

2. The surrounding countryside is a factor. The house should be designed to be built into and become part of the existing landscape.

3. The shape of the plot influences style. It is not wise, for instance, to build a long ranch style house on a narrow lot.

4. The contour of the plot must be considered. A split-level house blends into and becomes part of a lot that is located on a hillside.

5. The number of rooms is determined by what a family can afford. A house with less than three bedrooms, however, should be avoided as it is usually hard to sell.

6. The shape of the house reflects style and cost. If cost is important, a house with a square floor plan can be built at the lowest cost. A rectangular plan is also cheaper to build than others, but does not have the interesting appearance of L-, T-, or C-shaped plans. These, of course, cost more because of the extra corners and special roof construction.

7. The number of floors affects both style and cost. The average house has either one, one and one-half, or two floors.

   a. *One floor* homes have no stairs other than stairs to a basement or fold-down stairs to the attic. This style is economical in a small house, but expensive in a large house.

   b. *One and one-half floor* homes have all the advantages of a two-story house except there is less wall space.

   c. *Two floor* homes usually have the sleeping area on the upper floor and the dining, living, and cooking areas on the lower floor.

8. Always design for eventual expansion. Plan so a room or garage can be added. Using available attic or basement space for further expansion at a later date is cheaper than building additions to a home.

9. Zoning influences the style of a house. Zoning may limit the position, cubage, area, and height of a house on a given lot. Each city, county, and state has its own rules and regulations; thus, a study into each should be made before much designing is done.

10. In view of today's fuel shortages and spiraling costs, a house should be designed with energy-saving features such as:

   a. Compact rectangular plan

   b. Lower ceilings of 7 1/2 feet

   c. Fireplace that uses an air circulation method

   d. Limited use of or no windows facing north

   e. More windows facing south to pick up winter sunlight

   f. Triple-glazed windows

   g. 2 x 6 wall studs on 24-inch centers allow 6 inches of insulation to be added, such as insulation of R-19 in exposed walls and R-38 in ceilings

   h. Vapor barriers of polyethylene film behind exterior drywalls, beneath attic insulation, and above crawl space insulation.

   i. Water-saving fixtures and high-efficiency applicances

   j. Heating systems that can be shut off and zoned for areas not in use

Style dictates how many floors a house must have, whether to use a symmetrical design, the material used on exterior walls and roof, the type of windows and doors, and even the shade or color combinations. The style of a house should be in harmony with the people who own and live in it. Their furniture and room decorations should also agree with the house style.

HOUSE STYLES

There are two major kinds of house styles; traditional (conventional) and contemporary (modern).

Traditional architecture includes early American and colonial homes. Such basic designs as the simple Cape Cod, the saltbox, and garrison are some of the first American styles. Other popular styles are the southern colonial, dutch colonial, and french colonial. Each style has its own special features, figures 7-1 through 7-6.

Fig. 7-1 The traditional saltbox has two stories in front, one in the back, and a distinctive roof with a long rear slope. Adding dormers to the rear slope is a contemporary modification, however

Fig. 7-2 The Cape Cod is a compact house that usually has a central chimney and a steep gable roof

Fig. 7-3 The traditional style garrison house has a second story that overhangs first in the front elevation

Fig. 7-4 The southern colonial home is characterized by front columns and a giant portico

Fig. 7-5 The French colonial house has a mansard roof

Fig. 7-6 The Dutch colonial house has a gambrel roof with flared eaves

Fig. 7-7 This contemporary ranch home is an L-shape design

Contemporary architecture includes the ranch, raised ranch, split-level, and free-form styles, figures 7-7 through 7-10. These can be of various shapes, such as L, T, U, rectangular, etc. "Form follows function," a phrase coined by the 19th century American architect Louis Henri Sullivan and utilized by Frank Lloyd Wright, is often the case in contemporary architecture. This means that the function or purpose of a structure dictates how that structure will look.

Fig. 7-8 A split-level house has a main level, an upper level, and a lower level and is generally designed for a sloping or hilly lot

Fig. 7-9 The front entrance of a raised ranch opens onto a landing with stairs leading to the upper and lower levels

Fig. 7-10 A free-form style of contemporary architecture

COST ESTIMATE

Owners usually want to build as large a house as their salaries can afford. There are two commonly used methods of quickly estimating house cost. One method is based on the *cubage volume* of the building, the other on the *floor area*. In each of these methods the estimate is based on the average cost per unit (cubic foot or square foot).

Calculations by cubage volume include all enclosed areas, such as the garage, basement, attic, dormers, chimneys, and enclosed porches.

Calculations by area include all enclosed areas, but some are reduced in the following proportions:

Enclosed porch	2/3
Open porch	1/2
Unfinished basement	1/2
Finished basement—full area	full rate
Garage	2/3
Carport	1/2

The *unit cost* of a house by cubage or area varies considerably from one location to another and even from one year to another. Also, a small house costs more than a large one since some expenses, such as the heating plan, remain almost the same regardless of the size of the house.

Cost is the major consideration that influences all other factors when building a house, figure 7-11.

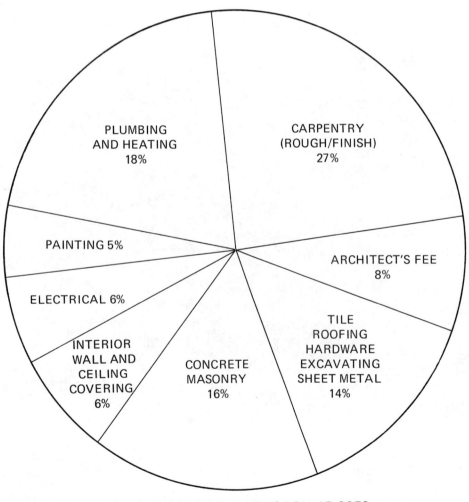

WHERE THE HOME BUILDER'S DOLLAR GOES

Fig. 7-11 Cost breakdown of a house, excluding land costs

To illustrate the effect of the number of floors and plan shape of the house on the total house cost, compare the two houses in figure 7-12. Each house has an identical floor area. The only difference between the two houses is the shape and the number of floors.

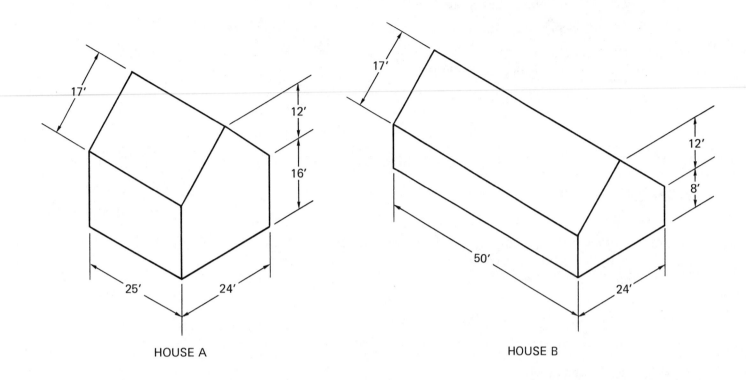

HOUSE A   HOUSE B

Fig. 7-12 Two homes of equal floor area, but different overall shapes

House A is a two-floor house with 25′ x 24′ (600 square feet) of floor area on each floor, giving a total of 1200 square feet. Its plan is nearly square. House B is a one-floor house with a floor area of 50′ x 24′ or 1200 square feet. Its plan is rectangular.

SURFACE	AREA	
	House A	*House B*
Front and rear elevations	800 sq. ft.	800 sq. ft.
End elevations	1056 sq. ft.	672 sq. ft.
Roof	850 sq. ft.	1700 sq. ft
Slab or cellar floor	600 sq. ft.	1200 sq. ft.
TOTAL	3306 sq. ft.	4372 sq. ft.

The total area of slab (or cellar floor), outside walls, and roof needed to enclose house A is 3306 square feet. The total area needed to enclose house B is 4372 square feet. There are some discrepancies in any comparison such as this. House A must have a heavier foundation and an additional interior floor. The increase in outside area needed to enclose house B over house A is:

$$\frac{(\text{area house B}) - (\text{area house A})}{(\text{area house A})} \times 100 = \% \text{ of increased outside area}$$

OR

$$\frac{4372 - 3306}{3306} \times 100 = 32\% \text{ more area}$$

FOUNDATION

The advantages of a basementless house are:

1. The furnace, water heater, laundry, workshop, storage area, and playroom are more convenient when located on the first floor.

2. A slight savings may be realized due to the lack of a celler floor and stairway.

The major advantage of a basement is:

1. The total cubage enclosed by a basement cannot be provided above ground at a comparable cost.

PLANNING THE HOUSE

The architect is responsible for designing a house which meets the needs of the client. In order to do this effectively, the needs and desires of the entire family must be evaluated. Information the architect must review before starting to design a family's home include:

- How much the family can afford to spend on a house
- The general style of house they wish to have (traditional or contemporary)
- The size of the family
- The ages of family members
- Recreational and social activities they enjoy
- The shape and slope of the lot where the house is to be built
- Building codes and deed restrictions
- The type of house desired, such as one-story, two-story, or split-level (governed by style)
- Basement, concrete slab floor, or crawl space
- The number and types of rooms
- Concrete block or poured concrete foundation
- Frame or masonry wall construction
- Type of room and roofing material
- Type of windows
- Type of heat and cooling
- Size of garage

Areas of the House

The house is designed around three major areas; eating, living, and sleeping areas. When designing a floor plan, these three areas of a house are usually separated.

The eating area must include food storage, room for food preparation, clean-up, and serving. All these activities involve the movement of food and dishes and a certain amount of odor and disorder. These activities should not conflict with other areas.

The living area includes noisy activities. The living room, family room, game room, or hobby area are typically found in this area of the floor plan. Noise, while a necessary part of living, would tend to disrupt those resting in the sleeping area.

The sleeping area includes all quiet activities. All bedrooms should be located in a quiet zone, isolated from the noisy areas of the house.

Bathrooms must be easily reached from all areas. It should not be necessary to disrupt activities in any area in order to reach a bathroom.

Program

Once the needs and desires of the family are evaluated, a list is made of everything that will go into the house. This is called a *program,* figure 7-13. This form should be filled out before starting a set of plans.

PROGRAM FORM

GENERAL REQUIREMENTS:

Overall Size _____

Approximate Cost _____

Style _____

Exterior Finish _____

Rooms _____

Number of floors _____

Basement _____

Orientation of building _____

ROOM REQUIREMENTS AND SIZE:

Living Room _____

Dining Room or Dining Area _____

Kitchen _____

Utility Room _____

Family Room _____

Master Bedroom _____

Other Bedrooms _____

Den or Study _____

Bathroom(s) _____

Laundry _____

Storage _____

Basement _____

Garage _____

Porch _____

MECHANICAL REQUIREMENTS:

Plumbing _____

Heating _____

Air Conditioning _____

Electrical _____

SITE:

Location _____

Size _____

Best View _____

Trees _____

Fig. 7-13 A sample program form

AREA PLANNING

Kitchen

Kitchens are the center of many activities, such as food preparation, dining, laundry, and sewing. They are usually arranged in I, L, U, and corridor shapes and planned around three appliances — the refrigerator, the sink, and the stove.

The sink is usually placed near the food storage area, the stove near the dining area, and the refrigerator near the sink. The total walking distance between the three major appliances should not be more than 22 feet. If it is, the kitchen plan should be revised.

Ideally, the kitchen should have at least 15 feet of free counter space in addition to the surfaces of the sink and stove. The sink and stove should have two or three feet of counter space on each side. Counter space beside the refrigerator is also helpful. If laundry facilities are located in the kitchen, they should not interfere with food preparation areas.

Dining Area

The dining area can be a separate room near the kitchen or part of the kitchen. It is sometimes combined with a family room or living room. The dining area must be large enough to hold the required furniture, including storage space for linen, china, and silverware. There must be enough space behind each chair so a person can be seated easily. The dining area should have a pleasant atmosphere. Large windows are helpful.

Living Area

The living area is one of the most frequently used rooms in a house if there is no family room. For some families the living room serves as a sitting room, music room, study, or library. It is even used as an extra bedroom for short periods of time. Usually this room faces the most pleasant outside view.

Large window areas are popular in living rooms. They do, however, reduce the amount of wall space available for furniture placement. The living room should have a central focal point, such as a fireplace or a picture window. Furniture is grouped for easy conversation. It is best if the front entrance does not open directly onto the living room as it makes part of the room the hall area, reduces the space available for living room use, and provides no protection from the weather.

Bedrooms

Bedrooms must be large enough to hold the required furniture. There must be aisles for traffic as well as space for dressing. Closets are essential. Windows provide proper ventilation. Some people prefer windows placed four to five feet above the floor for privacy and to free the space below the window for furniture placement.

Bedrooms must be entered from the hall. It should never be necessary to go through one bedroom to get to another. It is convenient to have a full or half bath off the master bedroom.

Closets

Closets are essential in every house for storage purposes. A closet near the front entrance provides a place to hang coats. Every bedroom should have a closet that is at least two feet deep with three to four feet of closet space per person using the bedroom. The bedroom closet should have a coat rod and at least one shelf above the rod. The average house needs a linen closet at least two feet long. It can be as shallow as one foot. Closet doors should open the entire width so space is not wasted. Sliding and folding doors are often used. A light in each closet is also desirable.

Bathrooms

Many houses have a bath and a half. Two full baths are common. A four-bedroom house should have two full baths. Houses built on several levels should have a bath or water closet on each level. It is economical to put two baths side by side. A bath which is backed up to a kitchen saves plumbing costs. A second bath can have a shower instead of a tub to save floor space. The door to the bath is placed so the water closet is not seen when the door is open. To prevent drafts, windows are not usually placed above a tub. It makes window and tub maintenance difficult too. The bath should be easily reached from other parts of the house without going through other rooms.

CIRCULATION PLAN

Another useful guide is a circulation plan of the house. This indicates how often members of the family travel from room to room, figure 7-14.

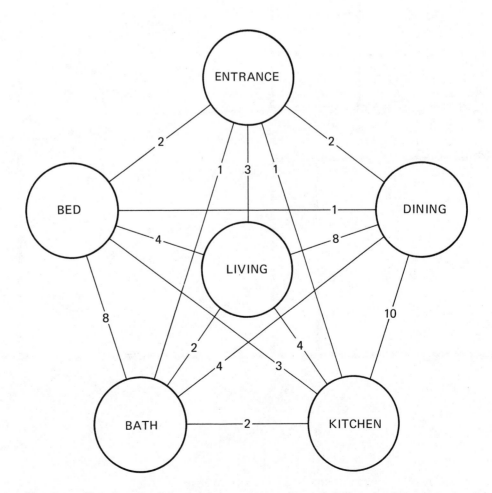

Fig. 7-14 Numbers indicate the average number of daily trips between rooms

The Traffic Pattern

A traffic pattern is a sketch that shows movement through the house. It should not be necessary, for instance, to walk through the living room to get to the bedroom area. Groceries should be carried directly into the kitchen. The stairs to the basement should be centrally located and reached easily from any area of the house.

The interior of a small house can appear larger by reducing the number of walls. This is called *open planning*. The kitchen and dining area, for instance, can be one large room. The family room and the laundry room can also be planned together.

Figure 7-15 shows a typical floor plan. The roughly sketched arrows indicate the traffic flow. If the traffic pattern shows that movement from room to room by family members is difficult, the floor plan must be redesigned.

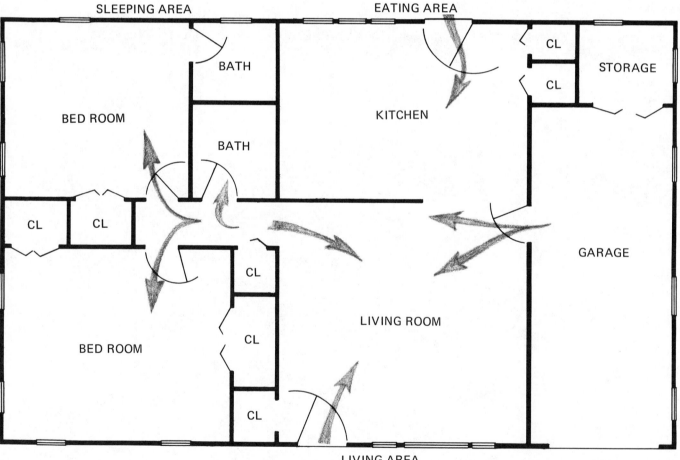

Fig. 7-15 Traffic pattern

HOUSE ORIENTATION

Orientation refers to the placement of the house on the lot and the location of rooms as related to the sun, wind, and view.

In the northern hemisphere, the south wall of the house receives the hot summer sun most of the day. The north wall receives very little sunlight. The west wall receives sun late in the day.

The living room can face east or south. If it faces south, it will be warmer in the evening. Generally, the garage, kitchen, or utility room is placed on the north side. Any room facing west will be hot in the summer. A porch or garage can be placed there to help break the sun's rays. It is important to shield the house on the hot sides. Sometimes a large roof overhang is used. Trees are also a good shield — evergreens on the north and deciduous on the south and west sides.

The direction of the prevailing wind must be considered. The summer breeze can be used to cool the bedroom area if it is located on that side of the house. Winter winds can be broken by placing the garage on that side.

APPROXIMATE ROOM SIZES

There are two major considerations in the design of the floor plan.

1. Each individual room must be designed so that it is pleasant, functional, and economical.

2. The rooms must be placed in correct relationship to each other.

This second consideration is similar to working out a jigsaw puzzle in which the pieces may change in shape and size to give various solutions.

Figure 7-16 gives minimum and average size suggestions for each room.

Room	Minimum	Average
Living room	12' x 16'	14' x 20'
Dining room	10' x 12'	12' x 13'
Dining area	7' x 9'	9' x 9'
Bedroom (master)	11½' x 12½'	12' x 14'
Bedroom (other)	9' x 11'	10' x 12'
Kitchen	7' x 10'	8' x 12'
Bathroom	5' x 7'	5½' x 8'
Unlived in basement	7' x 8'	8' x 11'
Hall width	3'	3½'
Closet	2' x 2'	2' x 4'
Garage (single)	9½' x 19'	12' x 20'
Garage (double)	19' x 19'	20' x 20'
Garage door (single)	8' x 6½'	9' x 7'
Garage door (double)	15' x 6½'	16' x 7'

Fig. 7-16 Suggested room sizes

UNIT 8

HOUSE CONSTRUCTION

HOUSE CONSTRUCTION PROCEDURES

This unit is designed to give the student an overall view of how a house is constructed. Note that the size and spacing given are examples only.

Step 1. Site at Start

The existing ground or *grade* at a construction site is first studied before any work begins. Water runoff and drainage, for instance, are very important, figure 8-1.

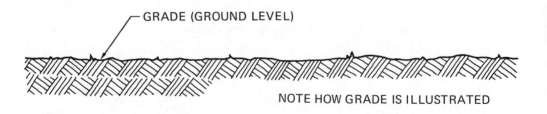

GRADE (GROUND LEVEL)

NOTE HOW GRADE IS ILLUSTRATED

Fig. 8-1 Ground level before construction begins

Step 2. Site Excavation

The cellar is excavated approximately 2'-0" to 3'-0" larger than the finished outside foundation wall, figure 8-2.

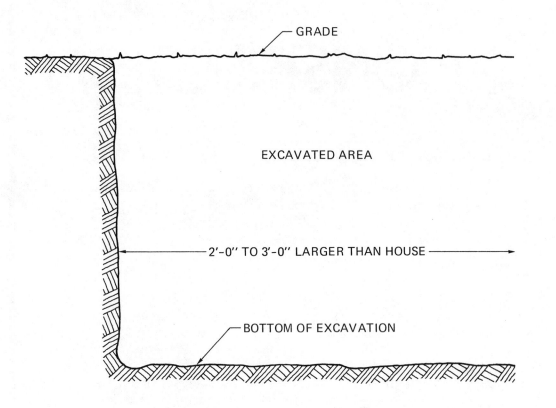

Fig. 8-2 Excavated area for foundation

Step 3. Footing with Key

A support for the foundation wall is called a *footing*. The footing has a 2 x 4 placed as shown in figure 8-3 while the concrete is still soft. After the concrete hardens, the 2 x 4 is removed leaving a cavity which is called a *key*. Notice the 2 x 10 form for the concrete. A key is used only if the foundation walls are to be poured concrete.

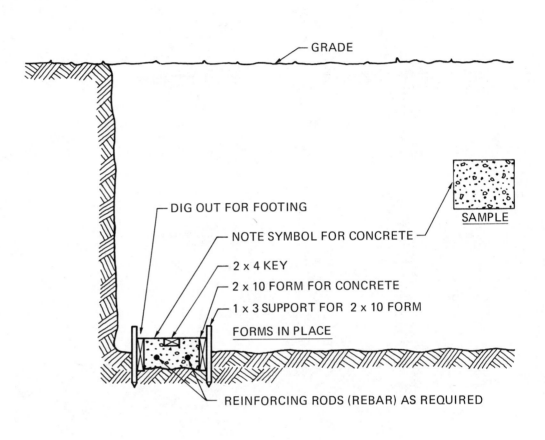

— GRADE

— DIG OUT FOR FOOTING

— NOTE SYMBOL FOR CONCRETE ⌐

SAMPLE

— 2 x 4 KEY

— 2 x 10 FORM FOR CONCRETE

— 1 x 3 SUPPORT FOR 2 x 10 FORM

FORMS IN PLACE

— REINFORCING RODS (REBAR) AS REQUIRED

Fig. 8-3 Foundation footing form

Step 4. Footings With Forms Removed

There should be adequate footings. The size of the footings needed varies according to soil conditions and applied load. Footings should be reinforced with long steel bars called *rebars*. Footings must meet local building code requirements.

In the absence of a code, the general practice is to build residential footings with a depth equal to the thickness of the foundation wall and a width equal to twice the wall thickness, figure 8-4.

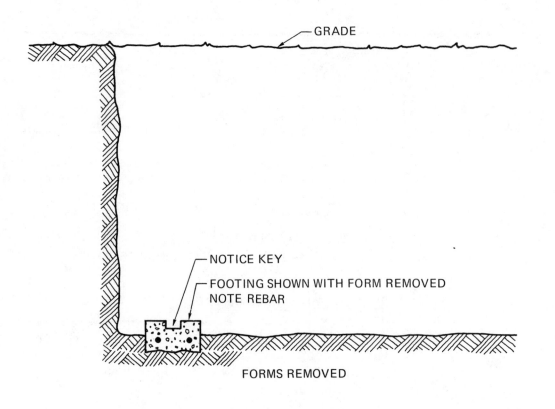

Fig. 8-4 Footing in place

Step 5. Foundation Wall Forms

The foundation wall forms are usually made of plywood sheets. These forms are extremely well braced and held together by timbers, called *wales,* that run vertically around the form. Strong wire ties hold the whole assembly together, figure 8-5.

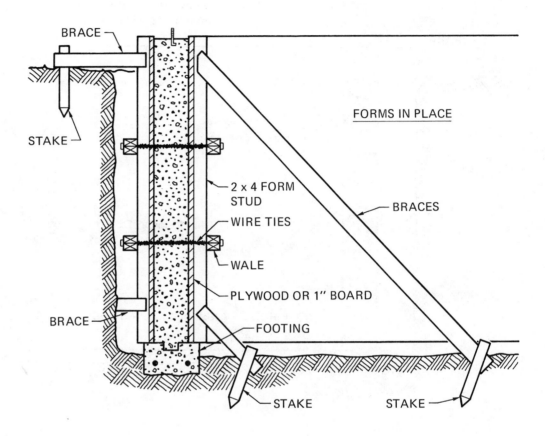

Fig. 8-5 Poured foundation with forms still in place

Step 6. Foundation Walls with Forms Removed

Anchor bolts are placed approximately 6 feet apart while the concrete is still soft. After the concrete sets for a day or two, the forms are removed and the wire ties broken off at the outside edge of the wall. Notice how the key holds the foundation wall, keeping it from shifting on the footing, figure 8-6.

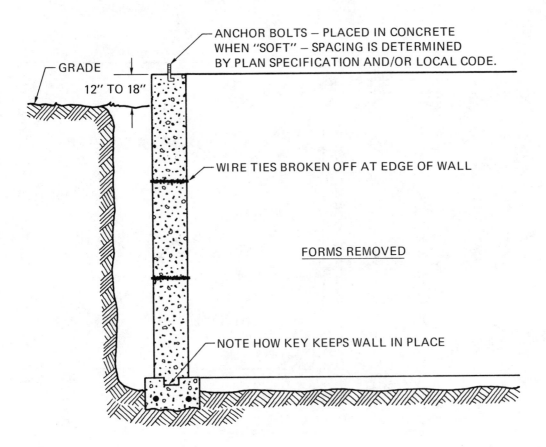

Fig. 8-6 Poured foundation with the forms removed

Step 7. Placement of Sill

A thin layer of mortar called *grout* is placed on top of the foundation wall. Sometimes a thin layer of insulation is used in place of the grout. Then the sill is bolted in place, figure 8-7. The grout or insulation keeps outside air or drafts from getting into the celler area.

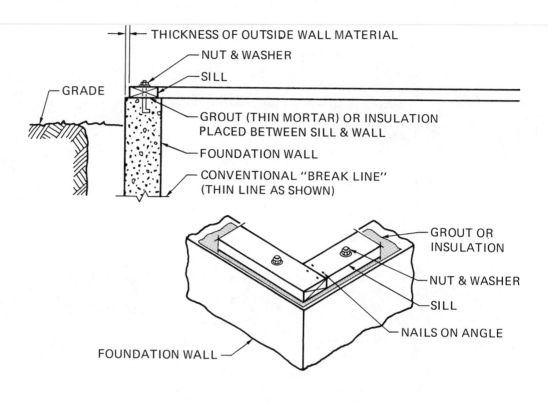

Fig. 8-7 Placement of sill

Step 8. Placement of Floor Joists, Headers, and Subfloor

The floor joist and headers are now nailed in place to the sill, followed by the subfloor. The subfloor is usually plywood, figure 8-8.

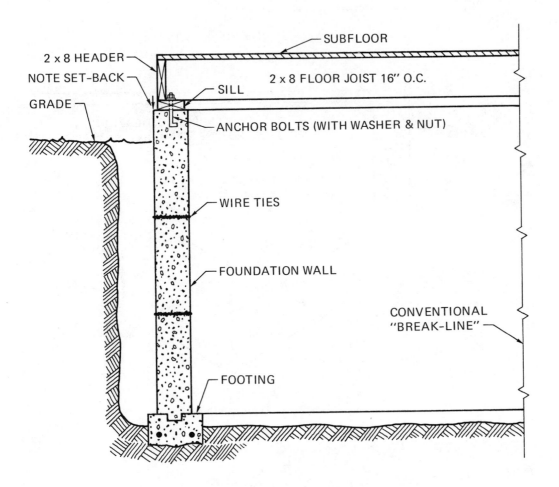

Fig. 8-8 Floor joists, header, and subfloor added

Step 9. Girder Construction

A floor joist is usually supported approximately halfway across the floor distance by a *girder*. Girders are constructed by one of the two methods illustrated in figures 8-9 and 8-10.

The first method, figure 8-9, requires a formed *pocket* in the foundation wall. The floor joist then rests on top of the girder. In the alternate method, figure 8-10, the floor joist butts up flush with the girder and is held in place by a *ledger strip*.

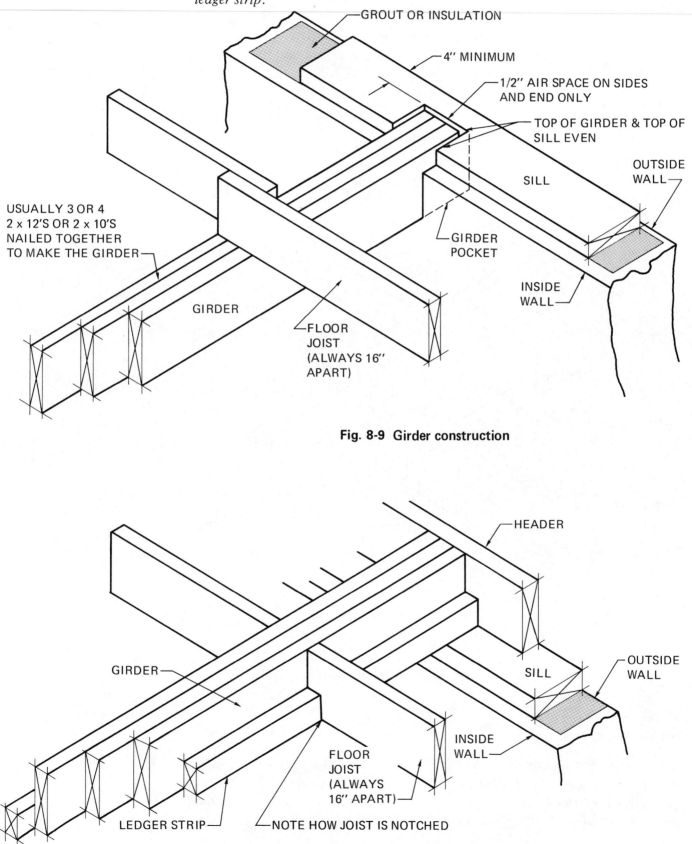

Fig. 8-9 Girder construction

Fig. 8-10 Girder construction, alternate method

Step 10. Bridging and Framing Openings

Stair openings, chimney openings, and openings in the floor must be strengthened by *framing* double headers around the openings, figure 8-11. Overall support for these internal double headers must be carefully designed. *Bridging* is an arrangement of small wooden or metal pieces between the joists. They stiffen the floor joists and eliminate warping of the joists.

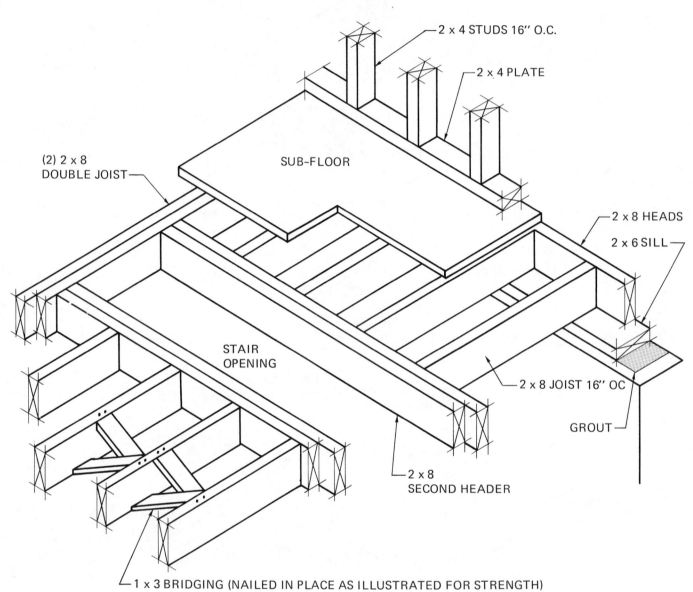

Fig. 8-11 Bridging and stair opening framing

Step 11. Plates, Posts, and Studs

The wall frame is usually constructed with 2" x 4" studs placed 16 inches on center (OC) around the outside and inside walls. The studs are held in place at the top and bottom by horizontal members called *plates*. At all corners and where one wall abuts another wall, a post must be constructed, figures 8-12, 8-13, and 8-14. A post is designed for extra strength and provides a nailing surface for the inside wall material.

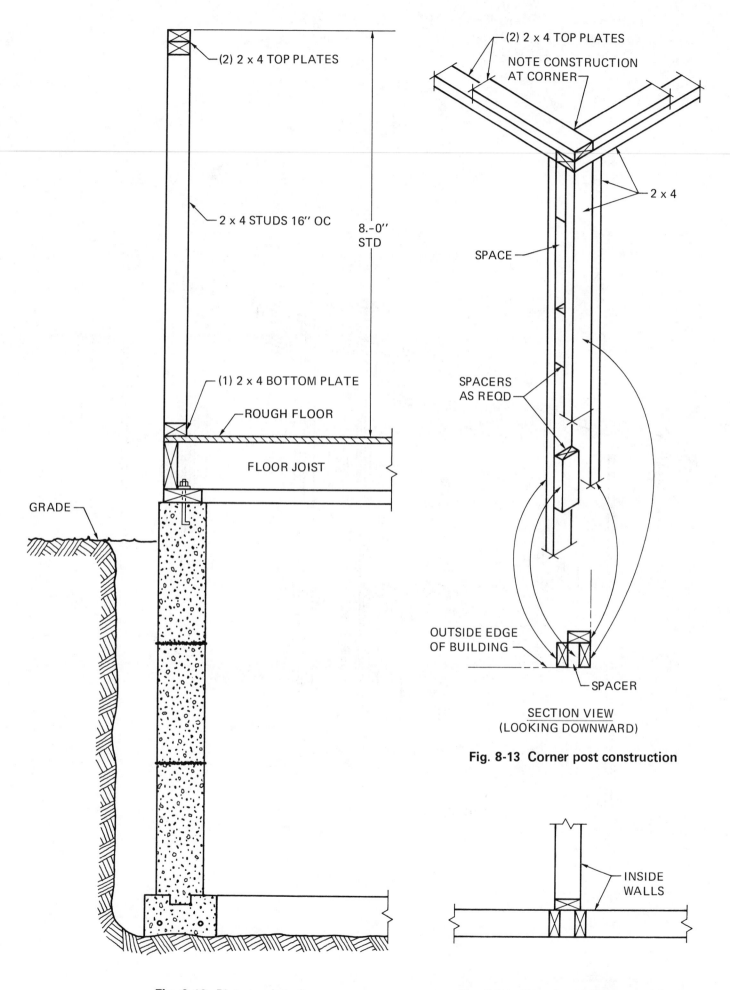

(2) 2 x 4 TOP PLATES

2 x 4 STUDS 16" OC

8.-0" STD

(1) 2 x 4 BOTTOM PLATE

ROUGH FLOOR

FLOOR JOIST

GRADE

Fig. 8-12 Plates and studs

(2) 2 x 4 TOP PLATES

NOTE CONSTRUCTION AT CORNER

2 x 4

SPACE

SPACERS AS REQD

OUTSIDE EDGE OF BUILDING

SPACER

SECTION VIEW (LOOKING DOWNWARD)

Fig. 8-13 Corner post construction

INSIDE WALLS

Fig. 8-14 Abutting wall construction

Step 12. Wall Studding

Figure 8-15 is a typical example of a studded wall. All studs are 16 or 24 inches on center, double headers are placed above all window and door openings, and the sides of windows and doors are double studded. Note the double top plate. This is for strength and to tie the corners together.

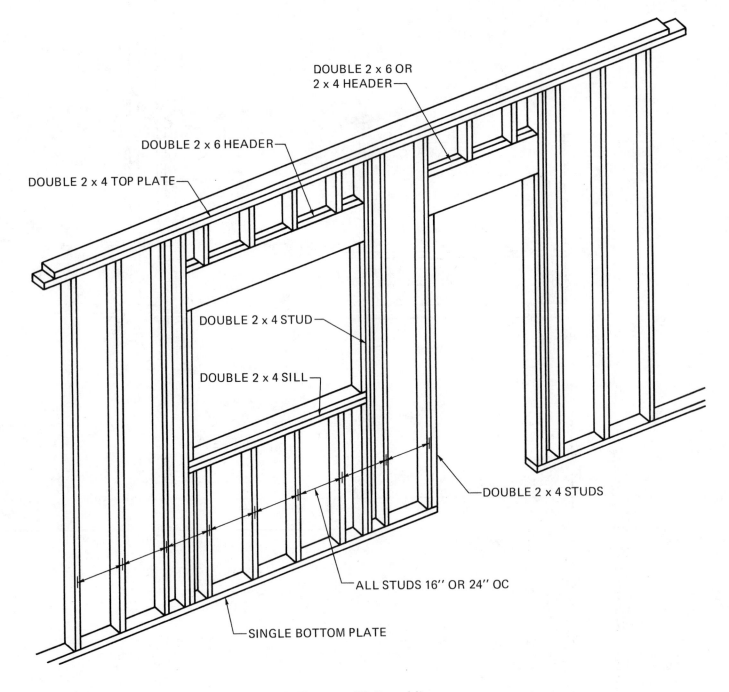

Fig. 8-15 Wall studding

Step 13. Roof Construction

The roof is an important factor in the overall house design, figure 8-16. In a traditional home the type of roof is determined by the house style. When the building is a contemporary design a wide variety of roof types may be used. The shape of the plan also affects the roof choice. A rectangular plan may have almost any type of roof. It is more economical, however, to cover a rambling plan with a flat roof. A hip roof on a rambling plan would require additional cutting and fitting, and the cost would therefore be much more.

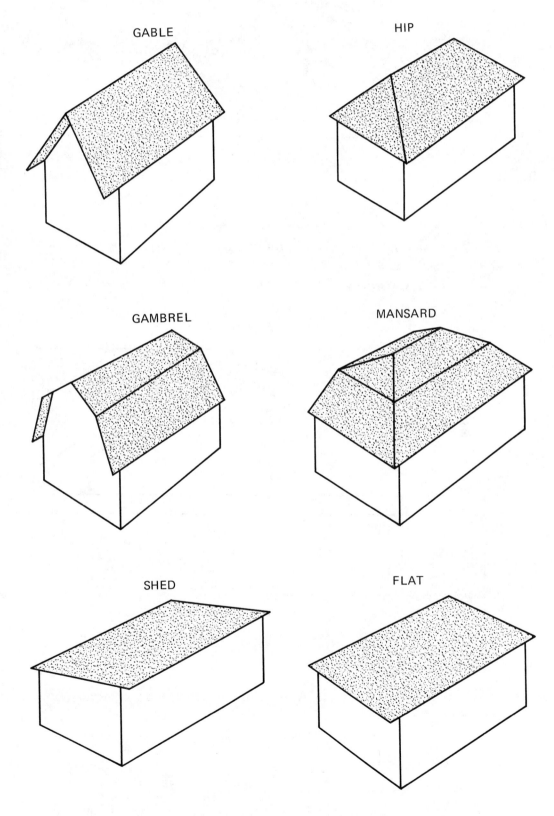

GABLE   HIP

GAMBREL   MANSARD

SHED   FLAT

Fig. 8-16 Examples of basic roof types used today

Truss Roof Construction. A *truss* is a lightweight, very strong roof support. It is usually manufactured at a factory and delivered to the site as a complete unit, figure 8-17. It is placed 2'-0" on center. A *gusset* is a brace or plate, usually made of plywood, that connects members of the truss construction. Metal framing plates are also used in place of wood gussets.

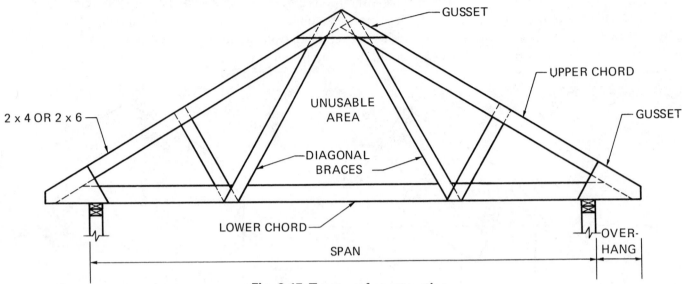

Fig. 8-17 Truss roof construction

Conventional Roof Construction. *Rafters* in conventional construction are usually cut at the site and put in place using the ridge board as a guide, figure 8-18. Construction time is longer, but this method has more flexibility and allows use of the attic area.

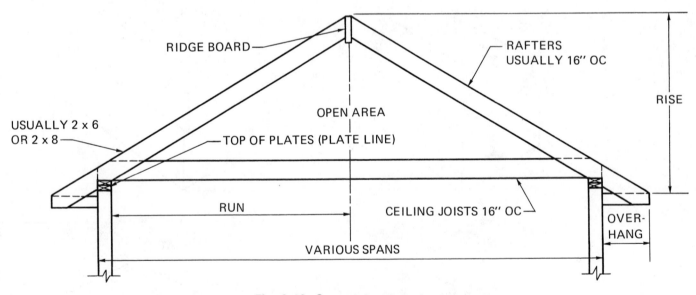

Fig. 8-18 Conventional roof construction

Roof Pitch Terms

Rafters support the roof sheathing (structural covering) and roofing material. The size of the rafter depends upon:

- Span
- Weight of roofing material
- Snow and/or wind loads

Span is the horizontal distance between the two supporting walls, measured to outside of the walls.

Total rise is the vertical distance from the top of the supporting plate to the ridge board.

Total run is the level distance each rafter covers, usually 1/2 the span.

Roof pitch is the slope or angle of the roof. It is expressed as the ratio of rise to span.

$$\text{Pitch} = \frac{\text{Rise}}{\text{Span}}$$

1/3 pitch means, for instance, that the vertical height from the top of the plate to the ridge board is 1/3 the total span.

Rafter length is the theoretical length of the rafter measured along its center line. The actual rafter length may vary due to cuts made at an angle for the ridge and tail.

Note: In northern areas where a greater snow load is a problem, a steeper pitch is recommended.

Figures 8-19 and 8-20 illustrate roof pitch.

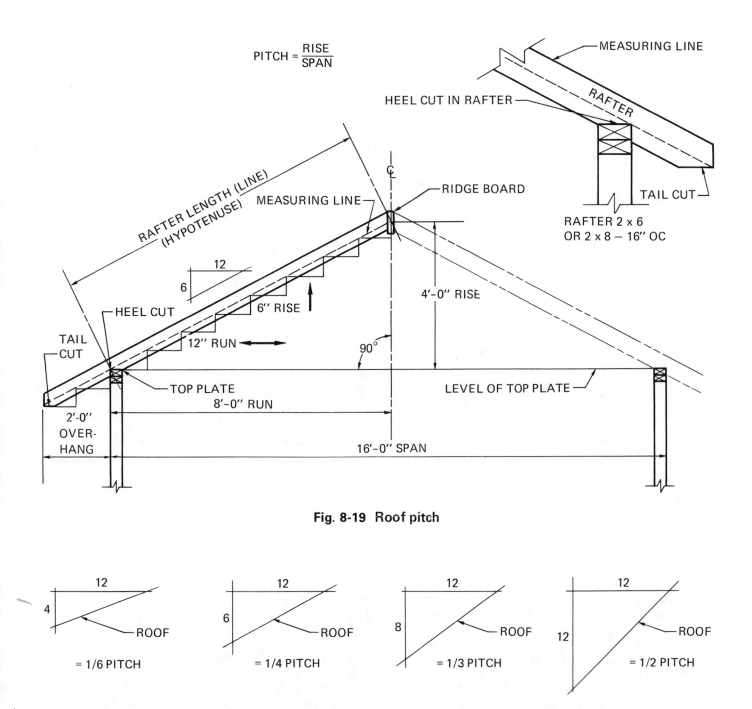

Fig. 8-19 Roof pitch

Fig. 8-20 Examples of roof pitches

The frame of the house is now ready for the ceiling joist and the roof rafters. The ceiling joists are usually nailed in place 16 inches on center, similar to the floor joists except a header is not used. Rafters are positioned and cut according to the required roof pitch and cornice, or overhang, style. Note the cutout in the roof rafter where the rafter rests upon the double top plates. This must be shown on the section drawings. Rafters are usually placed 16 inches on center also and nailed to the top plates and the ceiling joists, figure 8-21.

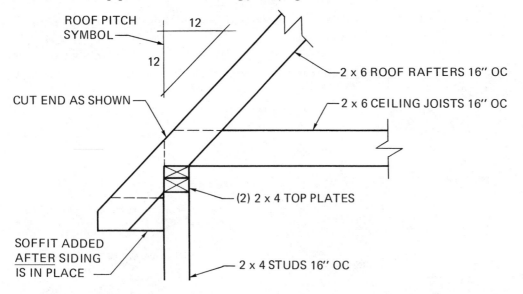

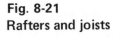

Fig. 8-21
Rafters and joists

The rafter overhang or *cornice* design should be in harmony with the style of the house. Figure 8-22 illustrates a few cornice styles.

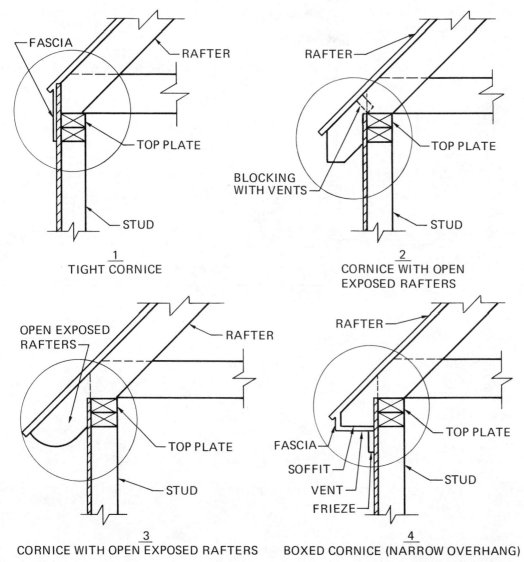

Fig. 8-22
Cornice styles

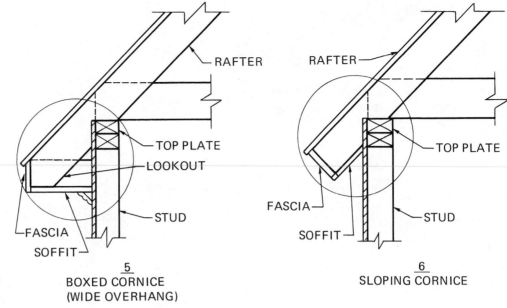

**Fig. 8-22 (continued)
Cornice Styles**

$\underline{5}$
BOXED CORNICE
(WIDE OVERHANG)

$\underline{6}$
SLOPING CORNICE

Study figure 8-23. The term *to the weather* means how much surface is exposed to outside elements. Notice how standard asphalt shingles are placed on the roof.

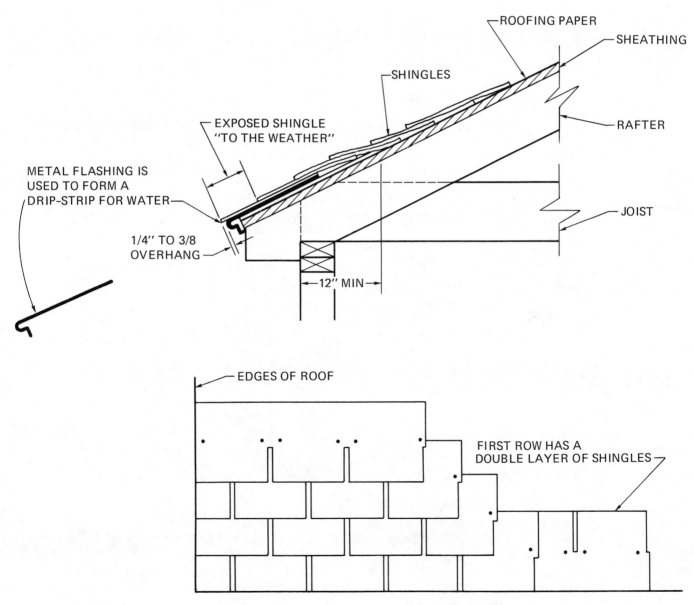

Fig. 8-23 Roofing

Step 14. Exterior Finishing

The house is now completely framed. Roof sheathing and roofing are now applied and the outside wall sheathing assembled. At some point during the construction, the outside foundation wall is coated with a bituminous material, and a 4-inch drain is placed around the footing. A layer of gravel or crushed stone is placed on top of the drain tile, figure 8-24, and the excavation around the outside wall is backfilled.

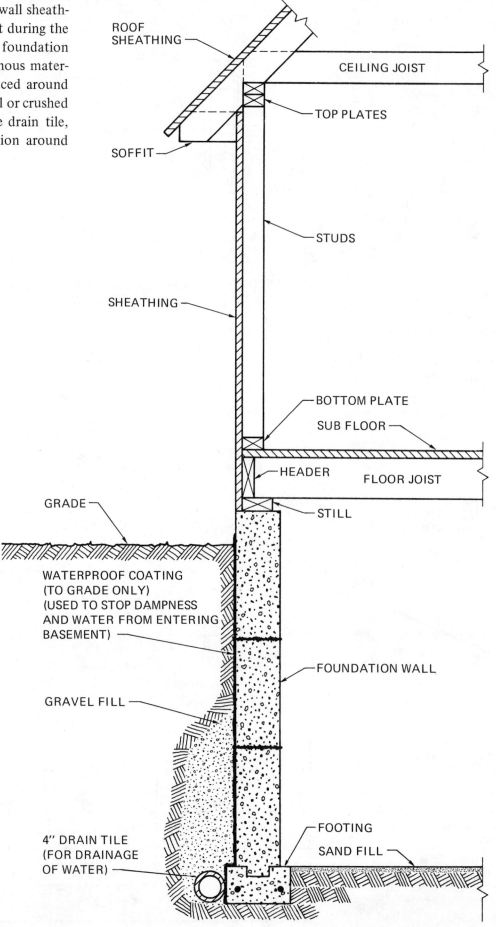

ROOF SHEATHING

CEILING JOIST

TOP PLATES

SOFFIT

STUDS

SHEATHING

BOTTOM PLATE

SUB FLOOR

HEADER   FLOOR JOIST

GRADE

STILL

WATERPROOF COATING (TO GRADE ONLY) (USED TO STOP DAMPNESS AND WATER FROM ENTERING BASEMENT)

FOUNDATION WALL

GRAVEL FILL

4" DRAIN TILE (FOR DRAINAGE OF WATER)

FOOTING

SAND FILL

Fig. 8-24 Roof boards, sheathing, tile, gravel, and foundation wall coating

Step 15. Detailed Drawing with Insulation Added

Generally, after the roof, side walls, windows, and doors are installed, a concrete basement floor is added. Rough electrical wiring and plumbing are installed next. The walls and ceilings, and in some cases the floor, are insulated.

Insulation comes in a variety of forms and types. They may be grouped into four broad categories:

- Flexible
- Loose fill
- Rigid
- Reflective

After the insulation is in place, the ceilings and inside walls are completed. The floor and the moldings around the windows and doors are then done, followed by the finished electrical and plumbing work. The kitchen and bathroom cabinets and counters are installed next, and all work is finished, figure 8-25.

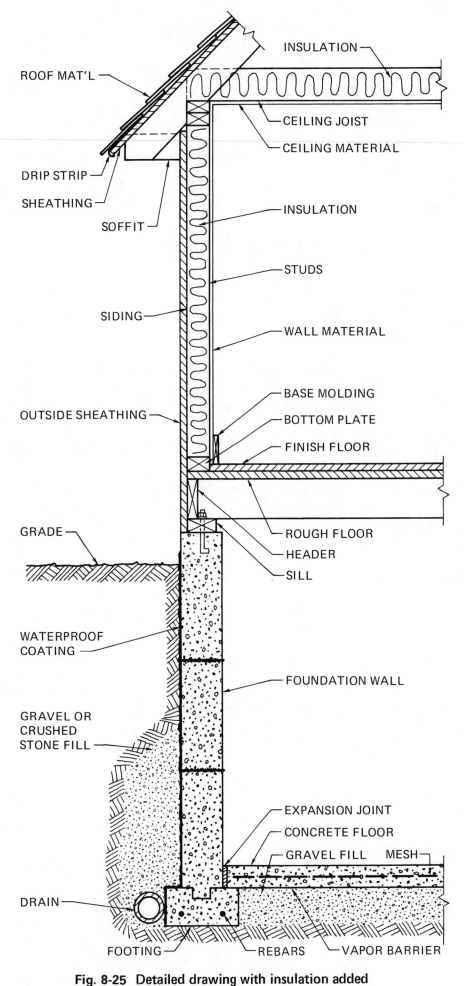

Fig. 8-25 Detailed drawing with insulation added

WINDOWS, DOORS, FIREPLACES & FIXTURES

WINDOWS AND DOORS

Windows and doors are completely assembled at a factory and shipped to the job ready to be installed. They are usually primed or painted. These finished units are simply installed in the rough stud opening (RO) after the outside sheathing is put in place and before the siding material is added. Usually the rough frame opening is 4 inches larger up and down and 3 inches larger left and right than the window unit to allow for adjusting, fitting, and leveling the unit. A *schedule*, figure 9-1, keyed to the working drawing, gives the number, size, and placement of windows and doors in a house.

DOOR SCHEDULE					
MARK	QUANTITY	SIZE	TYPE	MATERIAL	REMARKS
A	1	3'-0''x6'-8''x1 3/4''	See Elev.	Pine	Paint
B	8	2'-6''x6'-8''x1 3/8''	Flush	Birch	Hollow Core
C	3	2'-6''x6'-8''x1 3/8''	Louvered	Pine	
D	1	2'-6''x6'-8''x1 3/4''	10 Lights	Pine	
E	3	5'-0''x6'-8''x1 3/8''	Folding	Pine	Louvered
F	1	2'-0''x6'-8''x1 3/8''	Flush	Birch	Hollow Core
G	1	2'-6''x6'-8''x1 3/4''	Lights	Pine	See rear Elevation

Fig. 9-1 A sample docr schedule

Each window and door manufactured has its own size, style, and specifications. It is important that the window or door match the particular style of house under construction. Every drafter should have literature from various companies on file for reference purposes when choosing doors and windows.

Study the illustrations for windows and doors in this unit very carefully. A perspective, elevation, and plan view is given for each one. Memorize how to illustrate each style. Note line weight. It makes the view appear as natural as possible.

WINDOWS

Manufacturers and architects use certain standards when designing windows:

- Natural light, when required, must be provided by windows, glazed doors, skylights, transparent or translucent panels, or by any combination of these.

- Natural ventilation, when required, must be provided through openable windows, exterior doors, skylights, or other suitable openings in exterior walls or roofs.

- The total glass area needed to provide sufficient natural light must not be less than 10 percent of the floor area of the room or space.

The *sash* holds the glass and includes the top rail, meeting rail, and side rails or *stiles*. The *frame* holds the sash(es) and includes the top jamb, side jamb, sill, and blind stop. *Interior trim* is the material between the frame and the inside wall. *Exterior trim* is the material between the frame and the outside wall, figure 9-2.

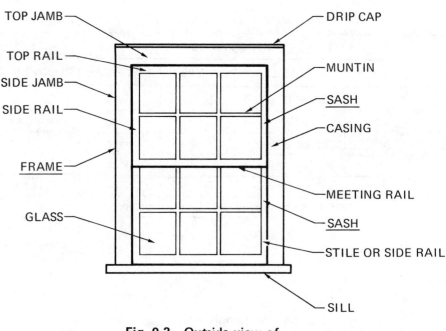

Fig. 9-2 Outside view of a double-hung window

Muntins are strips separating panes of glass in a sash.   Figure 9-3 illustrates the different types of muntins.

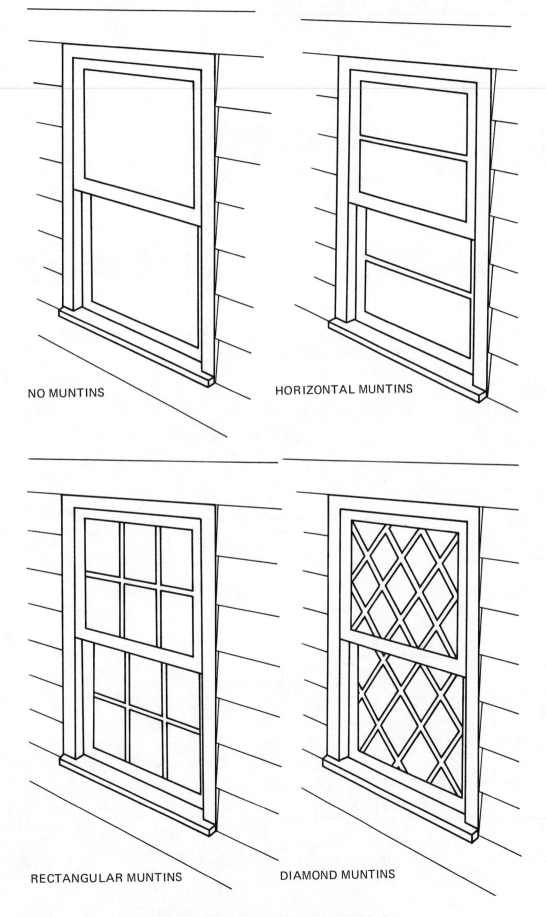

NO MUNTINS

HORIZONTAL MUNTINS

RECTANGULAR MUNTINS

DIAMOND MUNTINS

Fig. 9-3 Window units with muntins added

Standard Window Heights and Sizes

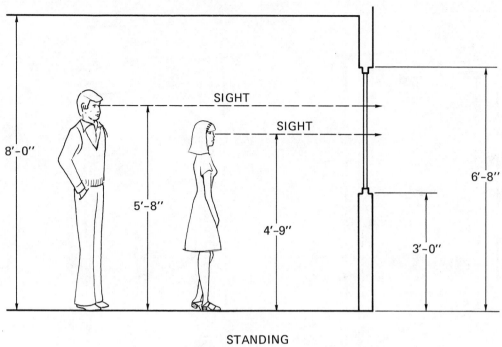

STANDING
BEDROOMS AND KITCHEN

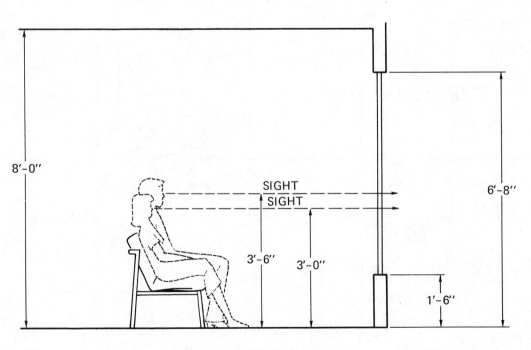

SITTING
DINING AND LIVING ROOMS

Fig. 9-4 Determining window height and size

Double-Hung Window

Double-hung windows are usually part of a colonial type house. These windows are spring-loaded and stay wherever placed. The sash is easily removed. They are sometimes used in groups of two or more, side by side, figure 9-5.

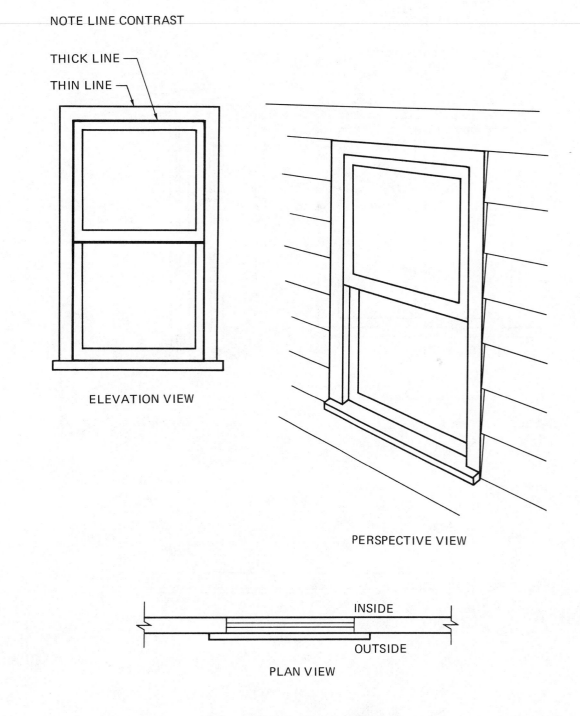

Fig. 9-5 Double-hung window

Fixed Window

A *fixed window* (not illustrated) does not move and is used for light and not for ventilation. If a fixed window is large, it is called a *picture window*. Fixed windows are becoming more popular as a result of the increased use of air-conditioning.

Casement Window

A *casement window* is hinged at one side and usually swings outward. Casement windows can be placed two or more, side by side. They can be hinged at the side, top, or bottom. Screens and storm windows are installed inside, figure 9-6.

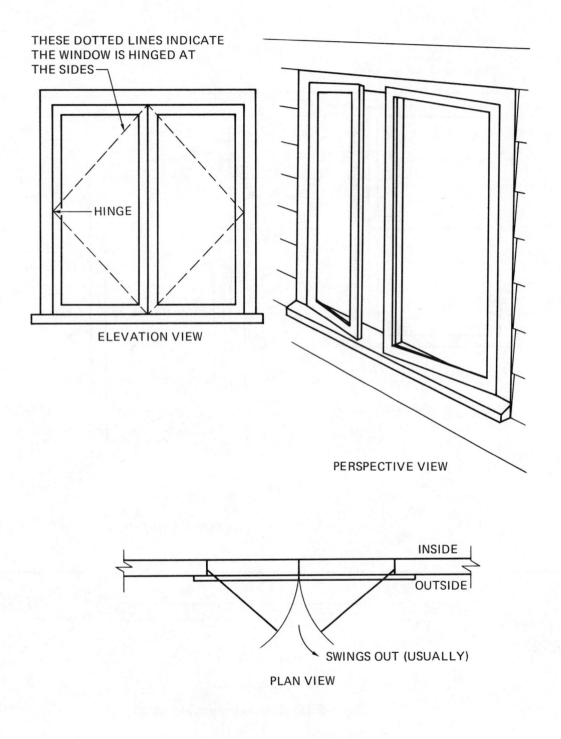

Fig. 9-6 Casement window

Awning Window

When a window is hinged at the top, it is called an *awning window*. Awning windows are used in more contemporary style houses. The bottom rail of one window interlocks with the top rail of the window below, figure 9-7.

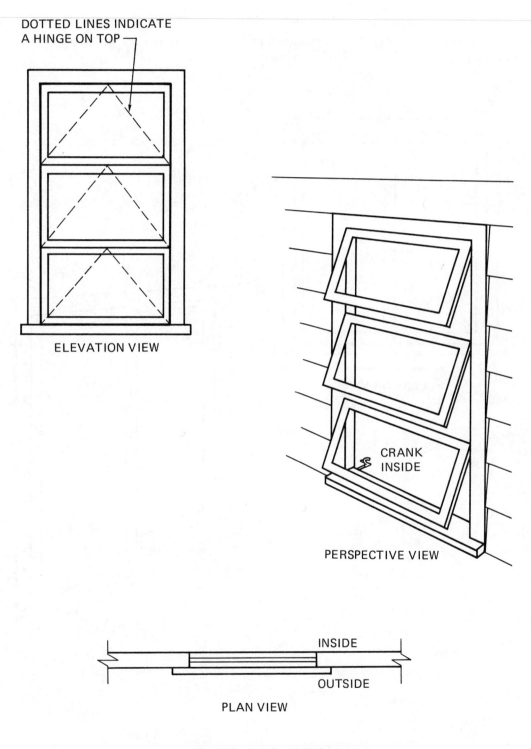

DOTTED LINES INDICATE
A HINGE ON TOP

ELEVATION VIEW

CRANK
INSIDE

PERSPECTIVE VIEW

INSIDE

OUTSIDE

PLAN VIEW

Fig. 9-7 Awning window

Hopper Window

When a window is hinged at the bottom, it is called a *hopper window* (not illustrated). Hopper windows are often used in foundations. They swing inward.

Sliding Window

Sliding windows open horizontally. They are sometimes called *gliding windows* as they run on tracks. The screen and storm windows are installed on the outside, figure 9-8.

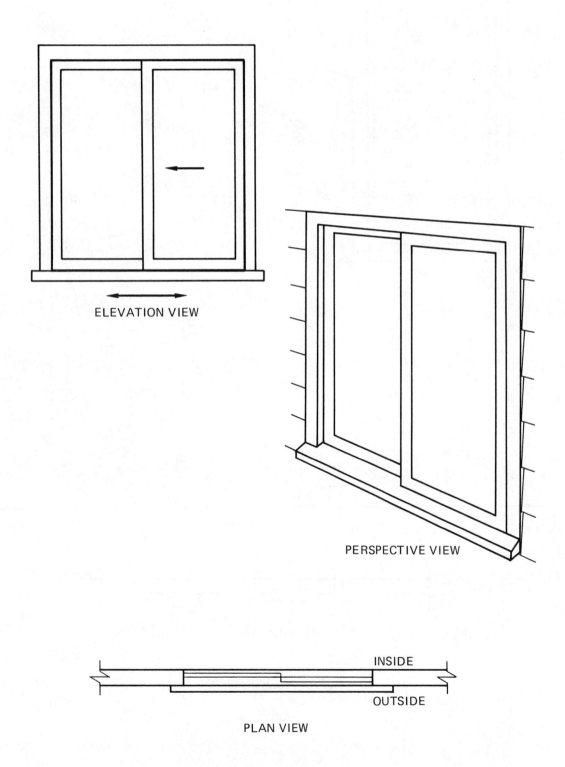

ELEVATION VIEW

PERSPECTIVE VIEW

INSIDE

OUTSIDE

PLAN VIEW

Fig. 9-8 Sliding window

Combination Windows

Various kinds of windows can be used in combination. Figure 9-9 illustrates a fixed window in combination with an awning window.

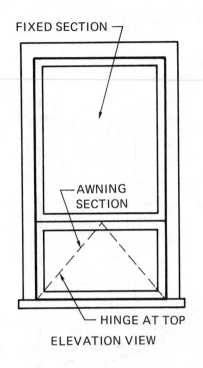

FIXED SECTION

AWNING
SECTION

HINGE AT TOP

ELEVATION VIEW

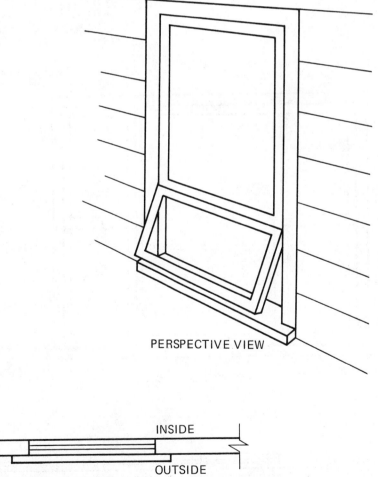

PERSPECTIVE VIEW

INSIDE

OUTSIDE

PLAN VIEW

Fig. 9-9 Fixed window and awning window combination

Any combination of windows can be put together. Figure 9-10 shows a fixed picture window with a double-hung window at each side. Casement windows could have been used in place of the double-hung windows.

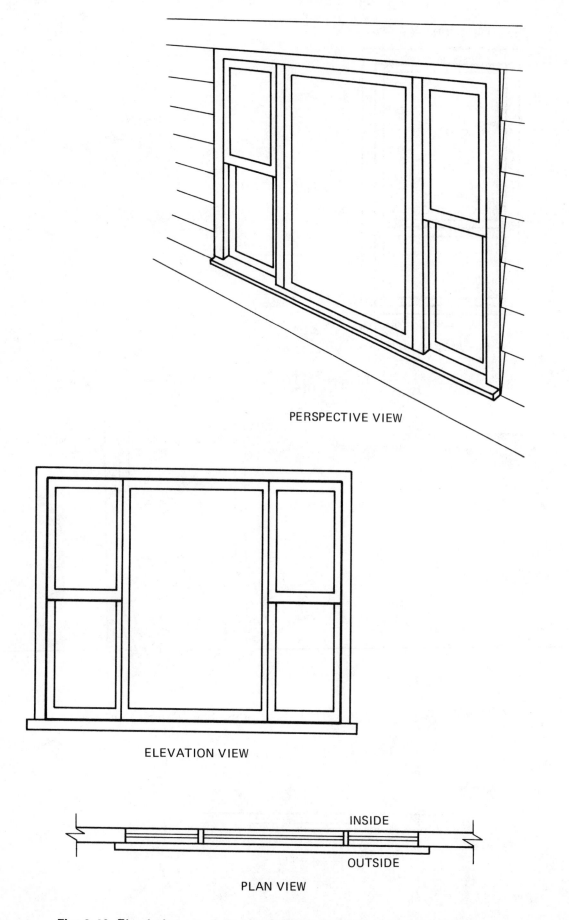

PERSPECTIVE VIEW

ELEVATION VIEW

INSIDE

OUTSIDE

PLAN VIEW

Fig. 9-10 Fixed picture window and double-hung window combination

Jalousie Window

Jalousie windows consist of many small, long panes that operate together with a crank. They are good for breezeways, porches, garages, and for house windows in warm climates, figure 9-11.

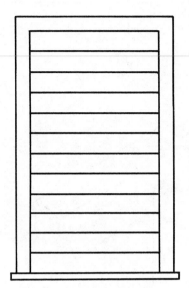

ELEVATION VIEW

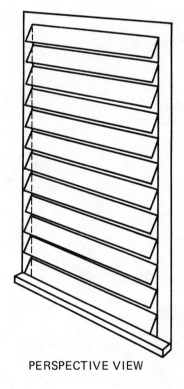

PERSPECTIVE VIEW

INSIDE

OUTSIDE

PLAN VIEW

Fig. 9-11 Jalousie window

Window Areaway

Window areaways are used to provide an open area around basement windows which are located partly below grade, figure 9-12.

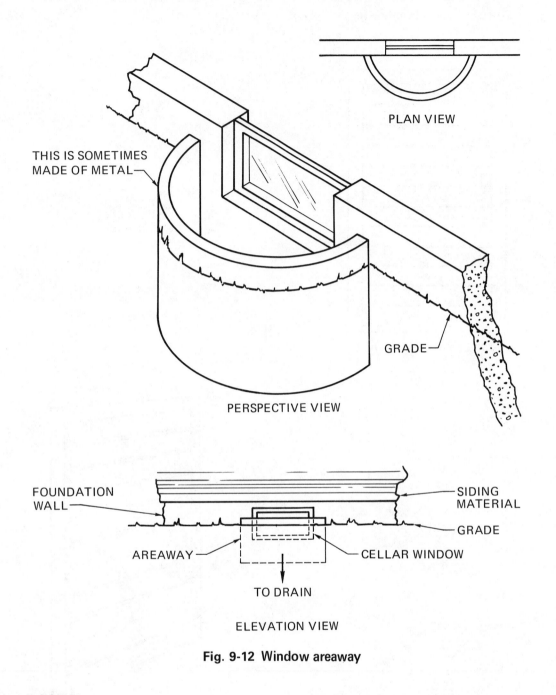

PLAN VIEW

THIS IS SOMETIMES
MADE OF METAL

GRADE

PERSPECTIVE VIEW

FOUNDATION
WALL

SIDING
MATERIAL

GRADE

AREAWAY

CELLAR WINDOW

TO DRAIN

ELEVATION VIEW

Fig. 9-12 Window areaway

DOORS

Exterior Doors

Manufacturers and architects use certain standards when designing doors:

- Minimum size:

	Width	Height
Main entrance door	3'-0"	6'-8"
Service door	2'-6"	6'-8"
Garage door, 1 car	8'-0"	7'-0"
Garage door, 2 cars	16'-0"	7'-0"

- Thickness of exterior wood doors must not be less than 1 3/4 inches, except service doors and garage doors which may be 1 3/8 inches.

- Doors must be made weathertight. A watertight threshold must be provided. Doors must be weather-stripped to prevent infiltration of dust and loss of heat.
- Provide screen doors in those areas where necessary. Minimum thickness for wood screen doors must be 1 1/8 inches.

Figure 9-13 shows an exterior view of a door.

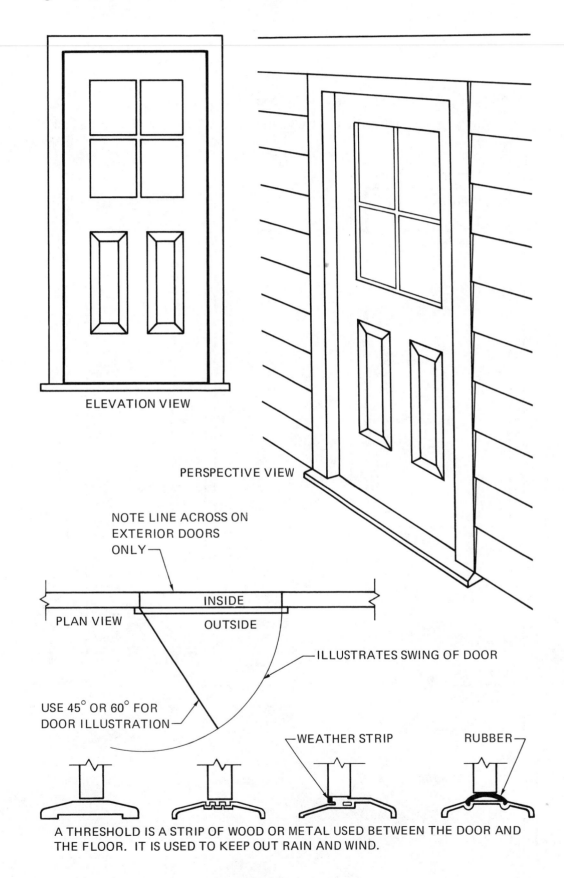

ELEVATION VIEW

PERSPECTIVE VIEW

NOTE LINE ACROSS ON
EXTERIOR DOORS
ONLY

INSIDE

PLAN VIEW   OUTSIDE

ILLUSTRATES SWING OF DOOR

USE 45° OR 60° FOR
DOOR ILLUSTRATION

WEATHER STRIP   RUBBER

A THRESHOLD IS A STRIP OF WOOD OR METAL USED BETWEEN THE DOOR AND
THE FLOOR. IT IS USED TO KEEP OUT RAIN AND WIND.

Fig. 9-13 Exterior door

Interior Doors

There are certain standards that manufacturers and architects use when designing interior doors:

- Provide a door for each opening to a bedroom, bathroom, and toilet compartment. Doors to bathrooms and toilet compartments must be a conventional hinged or sliding type and have locks.

- Minimum size:

  a. Habitable rooms — 2'-6" x 6'-8"

  b. Bathrooms, toilet compartments, and closets — 2'-4" x 6'-8"

  c. Linen and broom closets — 1'-4" wide

- Minimum thickness for interior wood doors must be 1 3/8 inches.

Figure 9-14 illustrates the elevation, perspective, and plan views of a *flush hollow core door*.

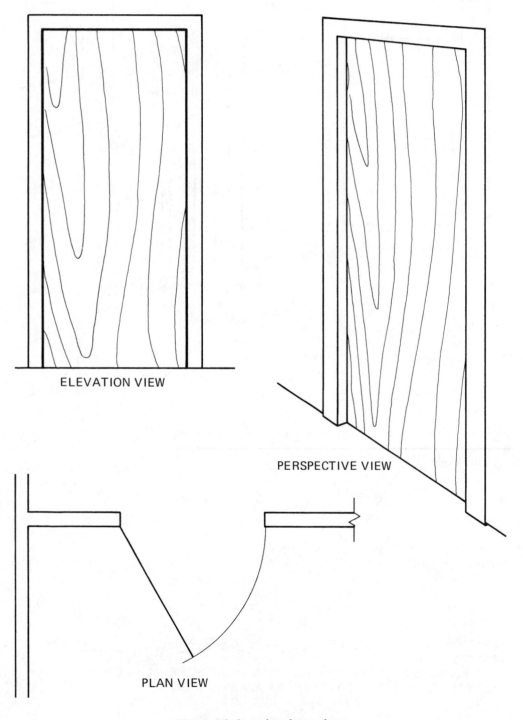

ELEVATION VIEW

PERSPECTIVE VIEW

PLAN VIEW

Fig. 9-14 Interior door views

Double Acting Door

A *double acting door* swings inward and outward, figure 9-15. The arched opening is illustrated in a plan view, figure 9-16.

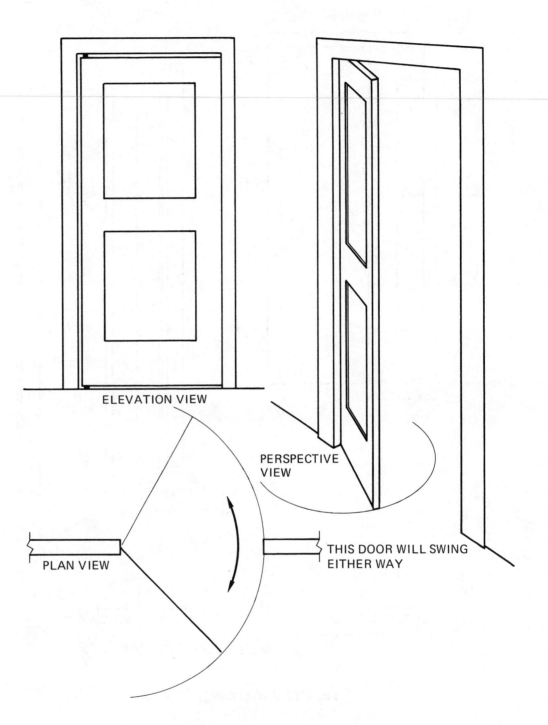

Fig. 9-15 Double acting door views

Fig. 9-16 Plan view for arched opening

Pocket Door

Pocket doors slide into the wall and out of sight. These make good closet doors, figure 9-17.

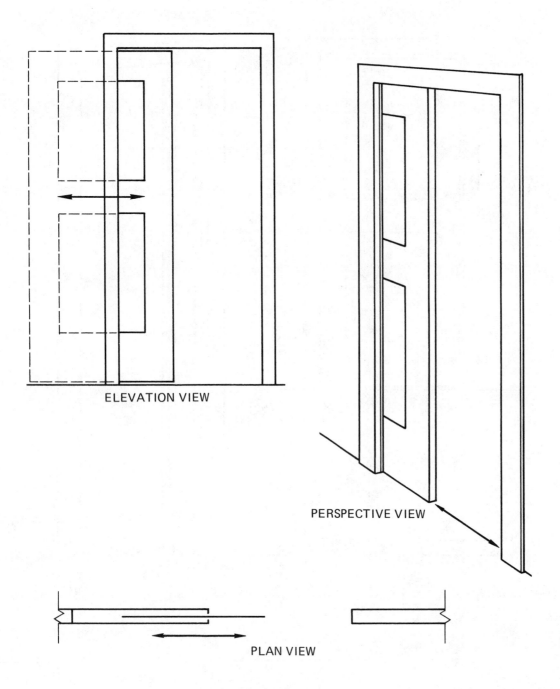

ELEVATION VIEW

PERSPECTIVE VIEW

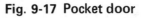

PLAN VIEW

Fig. 9-17 Pocket door

Double Sliding Door

A double sliding door is similar to a pocket door except that it does not slide into the wall. Double sliding doors slide past each other as illustrated in figure 9-18.

Fig. 9-18 Double sliding door plan view

Bi-fold Doors

There are many styles of folding doors. Figure 9-19 shows a colonial type *bi-fold door*.

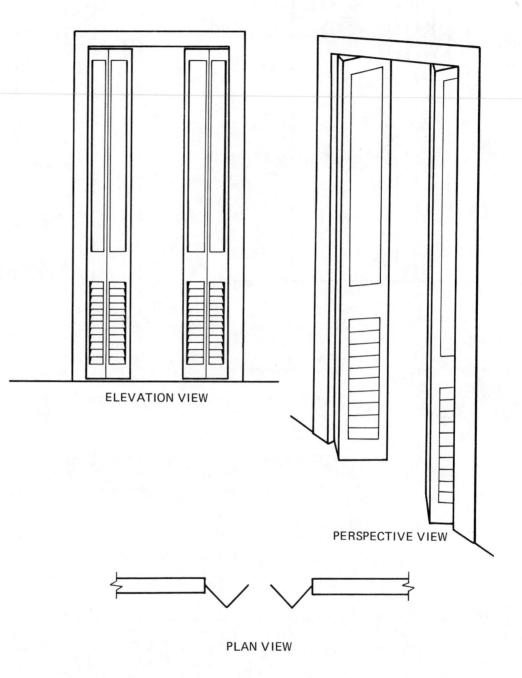

ELEVATION VIEW

PERSPECTIVE VIEW

PLAN VIEW

Fig. 9-19 Bi-fold door

A *single folding door* is drawn like figure 9-20. Folding doors may be made of wood, metal, or cloth and are usually used as closets, figure 9-21.

PLAN VIEW

Fig. 9-20 Single folding door plan view

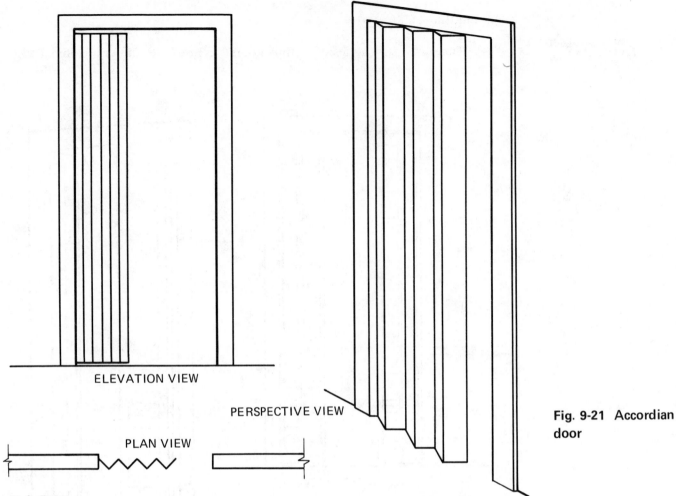

ELEVATION VIEW

PERSPECTIVE VIEW

PLAN VIEW

Fig. 9-21 Accordian door

Cafe Door

Cafe doors also come in many styles. They are usually used between the kitchen area and the dining area or for special effects in other parts of the house, figure 9-22.

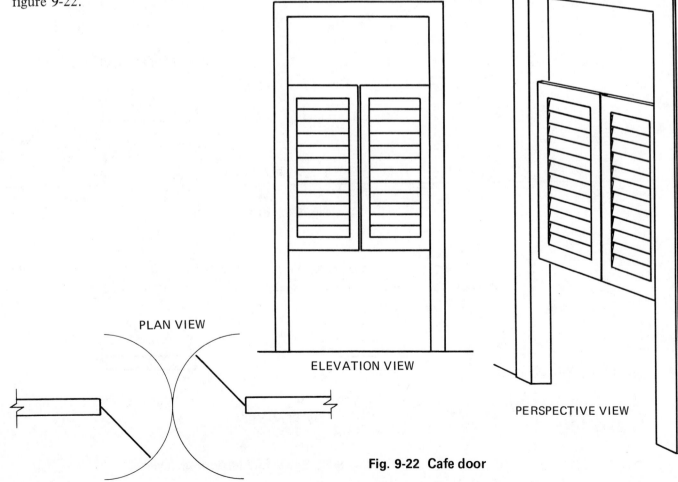

PLAN VIEW

ELEVATION VIEW

PERSPECTIVE VIEW

Fig. 9-22 Cafe door

Overhead Garage Door

Figure 9-23 illustrates an *overhead garage door* made up in four sections. One section has four windows. The standard size for a single garage door is 7'-0'' high x 8'-0'' wide. The standard size for a double garage door is 7'-0'' high x 16'-0'' wide. Use a door that blends with the style of the house. Be sure to leave 10 to 12 inches above the top of the door on the inside to the garage ceiling for installation of door hardware such as tracks.

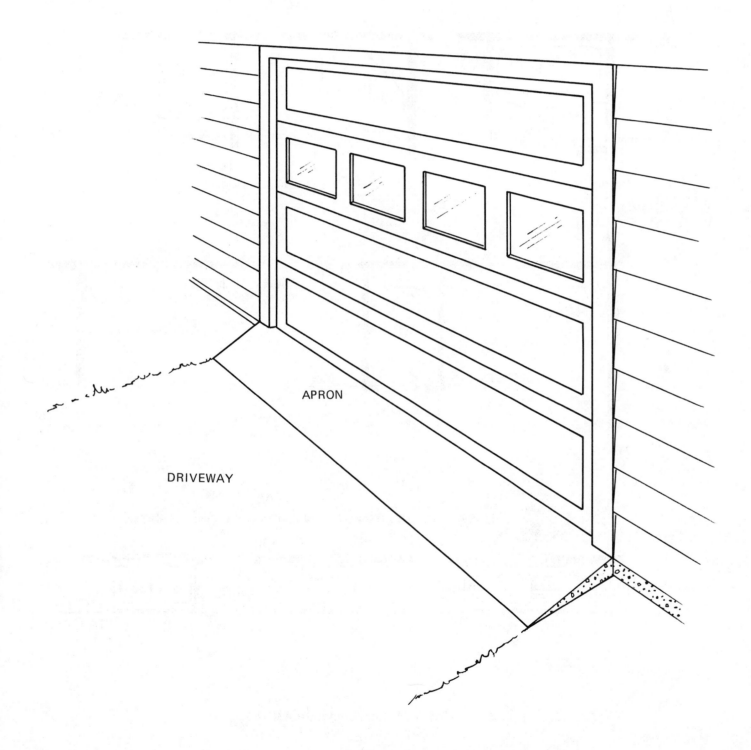

Fig. 9-23 Overhead garage door

ILLUSTRATING STANDARD FIXTURES

Figure 9-24 shows how to draw a few standard fixtures in the average home. These were drawn using a standard drafting template. Many standard dimensions are called out right on the template. Templates are very useful and save time when making plumbing drawings.

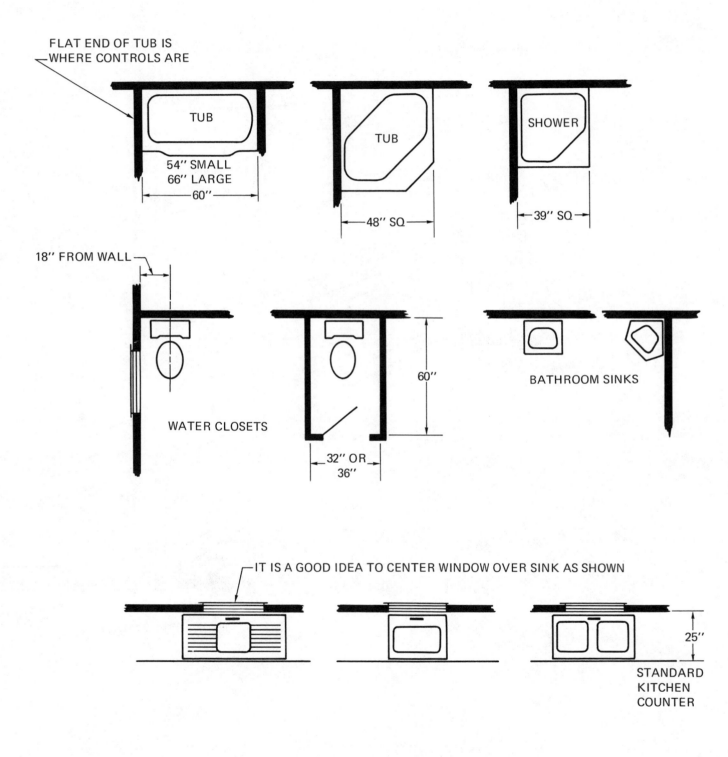

Fig. 9-24 Plumbing fixture sizes

CHIMNEYS AND FIREPLACES

With today's energy shortage, a fireplace is no longer a luxury. It provides an excellent backup heating system during an emergency or power failure, particularly if it has an air circulation system. The fireplace and chimney, like other architectural features, adds charm and conforms to the overall style of a house. It is designed and constructed to stand completely independent of the house, figure 9-25. For economy, a fireplace is located in the same chimney that is used for the main heating plant, but each has its own passage or *flue*.

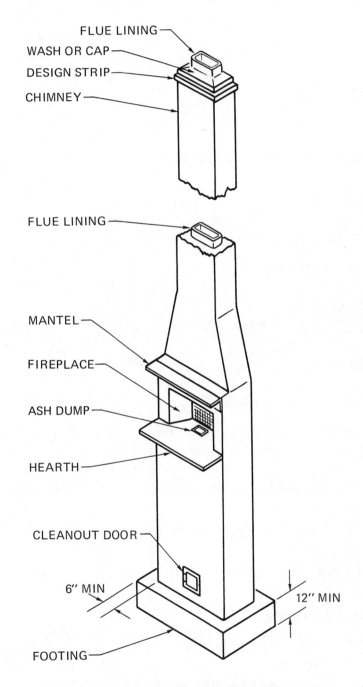

FLUE LINING
WASH OR CAP
DESIGN STRIP
CHIMNEY

FLUE LINING

MANTEL

FIREPLACE

ASH DUMP

HEARTH

CLEANOUT DOOR

6″ MIN   12″ MIN

FOOTING

A FOOTING APPROXIMATELY 12 INCHES THICK FOR A TWO-STORY BUILDING, OR 8 INCHES THICK FOR A ONE-STORY BUILDING, AND 6 INCHES LARGER THAN THE CHIMNEY BASE IS NECESSARY TO SAFELY SUPPORT THE WHOLE STRUCTURE.

Fig. 9-25 A chimney and fireplace is an independent structure

The fireplace and chimney are major elements in the overall appearance of a house, figure 9-26. Much thought must be given to:

- Location of the fireplace in the room with regards to placement of furniture and room arrangement.

- Coordination with the major heating plant for efficient design and layout of heating ducts or heating pipes

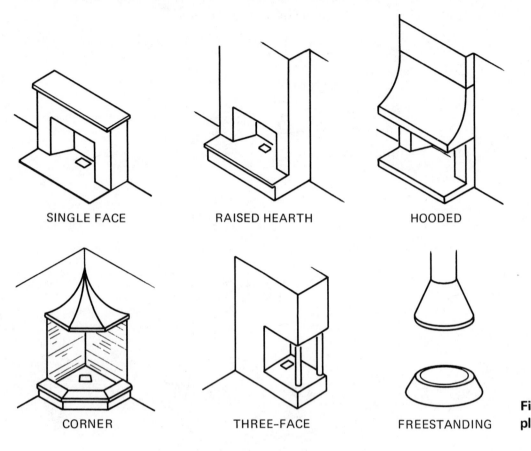

| SINGLE FACE | RAISED HEARTH | HOODED |

| CORNER | THREE-FACE | FREESTANDING |

Fig. 9-26 Styles of fireplaces

The fireplace may be located on a wall, in a corner, or be freestanding. Early American design usually has the chimney and fireplace located in the center of the house. Newer houses tend to locate the chimney and fireplace on an exterior wall. There are advantages and disadvantages to both systems.

Interior chimneys:

- *Lower in cost.* The brickwork cannot be seen, thus does not have to be finished.

- *Function better.* The flue is kept warm because it is sheltered by the house. Thus, it draws better.

- *Take up floor space.*

- *Best design* for heating plant in the basement.

Exterior chimneys:

- *Higher in cost.* All brickwork must be finished.

- *Do not function as well.* The outside air cools the flue, thus slowing down the draw.

- *Do not take up much floor space.* Most of the chimney is outside of the house.

- *Poorer design* for the heating plant in the basement. Some heating ducts or heating pipes must reach the length of the house.

Detail Drawings

Detail drawings of a fireplace and chimney, figure 9-27, usually consist of:

1. *a front view* showing the overall fireplace design and size of the opening.
2. *a section view* showing dimensions and construction of both the fireplace and chimney.

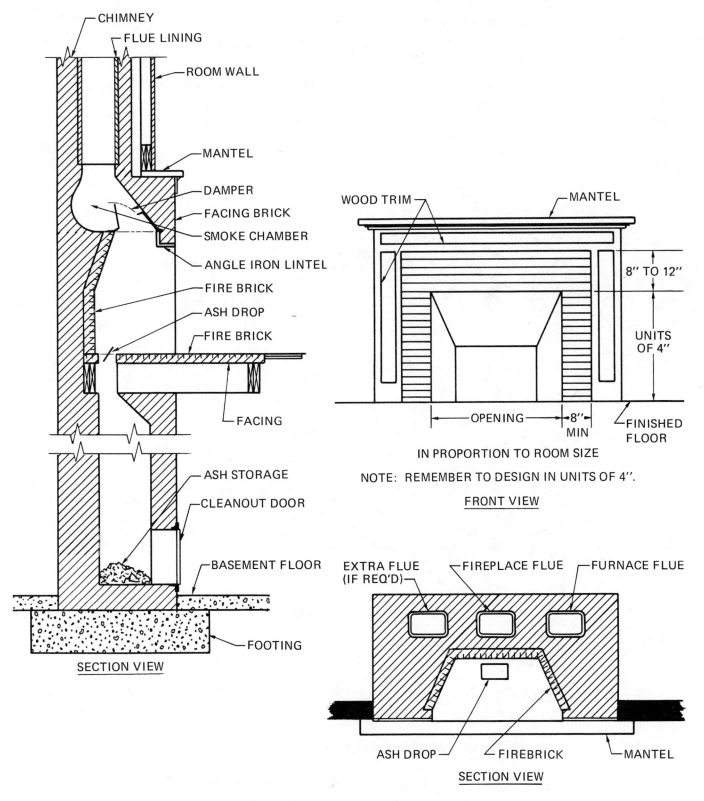

A WELL-DESIGNED CHIMNEY SHOULD BE SELF-SUPPORTING.

CHIMNEY

FLUE LINING

ROOM WALL

MANTEL

DAMPER

FACING BRICK

SMOKE CHAMBER

ANGLE IRON LINTEL

FIRE BRICK

ASH DROP

FIRE BRICK

FACING

ASH STORAGE

CLEANOUT DOOR

BASEMENT FLOOR

FOOTING

SECTION VIEW

WOOD TRIM

MANTEL

8″ TO 12″

UNITS OF 4″

OPENING

8″ MIN

FINISHED FLOOR

IN PROPORTION TO ROOM SIZE

NOTE: REMEMBER TO DESIGN IN UNITS OF 4″.

FRONT VIEW

EXTRA FLUE (IF REQ'D)

FIREPLACE FLUE

FURNACE FLUE

ASH DROP

FIREBRICK

MANTEL

SECTION VIEW

Fig. 9-27 Detail drawings of fireplace and chimney

Fireplace Openings

For best efficiency a fireplace opening must be in proportion to the size of the room. Recommended fireplace openings for various size rooms are noted in figure 9-28.

Room Size	Width of opening	Height of opening	Depth	Flue size
Small—250 Sq. Ft.	2'-8"	1'-9" to 2'-0"	1'-8"	8 1/2" x 13"
Medium—300 Sq. Ft.	3'-0"	2'-0" to 2'-2 1/3"	1'-8"	13" x 13"
Large—350 Sq. Ft.	4'-0"	2'-0" to 2'-2 1/3"	2'-0"	13" x 18"

Fig. 9-28 Proportion of fireplace opening to room size

A nominal size for a standard brick with mortar joint is 4" x 2 2/3" x 8". For a 3/8-inch joint, a 2 1/4" x 3 5/8" x 7 5/8" brick is used, figure 9-29. Call off brick dimensions in multiples of 8 inches, or at least in multiples of 4 inches. Remember that joint size determines the brick size and three courses always equals 8 inches. A *course* is a layer of stone or brick plus mortar joint.

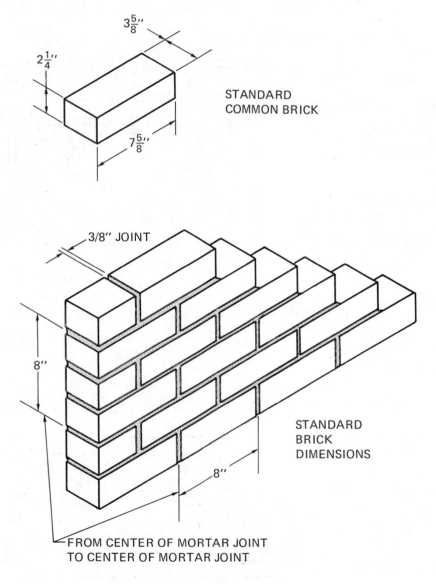

STANDARD
COMMON BRICK

3/8" JOINT

STANDARD
BRICK
DIMENSIONS

FROM CENTER OF MORTAR JOINT
TO CENTER OF MORTAR JOINT

Fig. 9-29 Standard brick dimensions

If a 1/2-inch joint is required, a brick size of 2 3/16" x 3 1/2" x 7 1/2" is used. For 1/4-inch joint, a brick size of 2 3/8" x 3 3/4" x 7 3/4" is used. Standard firebrick used inside the fireplace opening is 2 1/2" x 4 1/2" x 9".

Damper

The *damper assembly,* figure 9-30 is a manufactured part consisting of a metal frame and adjustable door. The damper opening is the same width as the fireplace opening width.

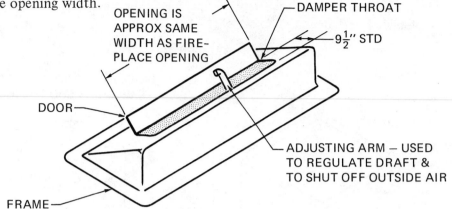

Fig. 9-30 Damper assembly

Ash Dump

The *ash dump* is a manufactured assembly consisting of a metal frame and a flush-fitting swivel door that allows ashes to drop to the ash storage area at the bottom, figure 9-31. It is manufactured in various sizes, but 5" x 8" is standard.

Cleanout Door

The *cleanout door* is a manufactured assembly consisting of a metal door mounted on a simple frame. It provides an opening to clean out the ashes and is located in the basement or on the exterior wall of the house. Cleanout doors come in various sizes, but 12" x 12" is standard, figure 9-31.

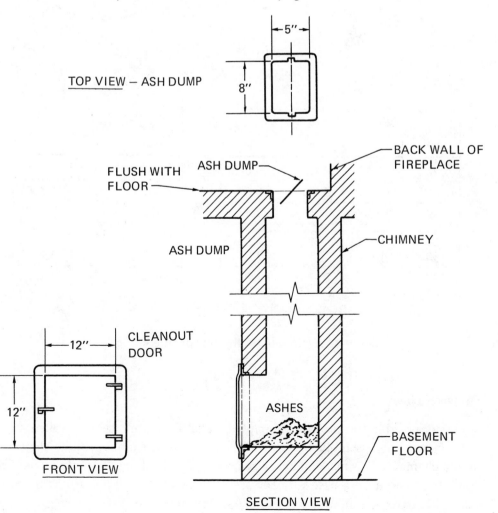

Fig. 9-31 Section view of an ash dump and cleanout door

Flue Lining

A *flue lining* is constructed of terra cotta. Its size, like the damper, is in direct relation to the size of the fireplace opening, figure 9-32. The area should not be less than 1/10 that of the fireplace opening. Flue linings are generally square or rectangular in shape.

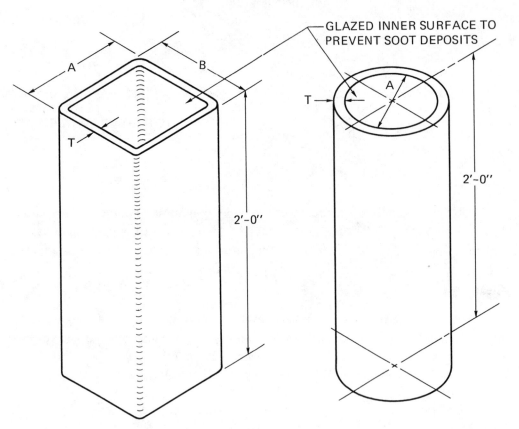

STANDARD SIZES: ALL 2'-0" LONG

Square/Rectangle Flue			
Area	A	B	T
22"	4 1/2"	8 1/2"	5/8"
51"	8 1/2"	8 1/2"	5/8"
79"	8 1/2"	13"	3/4"
125"	13"	13"	7/8"
168"	13"	18"	7/8"
232"	18"	18"	1 1/8"

Round Flue		
Area	A	T
26"	6"	5/8"
47"	8"	3/4"
75"	10"	7/8"
108"	12"	1"
171"	15"	1 1/8"
240"	18"	1 1/4"

AREAS SHOWN ARE NET INSIDE AREAS.

Fig. 9-32 Determining the size of flue lining

Fireplace Liner

It is possible to purchase a complete metal fireplace assembly called a *fireplace liner*. This assembly consists of the sides, back, damper, smoke shelf, and smoke chamber. It is made of heavy-gauge metal welded together into a complete unit. It is placed on a base with the facing brick or stone built around it. Some assemblies have built-in duct work to make them very efficient.

Standard Chimney

Figure 9-33 shows a standard chimney. The framing around a chimney is exactly like a stair opening; that is, a double header completely surrounds the opening.

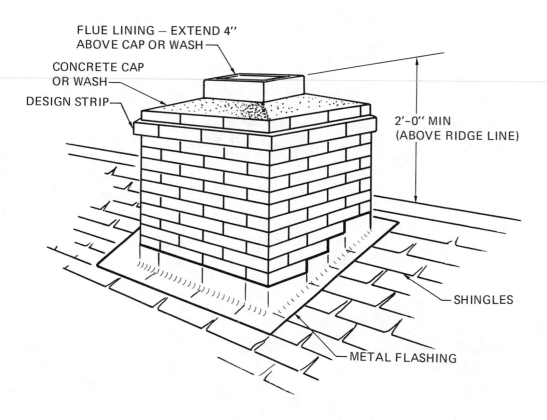

Fig. 9-33 Standard chimney

Chimney Hood

Chimney hoods, figure 9-34, prevent water from entering the chimney and stop down drafts due to nearby hills, buildings, trees, etc.

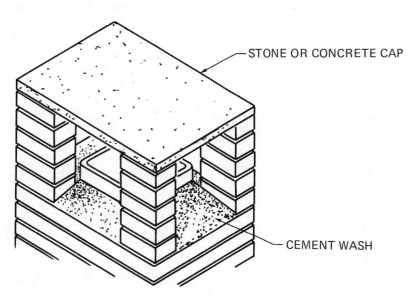

CHIMNEY HOOD

Fig. 9-34 Chimney hood

Height of Chimney Above the Ridge

On a flat roof, the top of a chimney should be a minimum of 3'-0" above the roof. Chimney heights for other roofs are illustrated in figure 9-35.

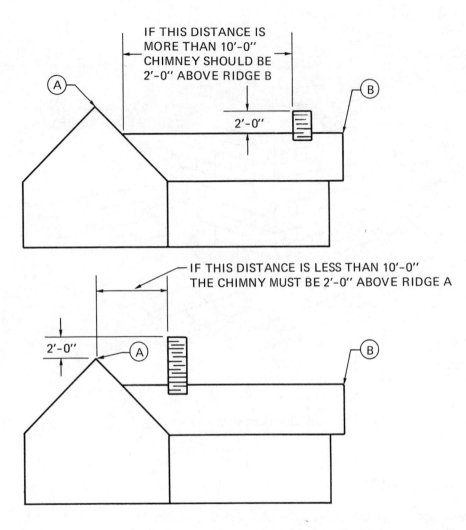

Fig. 9-35 Determining chimney height

UNIT 10

STAIR LAYOUT

Stairs provide access from one level to another. Some stairs lead from one level to the next without a change in direction, others turn 90 degrees, others a full 180 degree. Unit 10 shows the four major types of stairs, various terms associated with stairs, and how to layout each style of stair. It is important that thought be given to the stair requirements and length of required stair opening even at the floor plan sketching stage of design.

Note: The minimum width of stairs is 3'-0''; 3'-6'' to 4'-0'' is preferred.

Figure 10-1 shows the recommended angular measurement for stairs. Figure 10-2 shows the relationship between rise and tread.

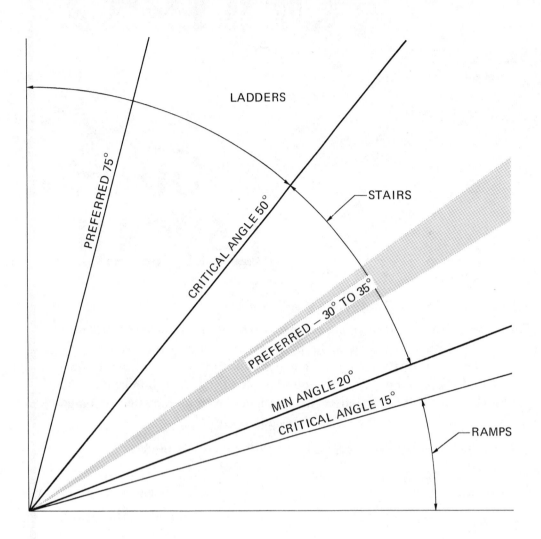

Fig. 10-1 Recommended angles

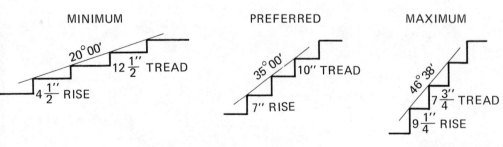

RISE + TREAD = 17 INCHES

Fig. 10-2 Recommended rise and tread relationship

TYPES OF STAIRS

Straight Stairs

Straight stairs go directly from one floor to the next without any turns, figure 10-3. These are the least expensive stairs to build. If the stairs have walls on both sides, they are called *closed stairs*. If they are open on one or both sides, they are called *open stairs*. Open stairs require a railing on the open side. Some stairs, such as those in the basement, may require a stair rail on both sides.

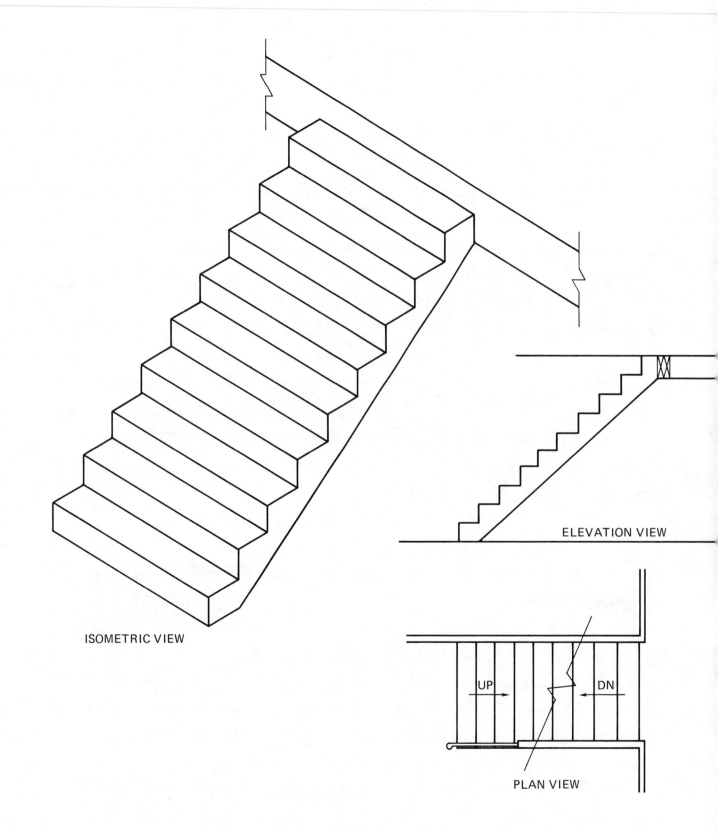

ISOMETRIC VIEW

ELEVATION VIEW

UP   DN

PLAN VIEW

Fig. 10-3 Straight stairs

L Stairs

An *L stair* has one landing somewhere in the stairway, figure 10-4. To be a true L stairway, the stairs must make a 90° turn at the landing. The landing can be located anyplace on the stair plan.

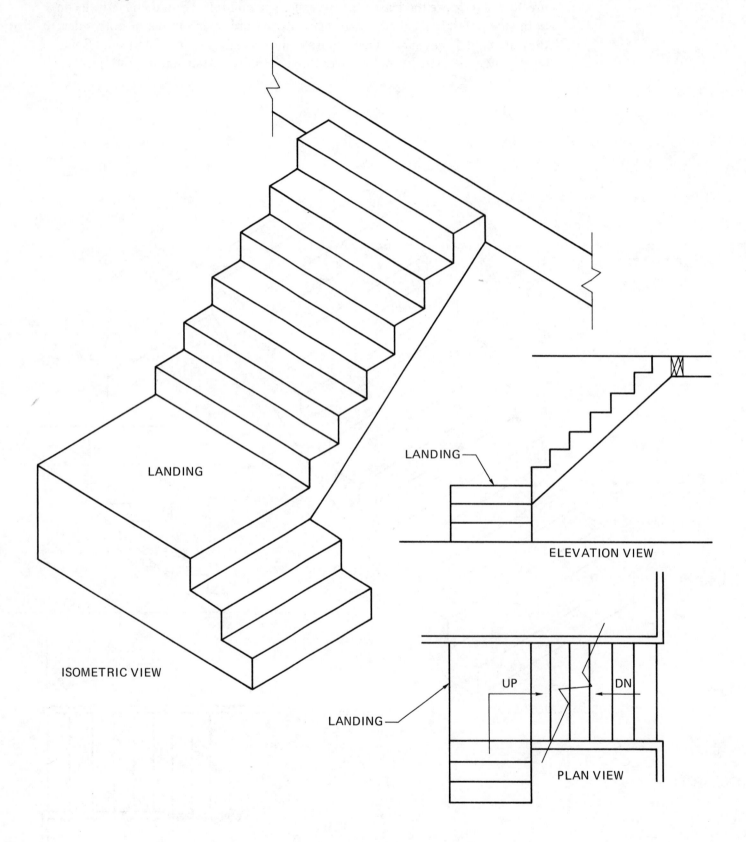

LANDING

ELEVATION VIEW

LANDING

ISOMETRIC VIEW

UP   DN

LANDING

PLAN VIEW

Fig. 10-4   L stairs

Winder Stairs

If space is short and there is no space for a landing, wedge-shaped stairs are used to form corners. Such stairs are called *winder stairs,* figure 10-5. These are more costly to make and could be a hazard as the narrow end is not large enough to step on safely.

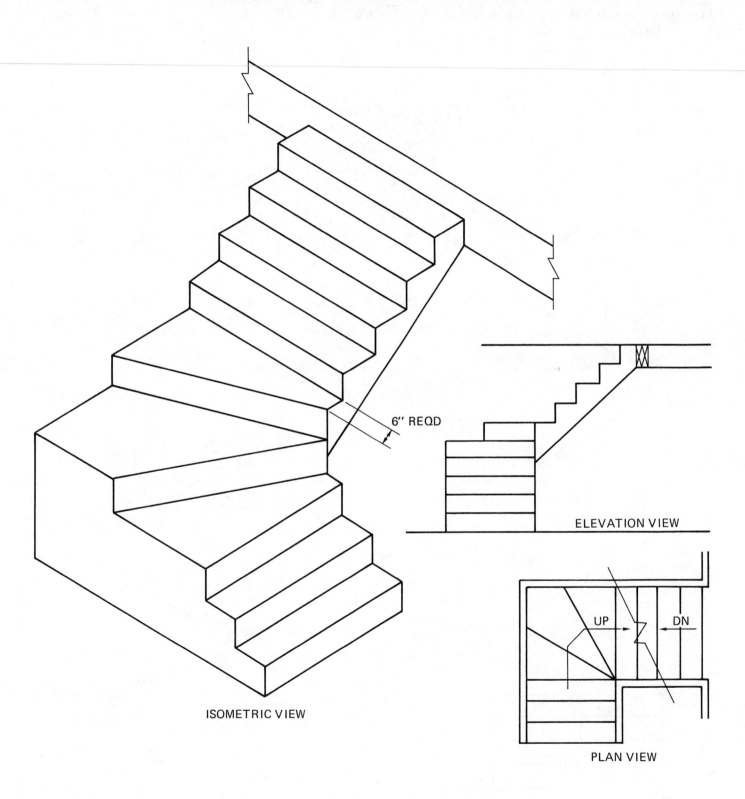

6″ REQD

ELEVATION VIEW

UP   DN

PLAN VIEW

ISOMETRIC VIEW

Fig. 10-5 Winder stairs

U Stairs

U stairs start with an entrance level and have two flights of steps going up and down parallel to each other. As seen in the plan view, figure 10-6, there may be little or no space between the flights of stairs. This type of stair is often used in split-level homes. The U stair is the hardest to visualize. Note the grade line and the placement of the footings in the raised ranch and the split-level in figure 10-7.

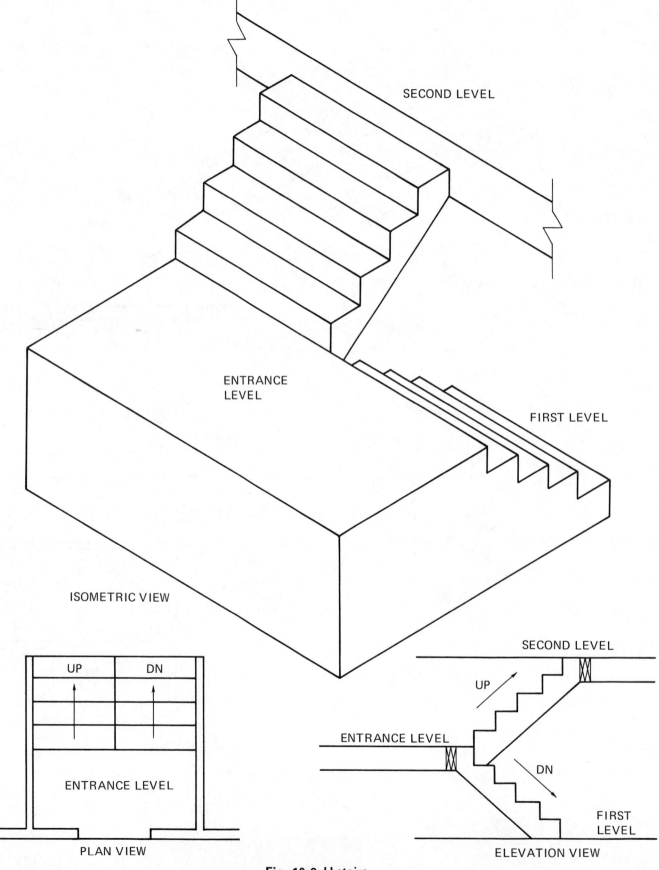

Fig. 10-6 U stairs

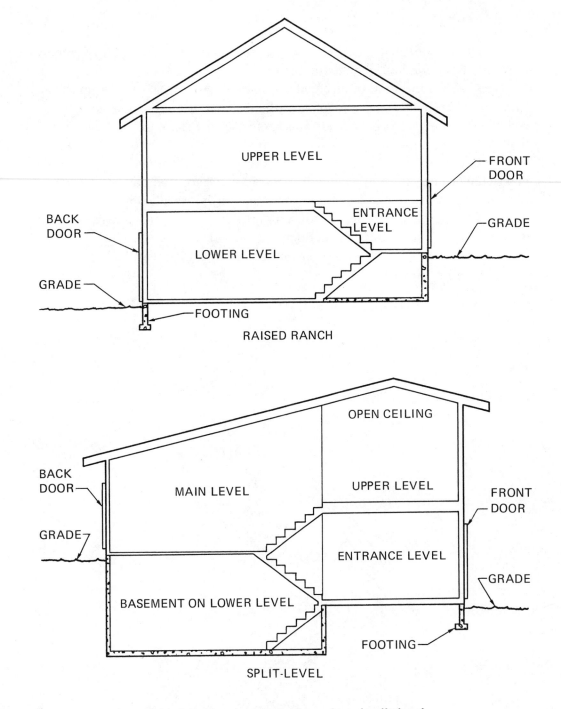

Fig. 10-7 U stairs in raised ranch and split-level

STAIR PARTS

It is important that a drafter know all stair parts, figure 10-8, and understand the basic method of constructing them.

Total run is the total of all treads. *Total rise* is the total of all risers from finish floor to finish floor. *Headroom* is the distance from the stair nose to the ceiling. The preferred distance for headroom is 7'-6", the minimum distance is 6'-8". *Handrails* should be a standard height of 2'-6" from nose of step. There is always one more riser than tread in a stairway as the landing or floor above makes the last tread. Study figures 10-8 and 10-9 to learn stair parts and terms.

One of the first important considerations in house planning is the stair design. In order to complete the house floor plans, the drafter must know the distance from finish floor to finish floor and the stair openings, figure 10-9. The stairway is the key to circulation for the whole house. A great deal of thought should be given to its location.

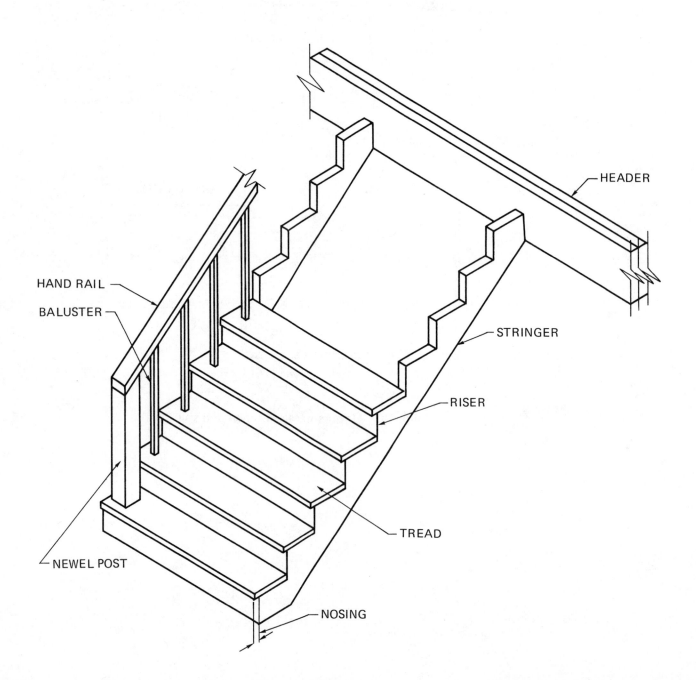

Fig. 10-8 Stair parts

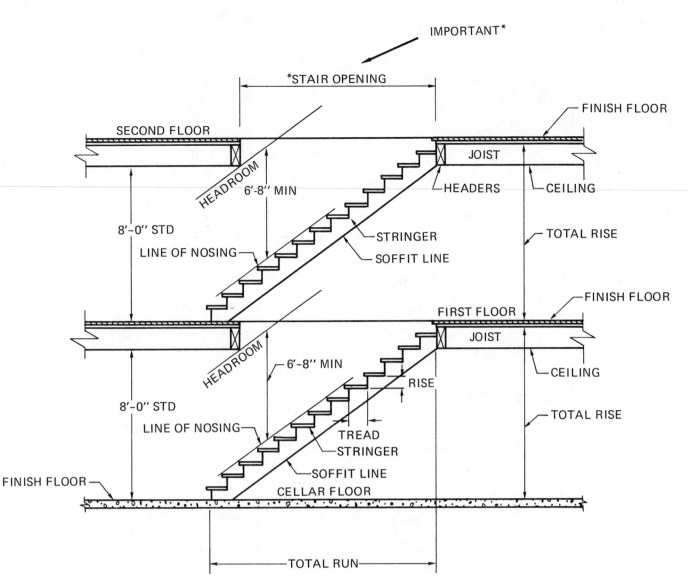

Fig. 10-9 Stair parts and terms.

MEASUREMENTS FOR STAIRS

When determining measurements for stairs, remember that as the tread decreases, the rise increases. The overall distance from step to step remains the same. A good rule to follow is to make the individual rise and tread measurements equal approximately 17 inches when added together.

STAIR FORMULA

Step 1. Using the measurements given in figure 10-10, find the exact distance from finish floor to finish floor. Note that floor joists are actually 3/4 inch thinner than stated. For instance a 2 x 8 floor joist has an actual thickness of 7 1/4 inches.

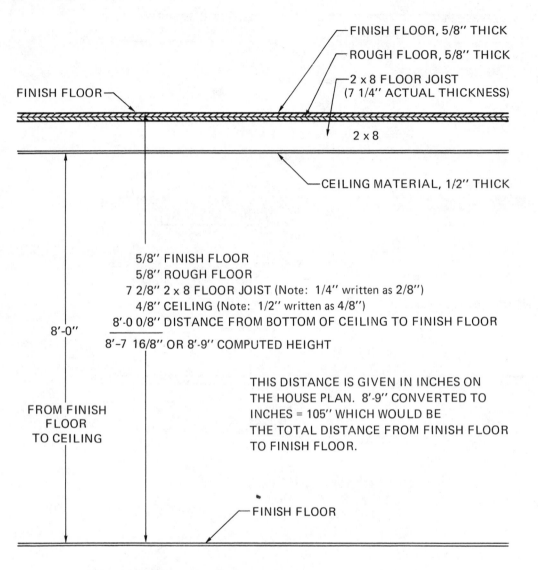

FINISH FLOOR, 5/8" THICK

ROUGH FLOOR, 5/8" THICK

2 x 8 FLOOR JOIST
(7 1/4" ACTUAL THICKNESS)

FINISH FLOOR

2 x 8

CEILING MATERIAL, 1/2" THICK

5/8" FINISH FLOOR
5/8" ROUGH FLOOR
7 2/8" 2 x 8 FLOOR JOIST (Note: 1/4" written as 2/8")
4/8" CEILING (Note: 1/2" written as 4/8")
8'-0 0/8" DISTANCE FROM BOTTOM OF CEILING TO FINISH FLOOR
8'-7 16/8" OR 8'-9" COMPUTED HEIGHT

8'-0"

THIS DISTANCE IS GIVEN IN INCHES ON
THE HOUSE PLAN. 8'-9" CONVERTED TO
INCHES = 105" WHICH WOULD BE
THE TOTAL DISTANCE FROM FINISH FLOOR
TO FINISH FLOOR.

FROM FINISH
FLOOR
TO CEILING

FINISH FLOOR

Fig. 10-10 Computing distance from finish floor to finish floor

Step 2. Each stair *riser* should be about 7 inches high. Divide 7 inches into 105 inches, which is the distance from finish floor to finish floor, step 1.

$$\begin{array}{r} 15 \\ 7\,\overline{)\,105} \end{array}\quad\text{APPROXIMATELY 15 RISERS}$$

Fig. 10-11 Computing stair rise

Step 3.   Using the scale 1/2" = 1'-0", two horizontal parallel lines are laid out 105 inches apart (8'-9"). Using the ruler method, this distance is divided into 15 parts representing the 15 risers needed, figure 10-12.

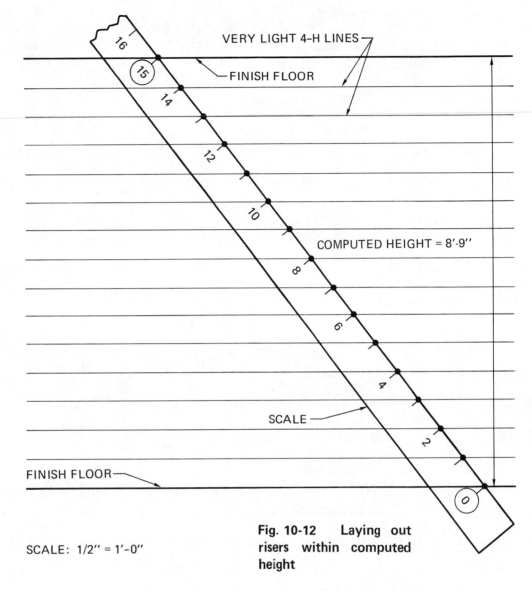

VERY LIGHT 4-H LINES

FINISH FLOOR

COMPUTED HEIGHT = 8'-9"

SCALE

FINISH FLOOR

SCALE: 1/2" = 1'-0"

Fig. 10-12   Laying out risers within computed height

Step 4.   A riser height of 7 inches is used to determine the total risers needed in a finish floor to finish floor height of 105 inches. The total of one riser and one tread (run) should equal approximately 17 inches. Therefore, the treads in this example should be 10 inches in width, since the riser (7 inches) plus tread (10 inches) equals 17 inches.

Stair Formula (continued)

Step 5. In this example the rise is 7 inches and the tread is 10 inches (step 4). There are 15 risers (step 2). Since there is always one less tread than riser, then 14 treads are required. This equals a run of 140 inches (10″ X 14). Change the 140 inches to feet and inches (140″ ÷ 12 = 11′-8″). Draw two vertical lines 11′-8″ apart, figure 10-13. This is the total run.

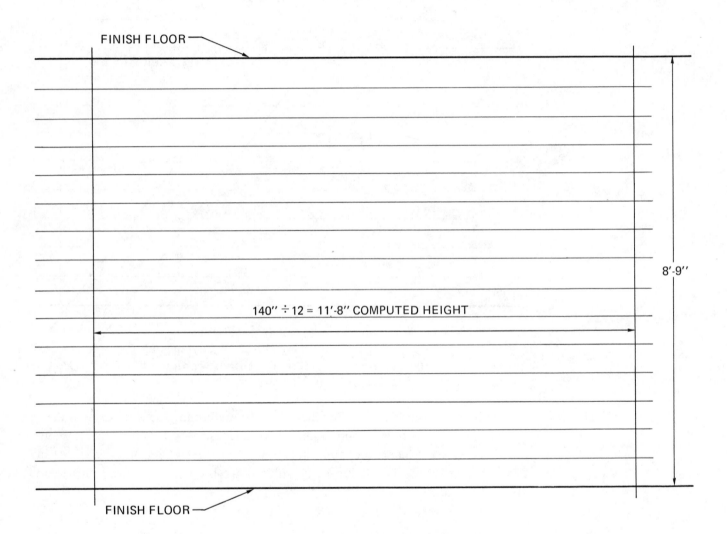

FINISH FLOOR

140″ ÷ 12 = 11′-8″ COMPUTED HEIGHT

8′-9″

FINISH FLOOR

Fig. 10-13 Computing run

Step 6. Using the same method as step 3, divide the total run section into 14 even spaces, figure 10-14. Carefully line up the drafting machine from point 'A' to point 'B' and check this angle. It should be between 30° minimum to 35° maximum (see figure 10-9). If it is not within this range, the layout must be redesigned. Draw a light line from point 'A' to point 'B.' Notice point 'A' is up one block and 'B' is on the finish floor above. This is the stair *nosing.* A protractor is used to determine this angle if drafting machines are not available.

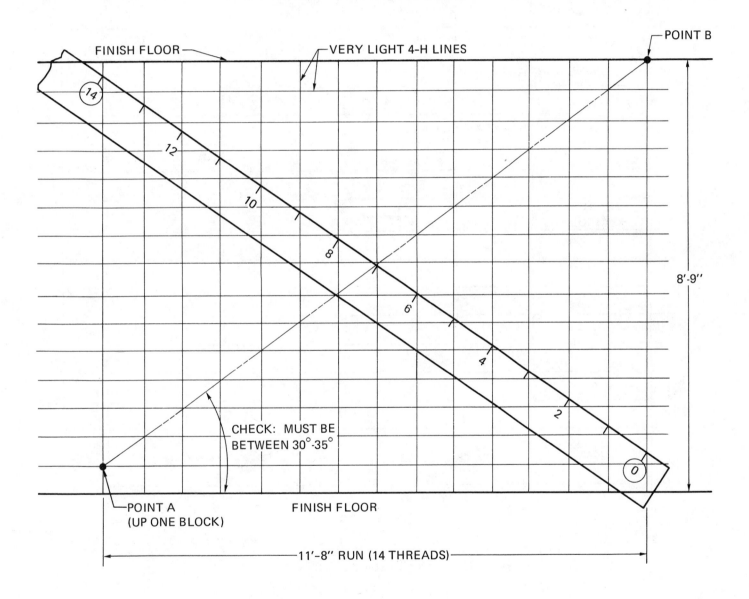

Fig. 10-14 Laying out treads within computed run

Step 7. Carefully draw in the stairs from point 'A' to point 'B.' From point 'A,' measure straight upwards to a distance equal to the *headroom* desired. 7'-0'' is used in this example. This locates point 'C'. Draw a line through point 'C' parellel to the *nosing line*. The resulting line represents the *headroom* of the stair well, figure 10-15.

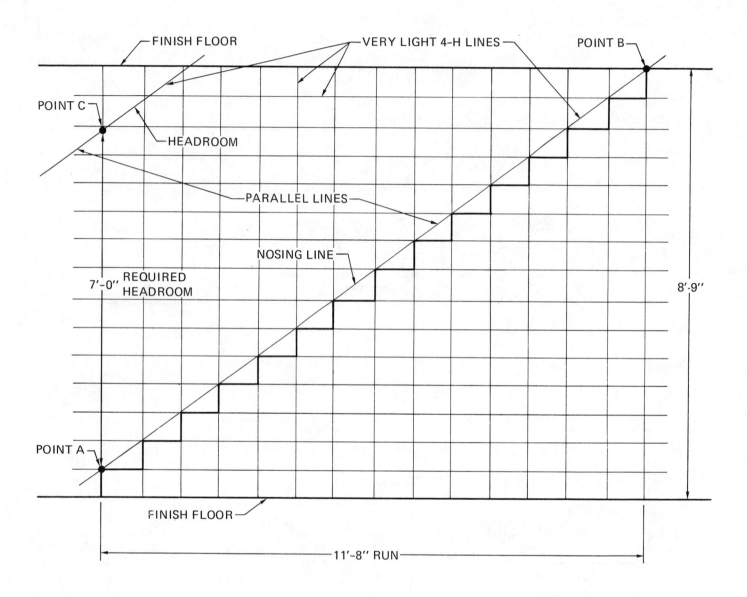

Fig. 10-15 Drawing in stairs

Step 8.   Lay out the finish floor, rough floor, floor joist, and ceiling so they stop or end on headroom line (point C). Measure the opening, figure 10-16. Before designing the floor plan, the stair opening size must be known. Basically, the same steps are followed to determine the stair openings for straight, L, winder, or U stairs.

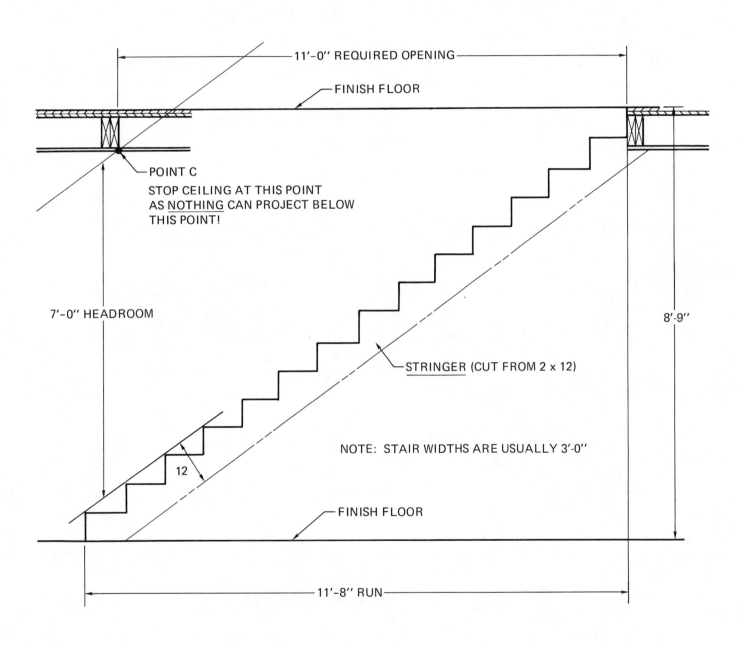

Fig. 10-16 Computing the stair opening

UNIT 11

STRUCTURAL MEMBERS & LOADING

BUILDING A STRUCTURE

The *architect* is the owner's representative. He designs the structure the owner wants and develops working drawings and specifications for the owner's needs. Most of the time the owner of the proposed structure cannot supervise the construction personally, nor has the knowledge to do so, so an architect is hired to check each step of construction. The architect's decisions are final as far as the building contractor is concerned.

The construction of any structure is described by a set of *drawings and specifications*. A set of house drawings shows the boundaries, contours, and outstanding physical characteristics of the site. Drawings give instructions for the excavation; erection of the foundations; installation of heating, lighting, and plumbing facilities; and whatever else is required to complete the structure.

The architect and engineer work together on the design of a structure. Together they determine the construction materials to be used and the methods of construction.

One of the principal factors influencing design is the intended use of the structure. Factors such as overall size; external appearance; arrangement of internal space; and the number, size and kind of doors, windows, and fittings are the responsibility of the architect. The engineer calculates the strength of the supporting members and the mechanical systems needed, such as plumbing, lighting, heating, ventilation, and air-conditioning.

Architectural working drawings consist of plans, elevations, sections, details, and a pictorial view of the building. Engineering drawings include structural, grading, electrical, plumbing, heating, ventilating, and site plans.

MEMBERS OF A STRUCTURE

A structure is built of parts, called *members,* intended to support and transmit loads. The points at which members are connected are called *joints.* All structures, such as bridges, towers, and buildings, have certain factors in common. It is important to understand these terms.

Loading

The main loads present in every structure are classified as dead loads and live loads.

Dead load is the weight of the structure itself. This weight increases gradually as the structure is built and remains constant once the structure is completed. The weight of all structural members plus the floors, walls, heating equipment, and all other nonmovable items in a building are considered when computing dead load.

Live load is the weight of movable objects on the floor of a building or deck of a bridge. This includes people and furniture in a building and the traffic across a bridge.

Structures are designed with the same basic theory of load distribution. All live loads are supported by horizontal structural members that, in turn, are supported by vertical structural members. The loads are transmitted from the horizontal members to the supporting vertical members. Vertical members are supported by footings, piers, or foundation walls that rest on the ground. All structural loads are therefore dispersed into the ground supporting the structure.

The ability of the ground to support loads is called its *soil bearing capacity.* The bearing capacity of the ground is measured in pounds per square foot. It varies for different soils. The area over which a footing extends is a factor in distributing the load received from a column in accordance with the bearing capacity of the soil. The size of a footing, therefore, is determined by the bearing capacity of the soil on which the structure is built.

The load on an individual structural member is classified as uniformily distributed or concentrated. A *concentrated load* is exerted at a particular point on a member as, for example, the load of a beam on a girder. A *uniformly distributed load* is one which is spread throughout a member, such as on a beam. *Eccentric loading* occurs when force on a member, such as a column, is applied off center instead of at the center of the column.

Stress

The loading of a structural member has a tendency to deform it. The ability of a member to withstand certain kinds of deformation is called *stress.*

Tension is the stress that resists the tendency of forces acting in opposite directions to pull a body apart.

Compression is the stress that resists the tendency of forces acting toward each other to push a member together.

Shear is the stress that resists the tendency of parellel forces acting in opposite directions to cause adjoining planes of a body to slide onto each other.

Torsion is the stress that resists the tendency of a body to twist.

Stiffness of a member is its ability to resist bending.

Strength of a member is its ability to resist breaking.

Vertical Structrual Members

Vertical members are in compression. They support loads acting downward from the top. Footings, columns, piers, posts, and studs are the most common vertical members.

Footings rest on soil and transmit their received load to the ground. The natural material on which a footing rests is called the *foundation bed.* Footings support columns, piers, pilasters, walls, and similar loads. In the case of masonry walls, however, spread footings are used. A *spread footing* extends the length of the structure. Footings are made of concrete with *rebar* (steel reinforcement bars) for strength.

Columns are of steel, timber, or concrete construction. They rest on footings and are the principal load-carrying vertical members.

Piers are of concrete, timber, or masonry construction. They rest on footings and support horizontal or vertical members.

Studs are vertical members used in wood frame construction for walls. *Posts* are also vertical members used in wood frame construction and are located at the corners.

Horizontal Structural Members

Horizontal members support live loads. They are supported by vertical members. Joists, beams, girders, and rafters are the most common horizontal structural members.

Joists are light beams. They take the load directly from the floor.

Beams, like joists, take the load of the floor directly.

Girders take the load of either joists or beams and are the heaviest horizontal members in a structure.

Lintels are beams which span door or window openings and support the structure above those openings.

Rafters are sloping members that support the roof covering. A *common rafter* fits between the valley and hip rafters. *Hip rafters* extend at an angle from the plates at the corner to the ridge. *Jack rafters* extend from the plate to the hip or valley rafter. *Valley rafters* extend from an inside corner of the plates to the ridge.

Purlins are horizontal timbers supporting several rafters at one or more points or the roof sheathing directly.

Trusses are wood or steel structural members connected together to span the space between the walls of a building to support the roof load.

Covering Members

Subflooring is attached to the floor joists. *Finish flooring* is attached to the subflooring with building paper between the sheathing and the finish materials.

Sheathing, siding, and *roofing* cover structural members to form the outside walls and roof. A *vapor barrier* is placed between the sheathing and the finish materials.

Mechanical systems of a building include heating, wiring, and plumbing.

MATERIALS

The various materials used in house construction must be understood by the drafter in order to prepare a drawing showing how those materials are assembled. Many materials are specified according to *nominal size* rather than actual size. For example, bricks which are considered to be 8 inches long are actually 7 5/8 inches long, allowing 3/8 inches for a mortar joint. The nominal size of the brick is 8 inches. Figure 11-1 lists common nominal and actual sizes of lumber.

Thickness		Width	
Nominal	Actual	Nominal	Actual
1	3/4	2	1 1/2
1 1/4	1	3	2 1/2
1 1/2	1 1/4	4	3 1/2
2	1 1/2	5	4 1/2
2 1/2	2	6	5 1/2
3	2 1/2	7	6 1/2
3 1/2	3	8	7 1/4
4	3 1/2	9	8 1/4
		10	9 1/4
		11	10 1/4
		12	11 1/4

Fig. 11-1 Nominal and actual sizes of lumber

Wood is the most common material and is used in every type of construction. Because of its wide use, a drafter must know the terminology; the names, function and location of structural members; and the various standard sizes of wood.

Concrete is the material used most frequently for footings and foundations. It may be strengthened by adding steel bars, in which case it is known as *reinforced concrete*. Reinforced concrete may be used to support heavy structural loads. Drafters must know the methods of building concrete structures and representing reinforced steel on drawings.

Masonry materials can be classified as material bonded together with mortar. This includes bricks, stone, concrete blocks, and various tile products. Each has specific uses, properties, and standard unit sizes.

Steel construction usually consists of assembling structural steel members that have been fabricated at the mill for the particular structure being erected. Drafters must know the shapes and sizes of standard members, the methods of connecting them, and the drawing practices pertaining to steel construction.

TRIBUTARY AREA AND WEIGHT

Each structural house member supports a certain part or area of the total building. The weight of this area is called *tributary weight:* Live load + dead load X total area = tributary weight. Figures 11-2, 11-3, and 11-4 explain tributary weight. Assume the total weight is evenly distributed across the floor as indicated by the arrows. Each wall supports half the weight.

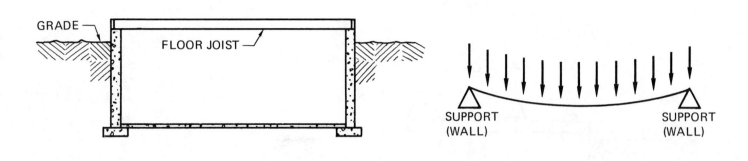

Fig. 11-2 Floor joist with no support

In figure 11-2, the floor joist has no support. A supporting member (beam) the length of the foundation is added, figure 11-3.

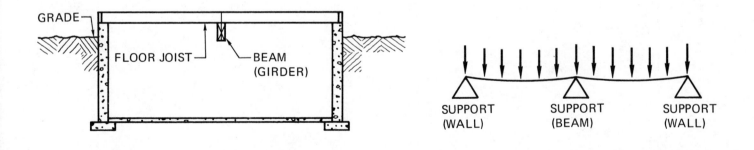

Fig. 11-3 Floor joist with beam added

Notice that *half the total load* (live load + dead load) is now on the beam, figure 11-4. The left wall supports one quarter of the weight, and the right wall supports one quarter of the weight. The other half is equally divided between the two walls. If there is a 4,000-pound load (live load + dead load) on the floor: 1,000 pounds are on the left wall, 1,000 pounds are on the right wall, and 2,000 pounds are supported or held up by the beam.

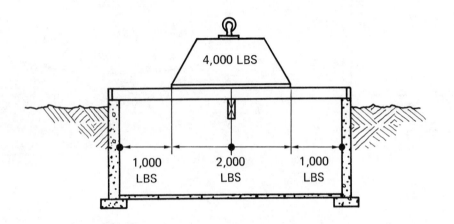

Fig. 11-4

Computing Tributary Weight

In order to find the tributary weight on any member, add the live load and the dead load together and multiply by the area of the tributary. To find the tributary weight of the beam in figure 11-5:

1. Live load + dead load = total load:
   40 lbs./sq. ft. + 20 lbs./sq. ft. = 60 lbs./sq. ft.

2. Total floor area = 26 ft. X 36 ft. = 936 sq. ft.

3. Total load X total floor area = total weight on the floor:
   60 lbs./sq. ft. X 936 sq. ft. = 56,160 lbs.

4. To find tributary weight on the beam, divide the total weight of the floor by 2:
   56,160 lbs. ÷ 2 = 28,080 lbs. tributary weight

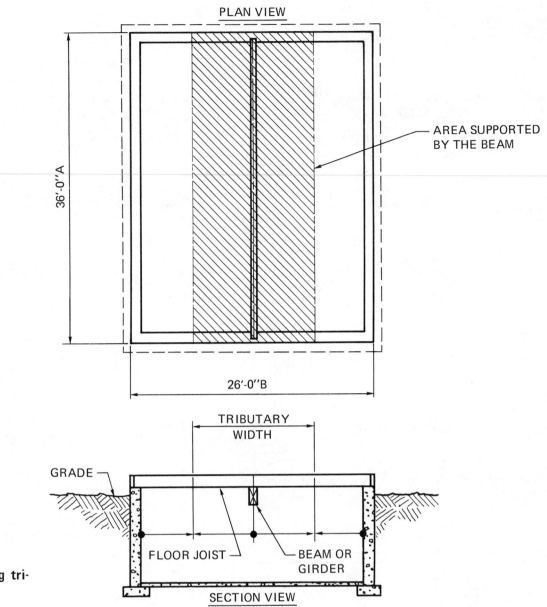

Fig. 11-5 Computing tributary weight

Estimating Loads

The total weight supported by the structural house members consists of the total dead load plus the live load. Dead load is the weight of all the materials that make up the building. Live load is anything that can come or go, such as people, furniture, snow, and wind. These loads will vary a little and it is assumed that the load is equally distrubuted around the floor. A simple method is to figure each floor with a live load of 40 pounds per square foot and a dead load of 20 pounds per square foot. Study figure 11-6 for other loadings:

Location	Dead Load	Live Load
Floor	20 lbs./sq. ft.	40 lbs./sq. ft.
Attic (storage)	20 lbs./sq. ft.	20 lbs./sq. ft.
Attic (not floored)	10 lbs./sq. ft.	0 lbs./sq. ft.
Roof (snow/wind)	10 lbs./sq. ft.	30 lbs./sq. ft.
Partitions/walls	20 lbs./sq. ft.	0 lbs./sq. ft.

Fig. 11-6 Estimating loads

Tributary Weight on a Column

Add a column in the center of the floor in figure 11-7. The column now acts like a wall to support the load and the same factors apply.

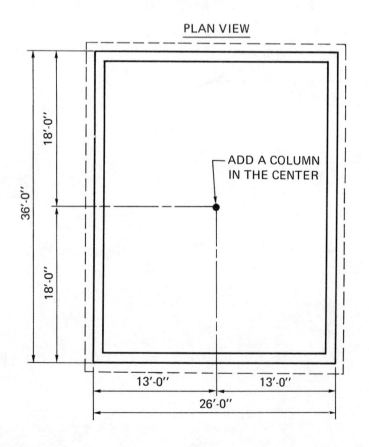

PLAN VIEW

Fig. 11-7

Notice in the section views, figure 11-8, how half the load is on the wall and the other half is resting on the column. Using the same loadings, what is the tributary area and weight supported by the column?

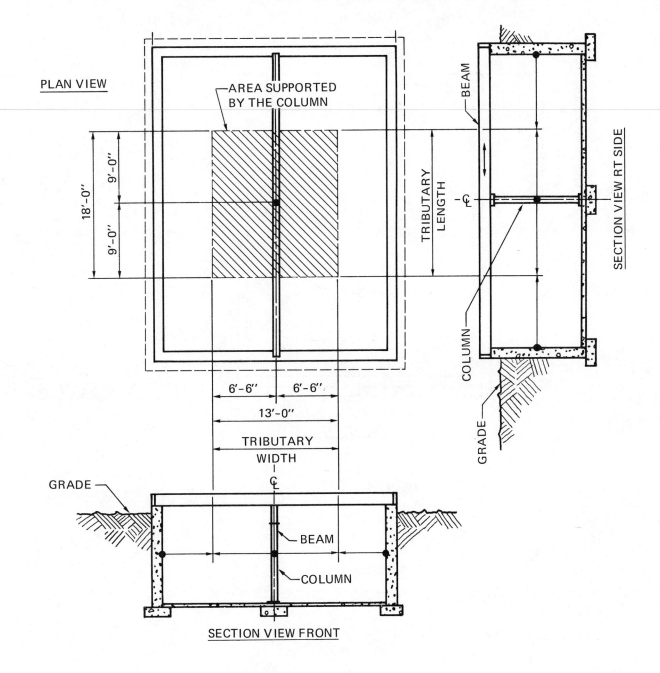

Fig. 11-8 Tributary weight of a column

1. Tributary area = 13 ft. × 18 ft. = 234 sq. ft.

2. Live load + dead load = total load:
   40 lbs./sq. ft. + 20 lbs./sq. ft. = 60 lbs./sq. ft.

3. Total load × tributary area = tributary weight
   60 lbs./sq. ft. × 234 sq. ft. = 14,040 lbs.

The total tributary weight placed on a column must be known in order to determine the correct size column to use.

Tributary Weight on a Beam Supported by a Column

Using the column in the center of figure 11-9, calculate the weight supported by the beam. In this example, figure 11-10:

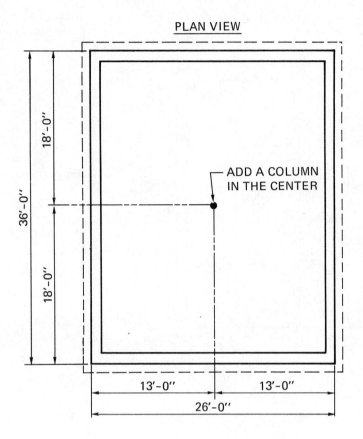

PLAN VIEW

Fig. 11-9

1. 18 ft. × 13 ft. = 234 sq. ft. tributary area

2. 40 lbs./sq. ft. + 20 lbs./sq. ft. = 60 lbs./sq. ft. weight of floor (live + dead)
    (live + dead)

3. 234 sq. ft. × 60 lbs./sq. ft. = 14,040 lbs. tributary weight

The tributary weight is usually converted to kips. One *kip* equals 1000 lbs. Therefore, 14,000 pounds equals 14 kips. Convert all weight (pounds) to kips.

PLAN VIEW

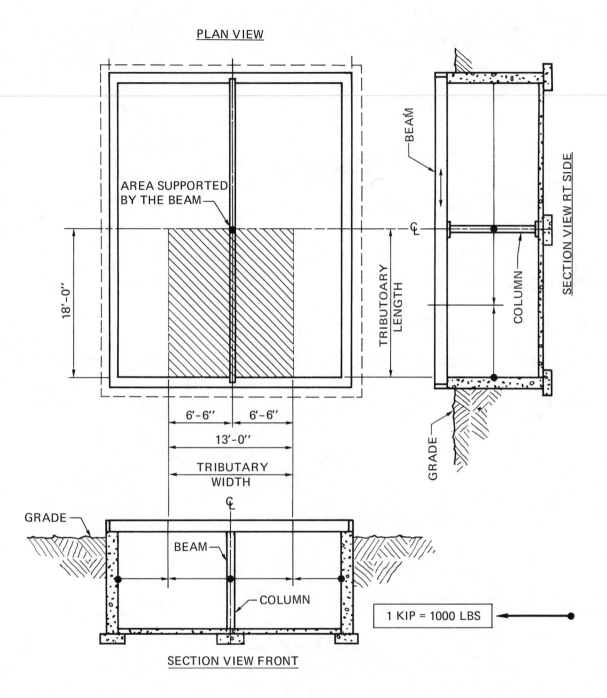

AREA SUPPORTED
BY THE BEAM

18'-0"

TRIBUTOARY
LENGTH

6'-6"   6'-6"

13'-0"

TRIBUTARY
WIDTH

BEAM

SECTION VIEW RT SIDE

COLUMN

GRADE

GRADE

BEAM

COLUMN

1 KIP = 1000 LBS

SECTION VIEW FRONT

Fig. 11-10

Size of Floor Joist (40 lb. live wt.)		
Max. Span	Spacing	Size of Joist
7'- 4''	16''	2 x 6
8'- 6''	12''	
10'- 4''	16''	2 x 8
12'- 0''	12''	
14'- 0''	16''	2 x 10
15'- 6''	12''	
16'- 6''	16''	2 x 12
17'-10''	12''	

Example: A span of 13'-8'' spacing, 16'' O.C., would use a 2 x 10 joist.

Fig. 11-11 Floor joists, span and spacing chart

Size of Ceiling Joist		
Max. Span	Spacing	Size of Joist
7'- 8''	16''	2 x 6
9'- 6''	12''	
10'-10''	16''	2 x 8
13'- 4''	12''	
14'- 8''	16''	2 x 10
18'- 0''	12''	

Example: A span of 10'-0'' spacing, 16'' O.C., would use a 2 x 8 joist.

Fig. 11-12 Ceiling joists, span and spacing chart

Size of Roof Rafter (over 3/12 pitch)		
Max. Span	Spacing	Size of Rafter
9'- 0''	16''	2 x 6
11'- 0''	12''	
12'- 8''	16''	2 x 8
15'- 6''	12''	
17'- 2''	16''	2 x 10
21'- 0''	12''	

Example: A span of 16'-0'' spacing, 16'' O.C., would use a 2 x 10 rafter.

NOTE: 16'' center to center spacing is standard and usually called off as: 16'' O.C. (example 2 x 8/16'' O.C.)

Fig. 11-13 Roof rafters, span and spacing chart

Size of Steel Beams

S 7 x 15.3 means a 7-inch high S beam that weighs 15.3 pounds per foot. *WF 8 x 17* means an 8-inch high, wide-flanged beam that weighs 17 pounds per foot. Other sizes of steel beams are listed in figure 11-14.

Size of Steel Beams							
Max Span							
8'	9'	10'	11'	12'	13'	14'	Size of Beam
17.3 kips	15.4 kips	13.9 kips	12.6 kips				S 7 x 15.3
24	21	18.8	17.1	15.7 kips			WF 8 x 17
28	25	22.6	20.6	18.9	17.4 kips		WF 8 x 20
36	32	29	26	24	22	21 kips	WF 10 x 21
44	39	35	32	29	27	25	WF 10 x 25

Fig. 11-14

Span for Headers

Headers are used above windows and doors. Figure 11-15 gives the maximum span for different sizes of wood headers.

Span for Headers (wood)		
No.	Size	Max. Span
(2)	2 x 4	3'- 6''
(2)	2 x 6	4'- 6''
(2)	2 x 8	6'- 0''
(2)	2 x 10	7'- 6''
(2)	2 x 12	9'- 0''

Fig. 11-15

Span for Steel Lintels

Lintels hold bricks or concrete in place over spans such as doors or fireplace openings. Figure 11-16 gives the maximum span for steel angle lintels per 4-inch thickness of material supported.

Span for Lintels (steel)	
Angle Iron Size	Max. Span
3 1/2 x 3 1/2 x 1/ 4	3'- 0''
4 x 3 1/2 x 5/16	5'- 0''
5 x 3 1/2 x 5/16	6'- 0''

Fig. 11-16

FOUNDATION FOOTING CALCULATIONS

Figure 11-17 shows how to calculate the weight a footing can support. Dimensions are added and all dead and live loads indicated. Wall or partition weights of 20 pounds per square foot are also added.

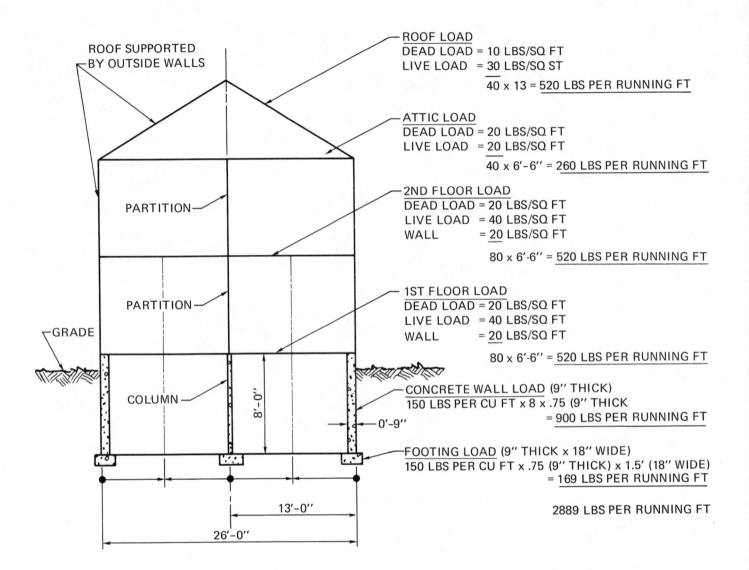

ROOF SUPPORTED BY OUTSIDE WALLS

PARTITION

PARTITION

GRADE

COLUMN

8'-0"

0'-9"

13'-0"

26'-0"

ROOF LOAD
DEAD LOAD = 10 LBS/SQ FT
LIVE LOAD = 30 LBS/SQ ST
40 x 13 = 520 LBS PER RUNNING FT

ATTIC LOAD
DEAD LOAD = 20 LBS/SQ FT
LIVE LOAD = 20 LBS/SQ FT
40 x 6'-6" = 260 LBS PER RUNNING FT

2ND FLOOR LOAD
DEAD LOAD = 20 LBS/SQ FT
LIVE LOAD = 40 LBS/SQ FT
WALL = 20 LBS/SQ FT
80 x 6'-6" = 520 LBS PER RUNNING FT

1ST FLOOR LOAD
DEAD LOAD = 20 LBS/SQ FT
LIVE LOAD = 40 LBS/SQ FT
WALL = 20 LBS/SQ FT
80 x 6'-6" = 520 LBS PER RUNNING FT

CONCRETE WALL LOAD (9" THICK)
150 LBS PER CU FT x 8 x .75 (9" THICK
= 900 LBS PER RUNNING FT

FOOTING LOAD (9" THICK x 18" WIDE)
150 LBS PER CU FT x .75 (9" THICK) x 1.5' (18" WIDE)
= 169 LBS PER RUNNING FT

2889 LBS PER RUNNING FT

Fig. 11-17 Foundation footing calculations

If an 18-inch wide footing is used, the load per square foot is: 12"/18" X 2,889 lbs./running ft. = 1,926 square feet. This is a safe footing for all kinds of soil as indicated in figure 11-18.

Safe Soil Loadings	
Type of Soil	Lbs. per Sq. Ft.
Ledge	30,000
Hard Pan	20,000
Gravel - compact	12,000
Gravel - loose	8,000
Sand - coarse	6,000
Sand - fine	4,000
Clay - stiff	8,000
Clay - med. stiff	6,000
Clay - normal	4,000
Clay - soft	2,000

Fig. 11-18   Safe soil load chart

COLUMN FOOTING CALCULATIONS

To determine the column footing weight, figure 11-19:

1. Calculate the column footing area;
    2'-0" X 2'-0" = 4 sq. ft.

2. Calculate tributary area:
    12'-0" X 13'-0" = 156 sq. ft.

3. Calculate weight load on cloumn:
    tributary area X total tributary weight
    156 sq. ft. X 200 lbs./sq. ft. = 31,200 lbs. on the column

4. Divide weight on a column by column footing area:
    31,200 lbs. ÷ 4 sq. ft. = 7,800 lbs./sq. ft.

Referring to figure 11-18, the size of the footing is satisfactory if it is built over loose gravel. It is not able to withstand the weight, however, if it is built on sand or clay soil.

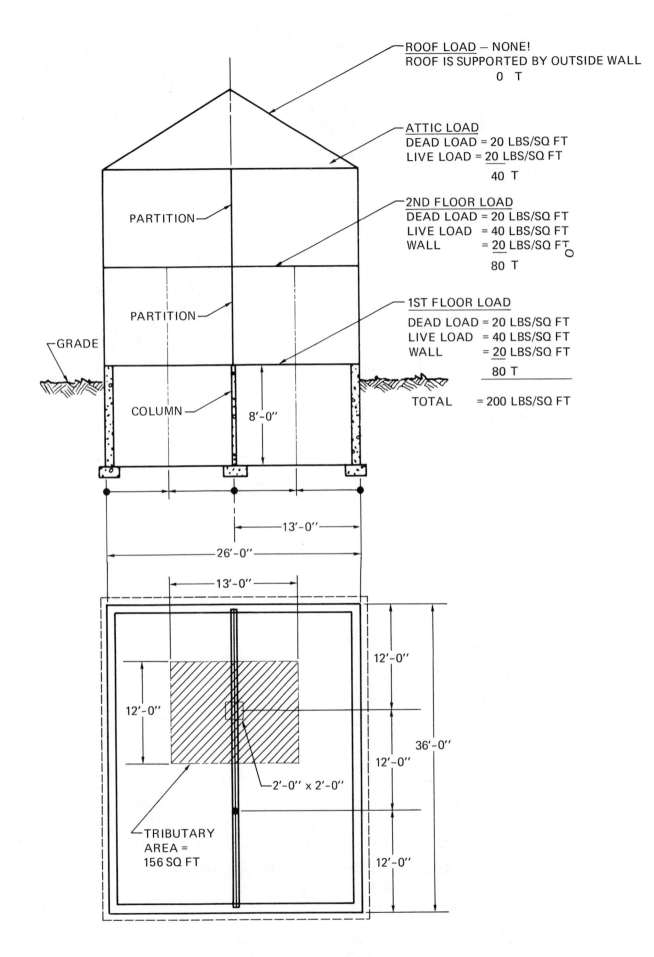

ROOF LOAD — NONE!
ROOF IS SUPPORTED BY OUTSIDE WALL
0   T

ATTIC LOAD
DEAD LOAD = 20 LBS/SQ FT
LIVE LOAD = 20 LBS/SQ FT
40 T

2ND FLOOR LOAD
DEAD LOAD = 20 LBS/SQ FT
LIVE LOAD = 40 LBS/SQ FT
WALL   = 20 LBS/SQ FT
80 T

1ST FLOOR LOAD
DEAD LOAD = 20 LBS/SQ FT
LIVE LOAD = 40 LBS/SQ FT
WALL   = 20 LBS/SQ FT
80 T

TOTAL   = 200 LBS/SQ FT

PARTITION

PARTITION

GRADE

COLUMN

8'-0"

13'-0"

26'-0"

13'-0"

12'-0"

12'-0"

36'-0"

12'-0"

2'-0" x 2'-0"

TRIBUTARY
AREA =
156 SQ FT

Fig. 11-19 Calculating column footing size

UNIT 12

WORKING DRAWINGS

DRAWINGS REQUIRED FOR DESIGNING A HOUSE

The sample house drawings in figures 12-1 through 12-9 of a split-level house illustrate the standard quality required in architectural drawing. All work should be of this same quality in terms of lines, lettering, and dimensioning and should include the same type of detail and notes.

Floor Plan

The floor plan is the first plan drawn when designing a house, figure 12-1. It includes:

- Overall size and shape of the house
- Size and location of each room
- Size and location of windows, doors, chimneys and fireplaces, and stairs
- Layout of kitchen and bathroom cabinets
- Electrical system
- Any special built-in features

A rough, in-scale layout should be done on another drafting sheet to determine exact stair opening. If a second floor is to be drawn, the outer walls, stair, and chimney locations should be traced directly from the first floor plan. These items must line up exactly in both plans.

Foundation Plan

The foundation plan is the second plan drawn, figure 12-2. It includes:

- Foundation wall and material
- Footings for foundation wall, columns, and chimney
- Location and size of all columns
- Size and location of windows, doors, chimneys, and fireplaces
- Heating plant location
- Electrical systems
- Any special built-in features

The foundation outer wall, stair, and chimney location should be traced directly from the first floor plan. These items must line up exactly in both plans.

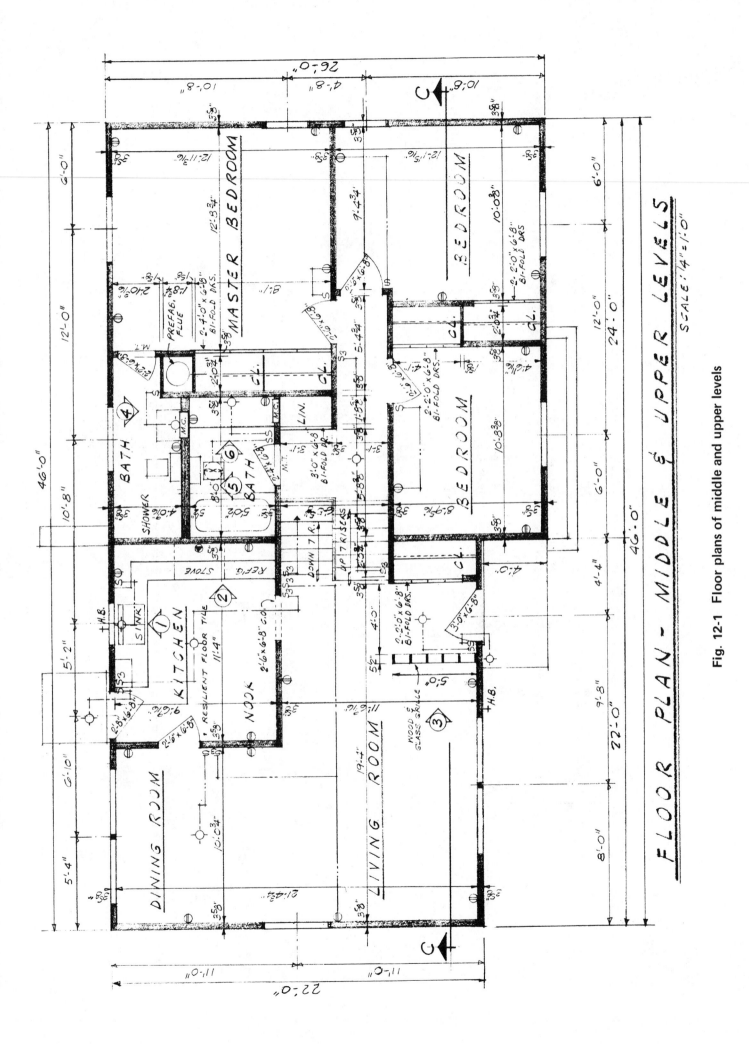

Fig. 12-1 Floor plans of middle and upper levels

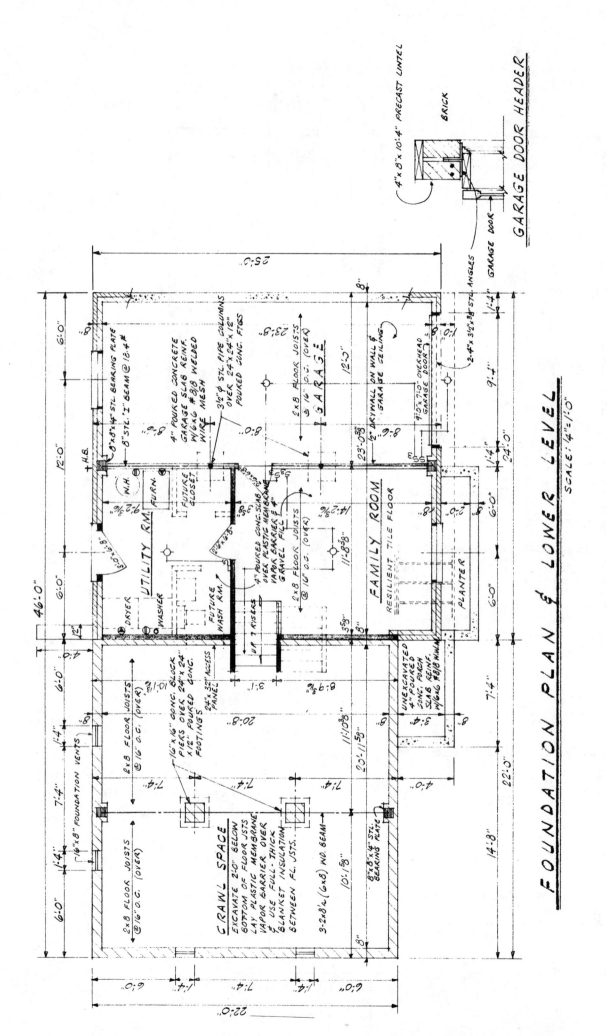

Fig. 12-2 Foundation plan and lower level

Section Views

Section views should be drawn next, figure 12-3. The section view should include:

- Footing
- Foundation
- Grade location
- Complete wall construction
- Roof pitch
- Style of eave
- Chimney size and height
- Window and door heights

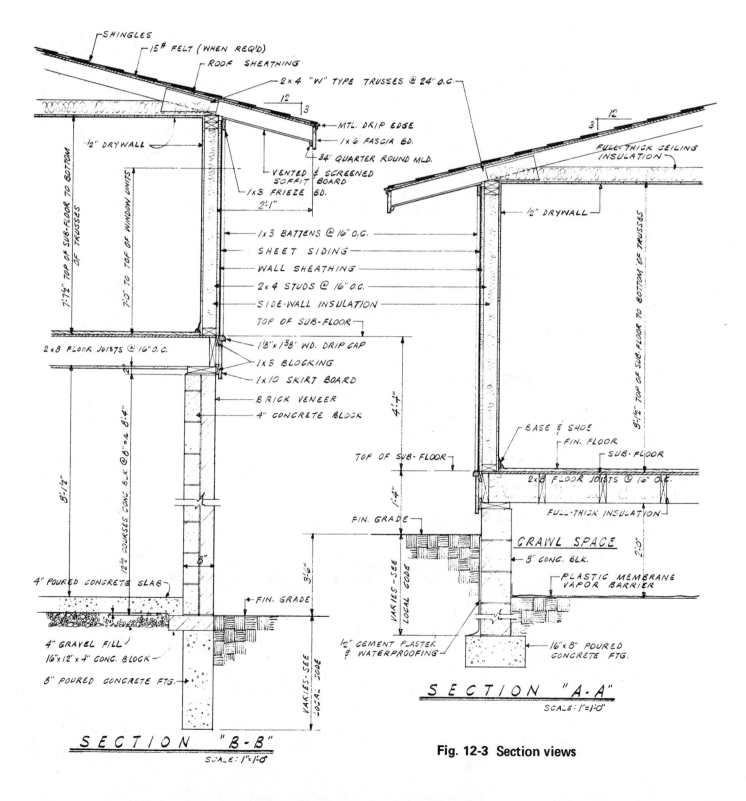

Fig. 12-3 Section views

Elevations

The front, back, right side, and left side elevations are drawn next, figure 12-4. These elevations must include all outside features and complete details, such as:

- Size and height of wall and roof
- Size, shape, style, and location of windows and doors
- Wall and roof materials
- Location and height of chimney
- A few dimensions for reference only

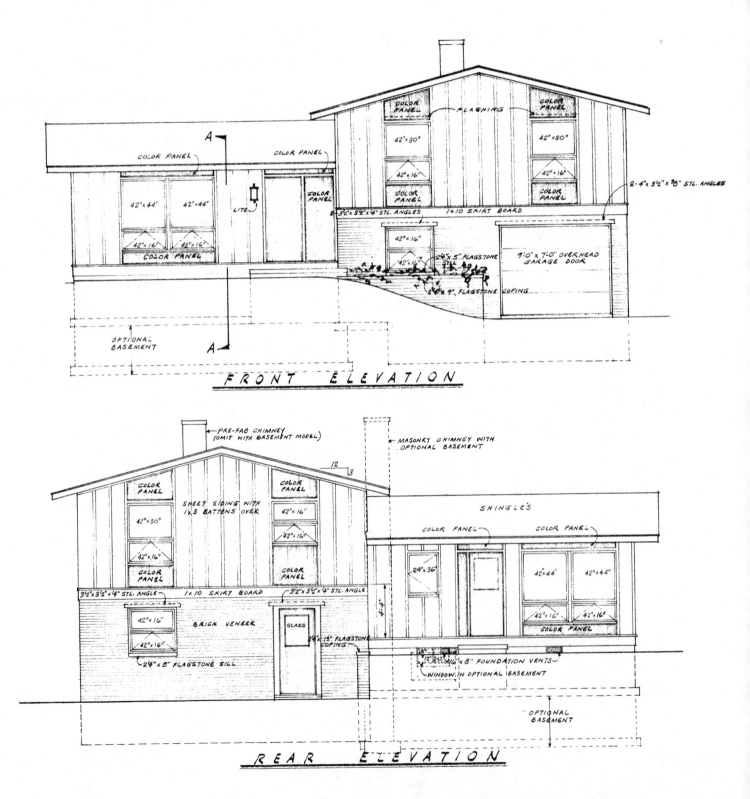

Fig. 12-4 Elevations

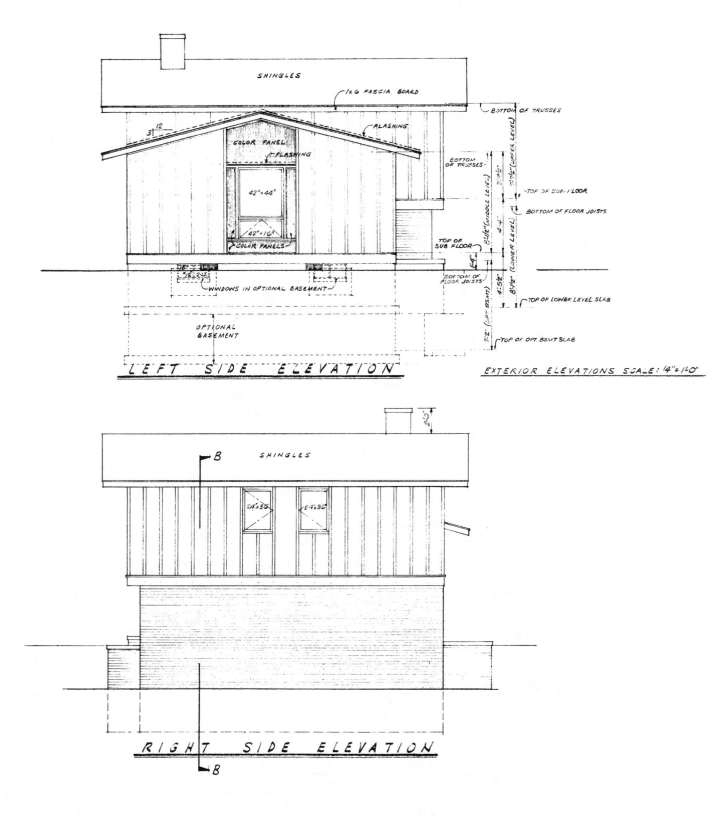

SHINGLES

1×6 FASCIA BOARD

FLASHING

3 | 12

COLOR PANEL

FLASHING

42"×44"

42"×16"

COLOR PANELS

WINDOWS IN OPTIONAL BASEMENT

OPTIONAL
BASEMENT

BOTTOM OF TRUSSES

BOTTOM
OF TRUSSES

TOP OF SUB-FLOOR

BOTTOM OF FLOOR JOISTS

TOP OF
SUB FLOOR

BOTTOM OF
FLOOR JOISTS

TOP OF LOWER LEVEL SLAB

TOP OF OPT. BSMT SLAB

LEFT SIDE ELEVATION

EXTERIOR ELEVATIONS SCALE: 1/4"=1'-0"

B

SHINGLES

24×36   24×36

RIGHT SIDE ELEVATION

B

Detail Drawings

Any assembly that should have clarification is detailed. Detail drawings are usually drawn to a larger scale. These drawings give complete information about components and subassemblies which would be difficult to interpret in smaller scale drawings. They may include:

- Details of construction
- Detailed layout of the roof, its construction, pitch, style of eave, materials, etc.
- Fireplace openings and trim
- Chimney layout
- Stair details and dimensions, figure 12-5
- Roof eave enlargement
- Cabinet layouts and sizes in kitchen and bathroom, figure 12-6
- Special molding details

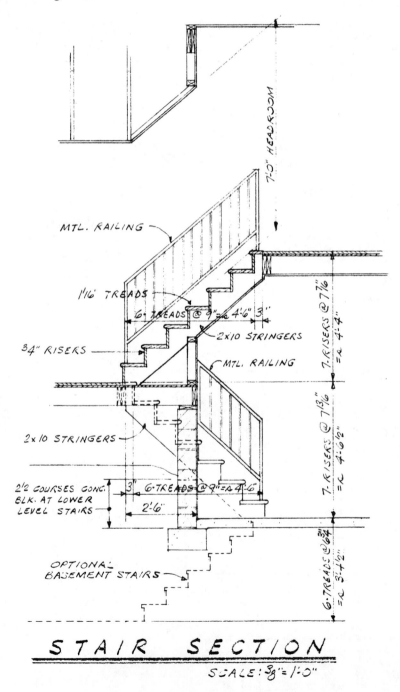

STAIR SECTION

SCALE: 3/8" = 1'-0"

Fig. 12-5 Detail drawings of stairs

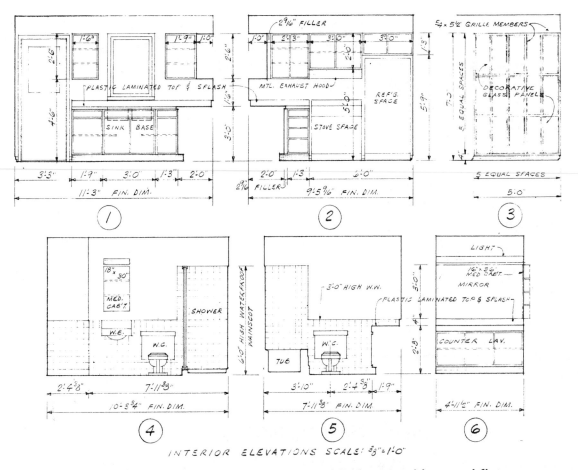

Fig. 12-6 Detail drawings of kitchen and bathroom cabinets and fixtures

Rendering

A *rendering* is a perspective drawing illustrating exactly what the house will look like when completed, figure 12-7. It is usually done by the architect or a rendering specialist. This drawing shows all exterior features exactly as they will appear in the finished house, as if a photograph had been taken of it. The rendering is often included on the title sheet.

DESIGN #1353 © HOME PLANNERS, INC., DETROIT

Fig. 12-7 Rendering of split-level house on title sheet

Title Sheet

The *title sheet* identifies the name and address of the owner of the plan, a rendering of the completed project, and any pertinent information, such as the name of the firm or person constructing the project, see figure 12-7.

Other Drawings

In addition to these standard drawings, other drawings are sometimes required, such as:

- Window and door schedules
- Electrical layout
- Plumbing details
- Heating and air-conditioning layouts
- Site or plot plan, figure 12-8
- Landscape plan

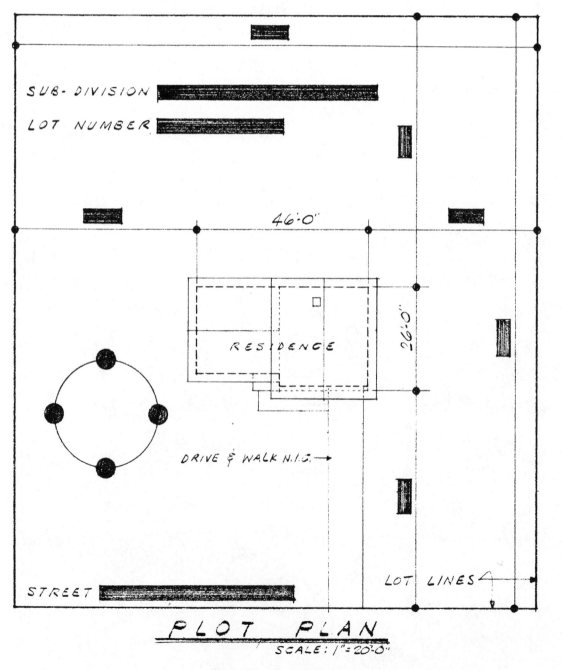

Fig. 12-8 Site plan

Specifications

It is impossible to include all the information on the working drawings that is necessary to complete a project. Therefore, construction specifications are needed. *Specifications,* or specs, are written documents that give detailed information not included on the working drawings.

In order to organize specifications into a standard form, the construction industry adopted the Construction Specification Institute's (CSI) *Format for Construction Specifications* in 1966. This format organizes all specifications into 16 *divisions:*

Division 1 - General Requirements

Division 2 - Site Work

Division 3 - Concrete

Division 4 - Masonry

Division 5 - Metals

Division 6 - Wood and Plastics

Division 7 - Thermal and Moisture Protection

Division 8 - Doors and Windows

Division 9 - Finishes

Division 10 - Specialties

Division 11 - Equipment

Division 12 - Furnishings

Division 13 - Special Construction

Division 14 - Conveying Systems

Division 15 - Mechanical

Division 16 - Electrical

Division 1, general requirements, describes such things as contracts; relationship between the owner, architect, and contractor; scheduling of work; temporary utilities; and project closeout. Divisions 2 through 16 detail the actual construction of the project and are arranged as nearly as possible in the order the work is to be done.

Each division is further divided into sections. A *section* contains all the detailed specifications for a particular phase of work within a division. For example, in Division 6 - Wood and Plastics, one section is: *06200 Finish Carpentry.* This section would contain all the detailed specifications needed to finish woodwork and related items, figure 12-9. The five-digit number identifies the section. It is useful when recording information for data processing.

The format for each section varies according to the job. If a section is not required for a certain project, it is omitted. A section may include such points as general conditions, scope of work, work performed by others, contract agreements, materials, application, guarantee, workmanship, etc.

The *CSI Format for Construction Specifications* is the most common standard used. Architects and specification writers may, however, choose to use their own method of recording specifications.

DIVISION 6 - WOOD AND PLASTICS

Section 06200 - FINISH CARPENTRY

General: This section covers all finish woodwork and related items not covered elsewhere in these specifications. The contractor shall furnish all materials, labor, and equipment necessary to complete the work, including rough hardware, finish hardware, and specialty items.

Protection of Materials: All millwork (finish woodwork*) and trim is to be delivered in a clean and dry condition and shall be stored to insure proper ventilation and protection from dampness. Do not install finish woodwork until concrete, masonry, plaster, and related work is dry.

Materials: All materials are to be the best of their respective kind. Lumber shall bear the mark and grade of the association under whose rules it is produced. All millwork shall be kiln dried to a maximum moisture content of 12%.

1. Exterior trim shall be select grade white pine, S4S.

2. Interior trim and millwork shall be select grade white pine, thoroughly sanded at the time of installation.

Installation: All millwork and trim shall be installed with tight fitting joints and formed to conceal future shrinkage due to drying. Interior woodwork shall be mitered or coped at corners (cut in a special way to form neat joints*). All nails are to be set below the surface of the wood and concealed with an approved putty or filler.

*(explanations in parentheses have been added to aide the student.)

Fig. 12-9 Sample section specification

UNIT 13

MAPS & SURVEYS

CARTOGRAPHY

Cartography is the art of mapmaking. A *cartographer* designs and draws maps using information obtained from various sources, such as surveyor's field notes and aerial photographs. Each map has a specific purpose. A cartographer chooses which features to include and how much detail to show, depending on the scale and use of the map. In order to draw an accurate map, a cartographer must know how an area is located on the earth.

The building should relate to the site and to the general area. A structure must become part of the environment and blend into the land, not simply indiscriminately placed on the land, thus a lot of thought must be given to style, shape and location. The structure should be oriented in regard to wind, sun, placement of trees, and surrounding buildings.

LATITUDE AND LONGITUDE

The earth's surface is divided into parallels of latitude and meridians of longitude. Where a base parallel and meridian intersect forms the coordinates of a point. They provide an accurate way of pinpointing an area on the earth.

Latitude is an arc distance measured in degrees from the equator, figure 13-1. A latitude north of the equator is called a north latitude, while one south of the equator is called a south latitude. The equator is the 0-degree latitude.

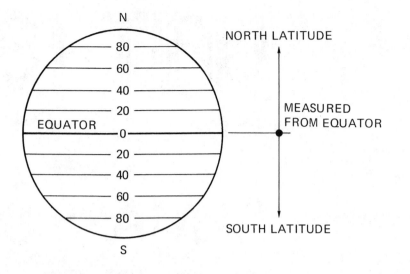

Fig. 13-1 Parallels of latitude

Longitude is an arc distance measured in degrees east and west from the prime meridian, figure 13-2. The *prime meridian* is an imaginary north-south line that passes through both geographic poles and through Greenwich, England. The prime meridian is the 0-degree meridian.

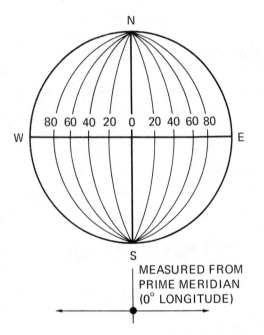

Fig. 13-2 Meridians of longitude

To pinpoint a place on the earth, simply call it out where the longitudinal line crosses the latitudinal line. New York City, for instance, is located where the 74°0′ west longitudinal line crosses the 40°45′ north latitude, figure 13-3.

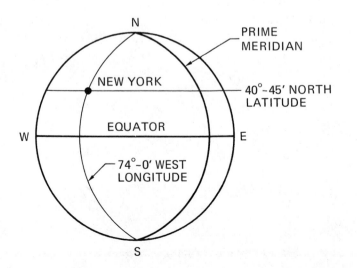

Fig. 13-3 Locating an exact point on the earth

MAGNETIC VARIATION OR DECLINATION

The earth's geographic poles are referred to as *true north* (or true south). In addition to these geographic poles, the earth has magnetic poles, figure 13-4. Magnetic poles are also connected by imaginary lines called magnetic meridians. A *magnetic meridian* is the direction a free magnet responds to the earth's magnetic pull.

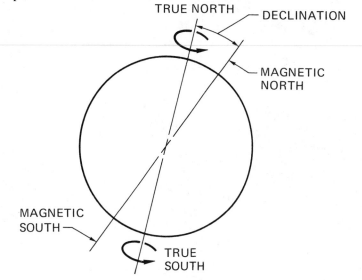

Fig. 13-4 The earth has a magnetic north and a true north

The distance between true and magnetic north is approximately 1300 miles. The position of magnetic north is influenced by changes in the earth and varies with time. True meridian, however, is constant.

The angle formed at any point between the magnetic meridian and the true meridian is called the *magnetic declination.* Variations of declination include secular, annual, diurnal, and other irregular variations.

True north is illustrated on a map by a full, solid arrowhead. Magnetic north is illustrated by a shorter, half arrowhead, figure 13-5. In surveying, the direction (or bearing) of a line is described by the angle it makes with either true north or magnetic north.

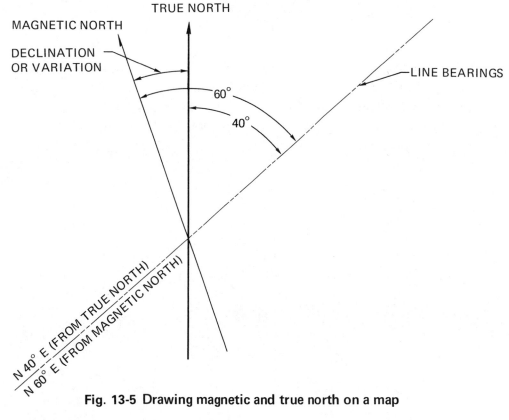

Fig. 13-5 Drawing magnetic and true north on a map

BEARING

The *bearing* of a line is the horizontal angle between the meridian plane through one end of the line and the vertical plane including the line. It is measured from the north or south up to 90 degrees, either right or left.

For example, a heading of N 60°E means from the north meridian plane, 60-degree horizontal angle, toward the east, figure 13-6.

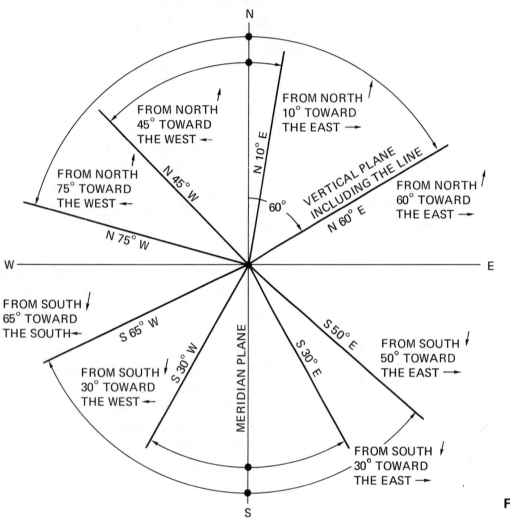

Fig. 13-6 Line bearings

Bearings are measured from the meridian. Therefore, all bearings are given as the number of degrees from a northerly direction or the number of degrees from a southerly direction. In figure 13-7, line OA heads south and is at a horizontal angle of 40 degrees from a south direction, so the bearing is S 40°. To

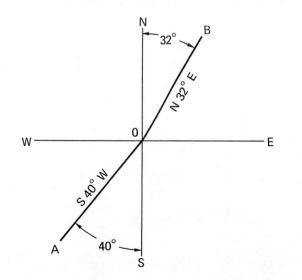

Fig. 13-7

indicate which side of the southerly line the bearing is on, an east or west is added: S 40° W. Line OB is 32 degrees to the east of a northerly direction, so its bearing is N 32° E.

It is suggested that the drafter rotate the drafting head 90 degrees counterclockwise so that 0 degrees is at the top, or north. All bearings can then be read directly from the protractor. A bearing angle may be from 0 to 90 degrees.

AZIMUTH

Another way to find the direction of travel of a line is to find its azimuth. An *azimuth* of any line is the direction it is deflected from either the north or south in a clockwise direction. In figure 13-8, the north azimuth was used. This is similar to determining bearings except azimuth angles go from 0 degrees to 360 degrees clockwise.

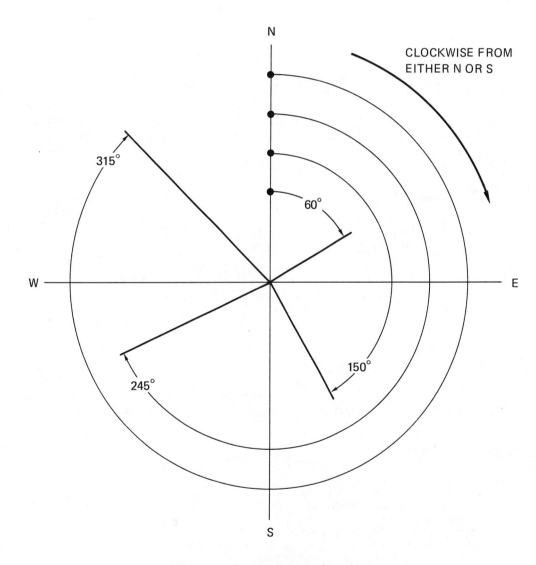

Fig. 13-8 Determining azimuths

To determine azimuth, start from either the north or south and head clockwise around to the direction of the line. The angle formed is the north or south azimuth. It is suggested that the drafter rotate the drafting head 90 degrees counterclockwise so the 0 is at the top or north. Then all degrees from 0 can be read directly from the protractor.

CIVIL MEASUREMENTS

There are many types of measuring systems used in the construction industry. Rulers and tapes are divided into common fractions. Decimal parts are used in map or civil drafting. With decimal parts, a foot is divided into tenths and hundredths of a foot instead of inches, figure 13-9.

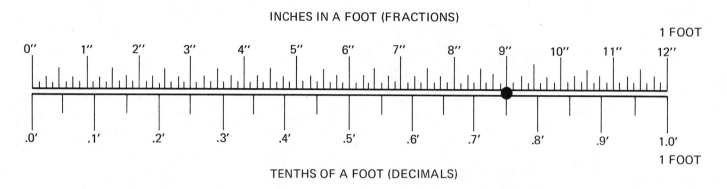

Fig. 13-9 Comparison between fraction and decimal scales

Use the bottom decimal scale for civil drawing in this text. The dot in figure 1-9 locates 9 inches on the fraction scale. This is written .75′ on the civil scale: (.75′ x 12″ = 9″).

Figure 13-10 lists conversions of inch dimensions to decimal dimensions. In order to find a dimension such as 8 1/2″, add 8″ (.67′) to ½″ (.04). Therefore, 8 1/2″ equals .71′.

1/8″ = .01′	1″ = .08′	7″ = .58′
1/4″ = .02′	2″ = .17′	8″ = .67′
3/8″ = .03′	3″ = .25′	9″ = .75′
1/2″ = .04′	4″ = .33′	10″ = .83′
5/8″ = .05′	5″ = .42′	11″ = .92′
3/4″ = .06′	6″ = .50′	12″ = 1.0′
7/8″ = .07′		

Fig. 13-10 Conversion chart changes inch dimensions to decimal dimensions.

1 MILE = 1760 YARDS = 5280 FEET = 1.6093 Km = 8 FURLONGS = 80 CHAINS
1 YARD = 3 FEET = 36 INCHES = 0.9144 m
1 FOOT = 12 INCHES = 0.3048 m
1 INCH = 2.54 cm
1 ROD (ALSO CALLED *POLE* OR *PERCH)* = 5.5 YARDS = 16.5 FEET = 0.5029 Dm

1 FURLONG = 10 CHAINS = 220 YARDS
1 CHAIN = 4 RODS = 22 YARDS = 66 FEET = 100 LINKS = 2.0116 Dm
1 LINK = 7.92 INCHES
1 SQUARE MILE = 640 ACRES = 6400 SQ. CHAINS
1 ACRE = 10 SQ. CHAINS = 4840 SQ. YARDS = 43,560 SQ. FEET
AN ACRE IS EQUAL TO A SQUARE, ONE SIDE OF WHICH IS 208.7 FEET

1 MILLIMETRE (mm) = 0.0393 INCH
10 MILLIMETRES (mm) = 1 CENTIMETRE (cm) = .3937 INCH
10 CENTIMETRES = 1 DECIMETRE (dm) = 3.9370 INCH
10 DECIMETRES = 1 METRE (m) = 39.3707 INCHES = 3.2808 FEET = 1.0936 YARDS
10 METRES = 1 DECAMETRE (Dm) = 32.8089 FEET
10 DECAMETRES = 1 HECTOMETRE (Hm) = 19.9278 RODS
10 HECTOMETRES = 1 KILOMETRE (Km) = 1093.61 YARDS = 0.6213 MILES
10 KILOMETRES = 1 MYRIAMETRE (Mm) = 6.2138 MILES

Fig. 13-11 Measurement Table

MAP SCALES

Map scales express the ratio between a map measurement and a corresponding ground distance. A scale of 1:125,000 means that one unit, such as an inch, represents 125,000 of the same such units on the earth's surface. Therefore, one inch on the map equals an actual distance of 125,000 inches, or approximately two miles, on the ground.

A *graphic scale* measures distances on a map, figure 13-12. It consists of a bar drawn at the same scale as the map. A portion of the map can be measured by gauging the distance with dividers, then comparing it to the graphic scale.

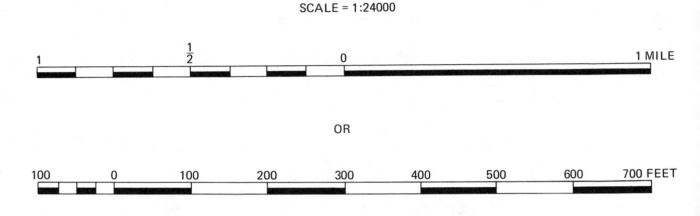

SCALE = 1:24000

1                    $\frac{1}{2}$ 0   1 MILE

OR

100   0   100   200   300   400   500   600   700 FEET

Fig. 13-12 Graphic scale

Quadrangle scales measure a standard four-sided area, set by the United States Geological Survey, that are bounded by lines of latitude and longitude, figure 13-13.

SCALE	1 INCH EQUAL
1:20,000	Approx. 1,667 feet
1:24,000	2,000 feet
1:30,000	2,500 feet
1:62,500	Approx. 1 mile
1:125,000	Approx. 2 miles
1:250,000	Approx. 4 miles

Fig. 13-13 Quadrangle scale

Study the *civil scale* (also called an engineer scale) in figure 13-14. Using a scale of 1″ = 100.0′ means that for every inch on the drawing there is 100.0′ on the ground. The scale of 10, as printed in the upper left-hand corner of the scale, could mean 1″ = 10.0′, 1″ = 100.0′ (illustrated), 1″ = 1000.0′, 1″ = 10,000′, and so on.

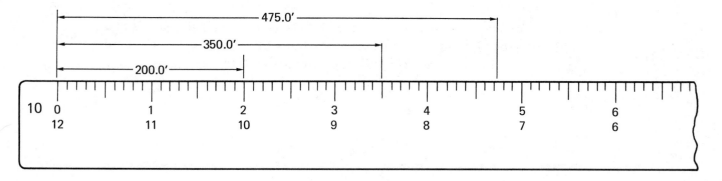

Fig. 13-14 Civil scale 1″ = 100.0′

Figure 13-15 shows a 1″ = 200.0 scale. Measurements are read directly from the scale. Study those given as examples.

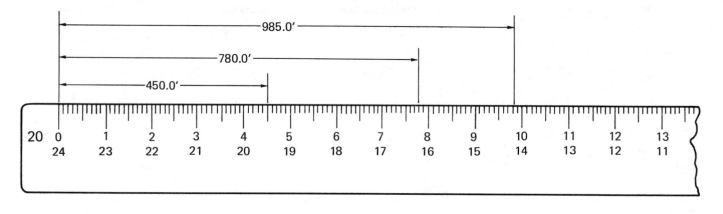

Fig. 13-15 Civil scale: 1″ = 200.0′

MAP FEATURES

The cartographer must decide what features to include on a map. The amount of detail depends on the scale of the map and its purpose. The most important features are emphasized by symbols, lines, or color. Only those features that pertain to the map are included.

Symbols

Features are represented on a map by symbols. Some standard symbols used by the United States Geological Survey are illustrated at the back of this text.

Symbols show where man-made features, such as railroads, bridges, buildings, roads, and public utilities, are located, including such utility equipment as gas mains, sewer systems, fire hydrants, electric poles, and telephone lines. Symbols indicate elevation and all types of boundaries. Natural surface symbols describe the terrain, the land's contour, and water features.

Symbols should never crowd a map. Too much detail makes a map difficult to read. Unnecessary features should not be included.

Color

A cartographer may add color to emphasize certain features on a map. Water may be colored blue, forests are green, mountains are brown, and icy regions are white. Color may distinguish one country from another.

The cartographer understands how to use color effectively and experiments with colored pencils, pastels, and water colors to get the desired effect.

Legend

A *legend* is a list that explains what certain symbols mean on a map. For instance, a legend may indicate what size city is shown by different symbols. Use of color is also described in a legend. Only those symbols that need an explanation are included in a legend.

KINDS OF MAPS

Each type of map has a specific purpose that governs the features included on it.

City maps are used to lay out cities and towns and show:

- Future planning and growth
- Records of land ownership
- Location of gas mains, water lines, sewer lines, and fire hydrants

Building site maps locate buildings on a lot and show:

- Orientation of buildings
- Ground elevation and contours
- Boundaries
- Utilities, walks, and driveways

Landscape maps are very much like building site maps and also include:

- All vegetation on a lot
- Location of shrubs, trees, grass, etc.

Plat maps are used as legal documents. They give a description of the land and show:

- All lengths and the bearings of all boundary lines
- Exact location of the plat in the township
- Acreage
- Name of abutting property owners

Topographic maps include all topographic features and show:

- Natural features such as lakes, streams, rivers, hills, and valleys
- Man-made features such as roads, houses, railroads, power lines, etc.

Nautical maps are used in sea navigation. They survey water and show:

- Shorelines
- Water depths
- Information about harbors
- Anchorage details
- Shipping approaches

Aeronautical maps are used in air navigation and show:

- Traffic routes
- Radio and electronic aids
- High points

Road maps are used by motorists and show:

- Roads
- Kinds of roads
- Location of towns

SURVEYS

A *survey* determines the shape, size, and location of an area by measuring distances and directions.

Plane surveying applies to small areas and ignores the curvature of the earth in its calculations. Most surveys are of this type.

Geodetic surveying takes the curvature of the earth into consideration. It is applicable to large areas and long lines, and precisely locates basic points suitable for controlling other surveys. It is used only when extreme accuracy is necessary.

Kinds of Surveys

A survey is made whenever certain features must be located precisely. Surveys establish boundaries for cities, lakes, forests, mines, and all types of construction sites.

Land or *boundary surveys* are the most common type of survey. Land surveys establish and locate property corners and lines. They are closed surveys; that is, they are surveys that start at one corner and end at the same corner.

Topographic surveys locate natural and artificial features and elevations of points on the ground. Cartographers use these surveys to prepare topographic maps.

Route surveys locate highways, railroads, pipe lines, transmission lines, canals, and other projects that do not close upon the starting point.

LAND SURVEYS

A land survey defines a tract of land by calling out the bearings and distances (metes and bounds) of each side, figure 13-16. This information is written into a *legal description*, figure 13-17. The description gives the location of the land, the point of beginning, the direction and length of the sides of the land, and pertinent information about adjoining (neighboring) properties.

The *point of beginning* is an established corner from which measurements are started. Established points are marked by a permanent object called a *monument*. A monument may be a natural feature, such as blazed tree, or artificial, such as a long iron pipe or wooden stake driven into the ground.

In figure 13-16, the point of beginning is a new iron pipe at the northwest corner of Henry Jones' 20-acre tract. Read the accompanying legal description and follow what it says about the land survey.

The legal description is attached to the deed of the property. The *deed* specifies the ownership of the land. It also includes such things as right of ways through the property; easements, such as water rights; and exceptions, reservations, restrictions, and convenants by the grantor (seller) and the grantee (buyer), such as timber conveyances, mineral rights, etc.

The deed is recorded at the county clerk's office and indexed according to the name of the grantor and the grantee. The recording is a public document and anyone may have access to it.

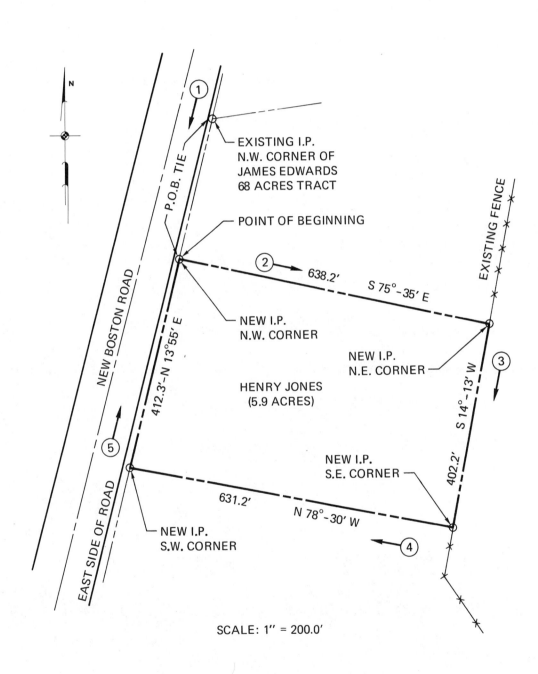

Fig. 13-16 A land survey

STATE OF VERMONT
COUNTY OF CALEDONIA

                    THIS IS TO CERTIFY: that we have made a careful examination of all records of the offices of the Clerks of the County and District Courts of this County and find as follows:

A good and sufficient legal description of the property is: All that certain real property situated in Caledonia County, Vermont described as follows, to wit:

    A certain tract of land containing 5.9 acres out of the James Edwards sixty-eight (68) acre tract; the said twenty acres being more particularly described as follows:

(1) Beginning at an existing iron pipe on the east line of the New Bosten Road, for the northwest corner of said twenty acres, being 280.3 feet along the east line of said road, South $13°-55'$ west from the northwest corner of said sixty-eight acres tract;

(2) Then south $75°-35'$ east; 638.2 feet to an iron pipe on fence line, the northeast corner of said twenty acres;

(3) Thence with fence along the east line of the James Edwards tract, south $14°-13'$ west, 402.2 feet to an iron pipe, the southeast corner of this tract;

(4) Thence with fence, north $78°-30'$ west, 631.2 feet to an iron pipe on the east line of New Boston Road, the southwest corner of this tract;

(5) Thence with the east line of the New Boston Road, north $13°-55'$ east 412.3 feet to the place of beginning.

We find the record title in:
    HENRY JONES

who acquired the above described land by deed from James Edwards to Henry Jones, dated January 6, 1975, recorded in Volume 3610, page 528, of the Deed Records of said County.

Tax Assessor's Records show present owner's address to be:
    Henry Jones
    Route 1 Box 105
    St. Johnsbury, Vermont

This property is subject to the following outstanding liens:
    NONE

Examination of Abstracts of Judgments and Federal Tax Liens has been made as to the following names only:
    NONE

Fig. 13-17 Legal description of the land survey in figure 13-16

UNIT 14

PLOTTING

PLOTTING DEFLECTION ANGLES

A *deflection angle* is an angle that is formed by a line to the right or left of the direction being traveled.

In figure 14-1, right is clockwise and left is counterclockwise. Follow the little footprints. Start at point A, work to point B, stand at point B looking ahead down the line of sight, turn to the right facing clockwise, and walk to point C. Stand at point C looking ahead down the line of sight, turn to the left facing counterclockwise to the next point. This is called *deflection angle plotting*.

It is suggested that the drafter line up the drafting machine on the line of sight with the arrow on the "head" set at 0 degree. Turn it either to the left or right and read the angle directly from the built-in protractor.

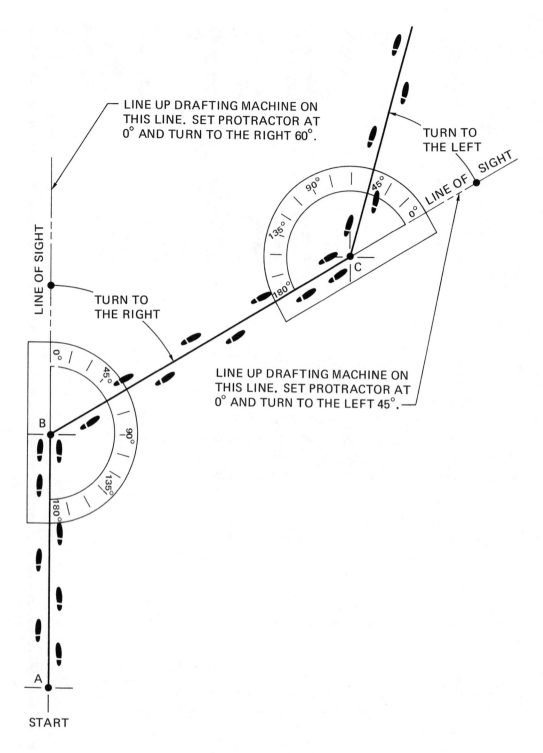

LINE UP DRAFTING MACHINE ON THIS LINE. SET PROTRACTOR AT 0° AND TURN TO THE RIGHT 60°.

TURN TO THE LEFT

LINE OF SIGHT

LINE OF SIGHT

TURN TO THE RIGHT

LINE UP DRAFTING MACHINE ON THIS LINE. SET PROTRACTOR AT 0° AND TURN TO THE LEFT 45°.

START

Fig. 14-1 Deflection angle plotting

TRAVERSE

A *traverse* is a series of connected lines of known lengths and directions. Connecting lines with known lengths and known directions form a traverse, figure 14-2. An *open traverse* is shown at the left, and a *closed traverse* is shown at the right. A closed traverse is easier to check as it must close upon itself and end where it started. An open traverse is more difficult to prove unless the drafter can sight back as illustrated by the dotted line, E to A, which would be just like a closed traverse.

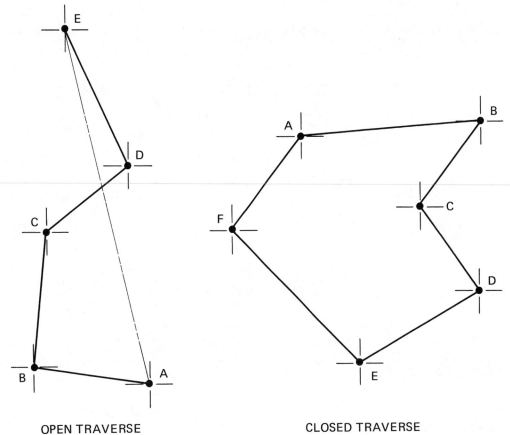

Fig. 14-2 Open and closed traverse

OPEN TRAVERSE

CLOSED TRAVERSE

ARROWHEAD

Figure 14-3 shows a sample of a properly drawn *directional arrowhead*.

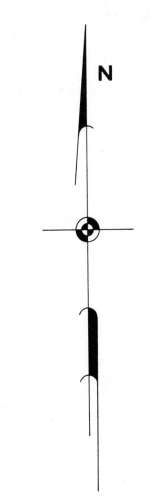

Fig. 14-3 Directional arrowhead

Always try to position the north arrow facing up on the drawing paper, figure 14-4. That way east will always be to the right, south at the bottom, and west to the left of the paper.

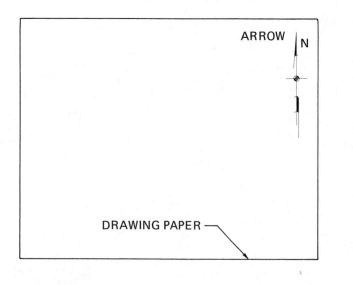

ARROW | N

DRAWING PAPER —

Fig. 14-4 Positioning the north arrow

DRAFTING STANDARDS

Line Weight. Use the same line contrast as in other drafting areas in order to make the drawing easier to understand.

Callouts. Each line must include the distance in feet and/or tenths and hundredths of a foot. Actual inches are not used. The bearing must also be included in the callout, figure 14-5.

650.0'   (DISTANCE)

N 60°5' E   (BEARING)

Fig. 14-5 Callout for lines

Corners. Neatly make each corner or turning point as illustrated in figure 14-6.

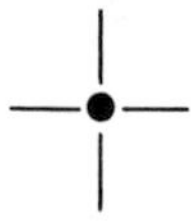

Fig. 14-6 Corner or turning point

A line from point (corner) A to point B is drawn exactly as shown in figure 14-7. All callouts must be parallel to the line, 1/8 inch high, and read from the bottom of the page.

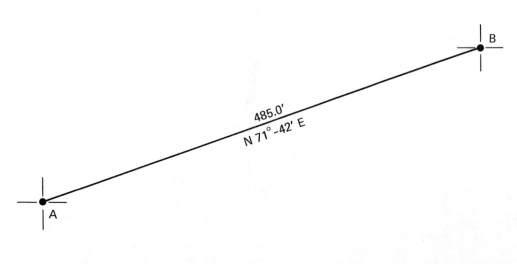

485.0'
N 71°-42' E

B

A

Fig. 14-7 Drawing a line from corner to corner

FINDING ANGLES BETWEEN BEARINGS

With One Quadrant

If there are two bearings such as those given in figure 14-8, the angle between the bearings can be calculated by adding the quadrant north to east. It is 80 degrees to the one bearing and 15 degrees to the other. Subtract 15 degrees from 80 degrees. The included angle between the bearings is 65 degrees.

Given:

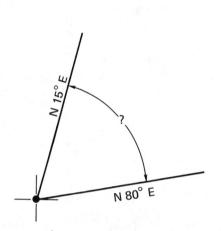

Method:

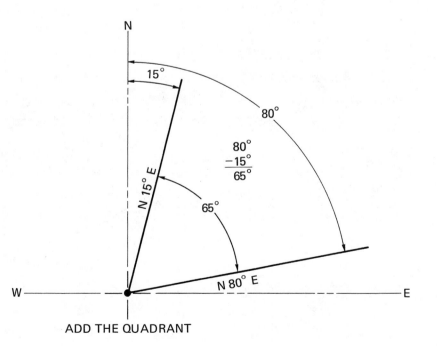

ADD THE QUADRANT

Fig. 14-8

With Two Quadrants

If there are two bearings such as those given in figure 14-9, the two quadrants must be added together, north to south (180 degrees). Use the same method as in figure 14-8.

Given:

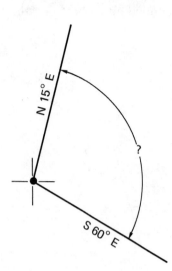

Method:

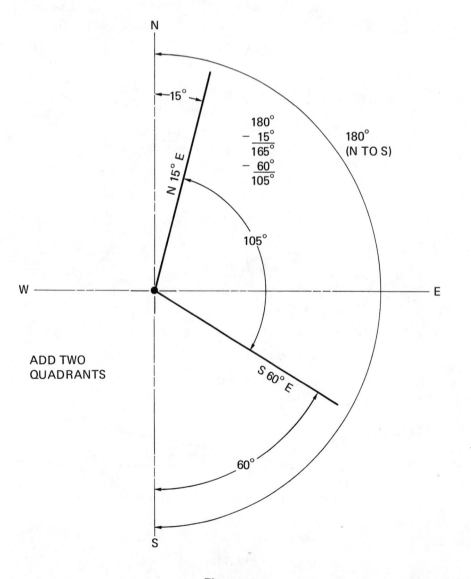

ADD TWO
QUADRANTS

$$\begin{array}{r} 180° \\ - \ 15° \\ \hline 165° \\ - \ 60° \\ \hline 105° \end{array}$$

180°
(N TO S)

Fig. 14-9

With Three Quadrants

If there are two bearings such as those given in figure 14-10, the three quadrants must be added. Add: 15° + 90° + 30° = 135°.

Given:

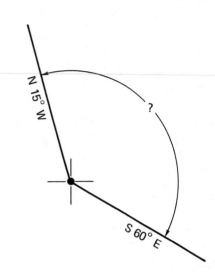

Method:

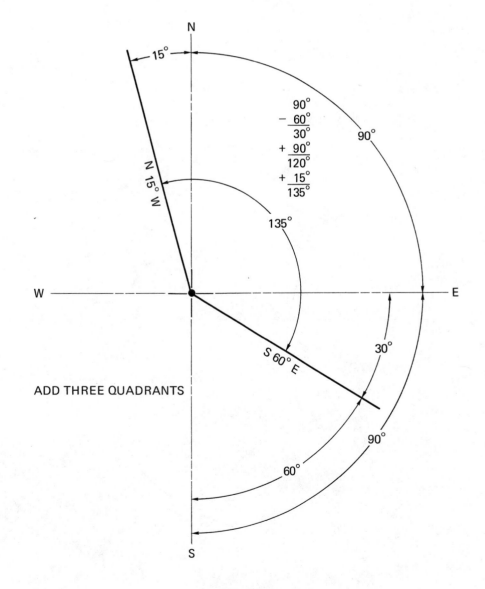

ADD THREE QUADRANTS

Fig. 14-10

With Four Quadrants

If there are two bearings such as those given in figure 14-11, all four quadrants are added. Add: 15° + 180° + 30° = 225°.

Given:

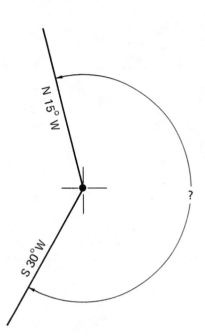

Method:

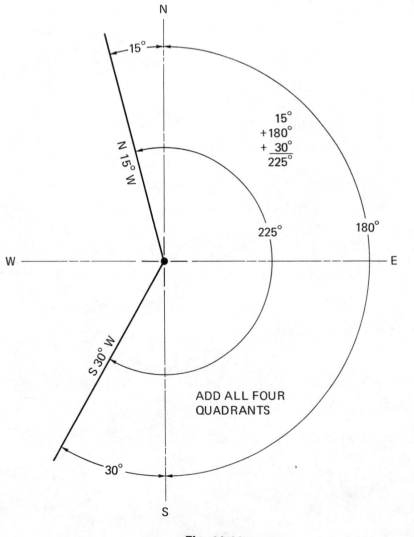

Fig. 14-11

VERNIER

Study the vernier scale on a drafting machine. Inside there is a fixed scale graduated in full degrees; outside there is a vernier scale with twelve divisions of a degree, in five minute graduations, equaling one degree (12 x 5' = 60' = 1°).

Examples A through G show how to read a straight vernier scale graduated in inches and tenths of an inch. The vernier scale illustrated in figure 14-12 is read in exactly the same manner except that it is divided into degrees and minutes.

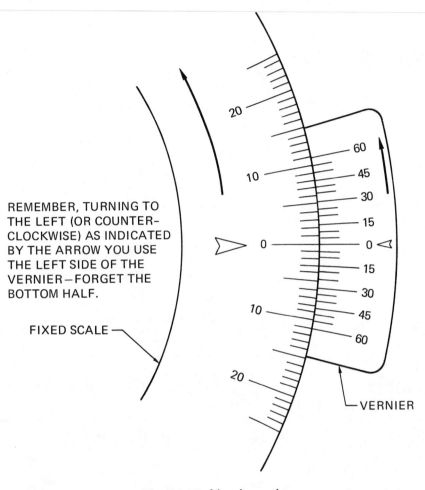

REMEMBER, TURNING TO THE LEFT (OR COUNTER-CLOCKWISE) AS INDICATED BY THE ARROW YOU USE THE LEFT SIDE OF THE VERNIER — FORGET THE BOTTOM HALF.

FIXED SCALE

VERNIER

Fig. 14-12 Vernier scale

On the drafting machine's vernier scale, readings can be taken from either the right or left of 0 degree. If the angle turns to the right, only the right side of the scale is used.

The fractional part of any division can be read exactly by means of a vernier scale.

Example A: The arrow indicates the nearest *full* division, in this case "0."

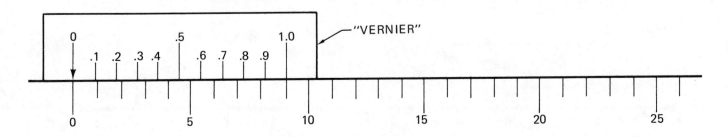

Example B: Moving from left to right, the arrow indicates 10, the nearest full division. On the vernier scale, find a line that lines up with another line; in this case it is .5. This reading is 10.5.

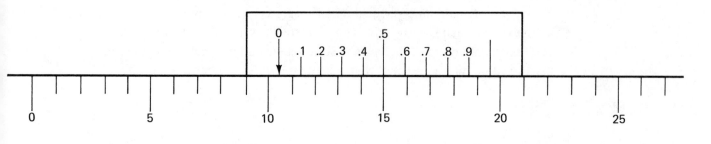

Example C: Moving from left to right, the arrow indicates 15. The .2 lines up with a line below. The reading is 15.2.

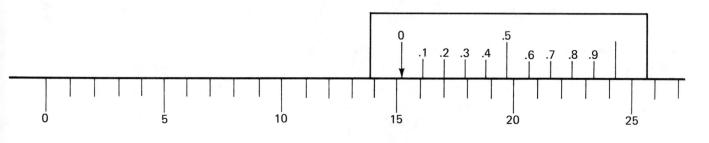

Example D: Moving from left to right, the arrow shows 7 full divisions with .4 lining up with another line. The reading is 7.4.

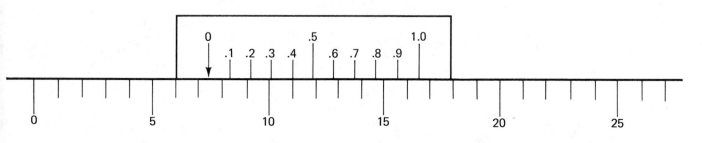

Example E: Fourteen full divisions with .6 lining up. Reading is 14.6.

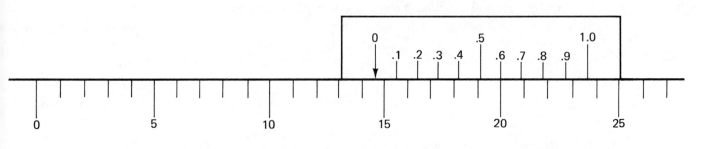

Example F: Moving from left to right, one full division; .8 fractional part. Reading = 1.8.

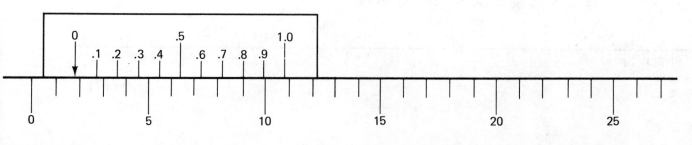

DEFLECTION PLOTTING

There are three ways to plot.

- Bearings
- Azimuths
- Deflection

Figure 14-13 illustrates *deflection*. Start with a point (point A) and have a heading (N 60°E) or some other point to head towards (point B). From then on it is simply measuring distances, finding points, and turning either left or right from the line of sight.

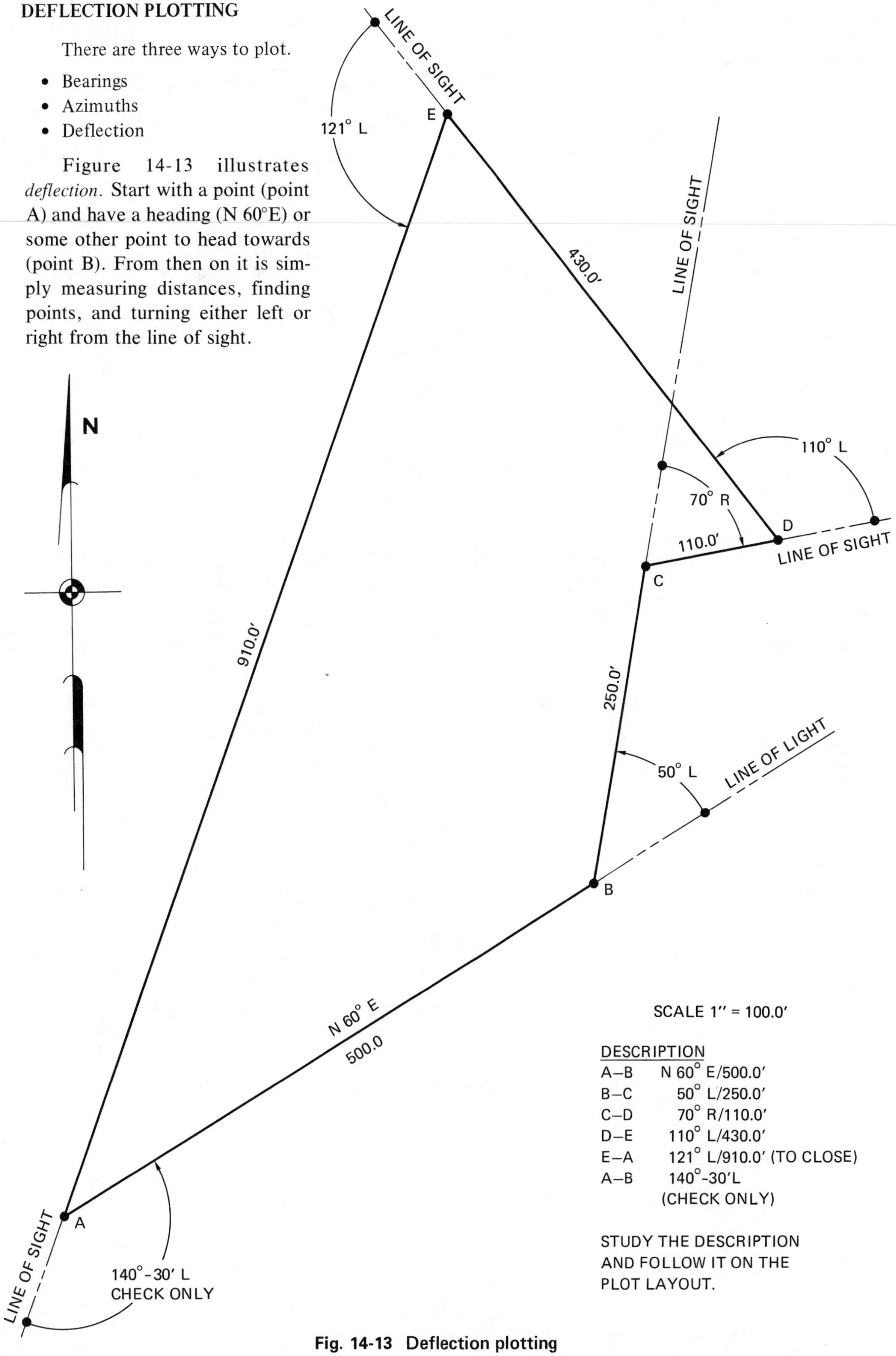

LINE OF SIGHT

121° L

E

430.0'

LINE OF SIGHT

110° L

70° R

D

110.0'

LINE OF SIGHT

C

910.0'

N

250.0'

50° L

LINE OF LIGHT

B

N 60° E

500.0

SCALE 1" = 100.0'

A

140°-30' L
CHECK ONLY

LINE OF SIGHT

DESCRIPTION

A–B	N 60° E/500.0'
B–C	50° L/250.0'
C–D	70° R/110.0'
D–E	110° L/430.0'
E–A	121° L/910.0' (TO CLOSE)
A–B	140°-30'L
	(CHECK ONLY)

STUDY THE DESCRIPTION
AND FOLLOW IT ON THE
PLOT LAYOUT.

Fig. 14-13 Deflection plotting

UNIT 15

SURVEYING

MEASURING IN THE FIELD

A survey crew is a group of people who work together to take the necessary measurements for a survey map. The leader of the crew is called the party chief. Working for the party chief are a clearing crew, a head chainman, a rear chainman, an instrument person, and a recorder or record keeper. Sometimes workers in a survey crew perform more than one duty.

The head chainman proceeds along the line to be measured carrying the head of the steel tape, called a *chain,* figure 15-1. The rear chainman follows with the end of the chain which has the higher numbers. When the tape is in position for measuring the line, the rear chainman calls out the even foot distance. The head chainman calls out the fractional part of a foot. The recorder marks the measurement in a log.

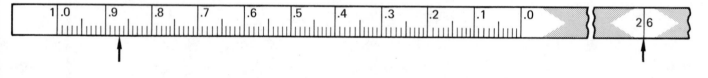

Fig. 15-1 Chain

The following callouts are made by the surveying crew for the measurement shown in figure 15-2.

    Rear: "26" (indicates even footage at the rear of the tape)
    Head: "Point 87" (indicates part of a foot at the front of the tape)
    Rear: "26 point 87" (indicates total footage)
    Head: "Check" (indicates agreement)

Fig. 15-2 Chain measurement of 26.87 feet

Figure 15-3 illustrates this conversation between the workers at the head and the rear of the chain.

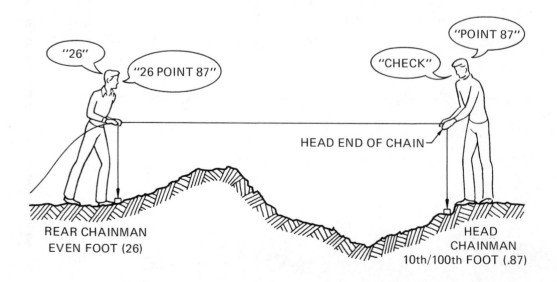

Fig. 15-3

In chaining, the workers must:

1. Measure in a straight line.

2. Pull at a standardized tension. The chain must be supported to prevent sag.

3. Hold the chain horizontally.

4. Allow for temperature.

5. Call off measurement correctly, see figure 15-3.

Errors in taping may be classified by the following:

1. Incorrect length of tape
2. Pull or tension not consistent
3. Sag due to weight and wind
4. Poor alignment
5. Tape not horizontal
6. Temperature other than the standard 68° F
7. Improper plumbing
8. Faulty marking
9. Incorrect reading or interpolation

Breaking the Chain

The chain must be held horizontal even while chaining up or down a hill. Usually the chain is held between waist and chest level. This is accomplished while measuring on a slope by taking only short distance measurements, figure 15-4. This procedure is called *breaking the chain.*

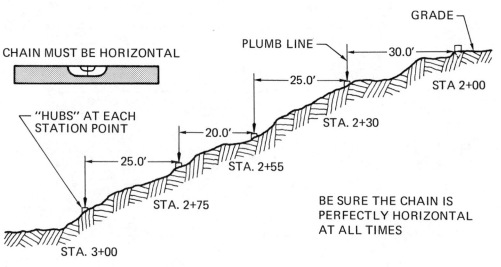

Fig. 15-4 Breaking the chain

Stadia Theory

The term *stadia* is a Greek word for a unit of length. It was originally a distance in an athletic contest that equalled approximately 600 feet. Stadia now refers to the top and bottom cross hairs that are aligned with an object through a transit sight, figure 15-5. A *transit* is a basic surveying instrument used to measure horizontal and vertical angles.

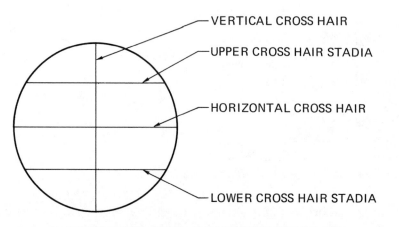

ADJUST (FOCUS) CROSS HAIRS BEFORE STARTING

Fig. 15-5 Cross hairs in a transit sight

The stadia theory is illustrated in figure 15-6. Set the level, though it need not be exact. Then adjust the bottom cross hair on an even foot mark and lock. Read the top cross hair to calculate distance.

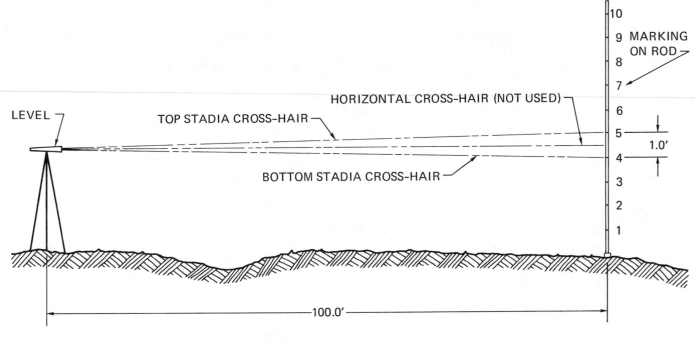

Fig. 15-6 Stadia theory

The level in figure 15-6 is placed 100.0 feet from the rod. The vertical distance between rod marking four and five is 1 foot, so a 100.0-foot horizontal distance measures exactly 1.0 foot on the rod. Example: A reading of 2.5 feet between stadia cross hairs means 250.0 feet from transit to rod.

This is an efficient way to obtain distances. It is not 100 percent correct, but it is close enough for surveys of a low precision, for topographic work, and general location of points.

LEVELING

Leveling is a very simple process. The only equipment needed is a level (transit), tripod, and leveling rod, figure 15-7. The level, as its name implies, is level at all times and simply transfers a height or reading from one plane to another.

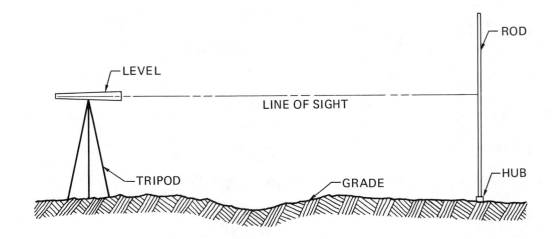

Fig. 15-7 Sighting a level

There are basic terms associated with the leveling process:

Bench mark — B.M.
Temporary bench mark — T.B.M.
Height of instrument — H.I.
Backsight — B.S.
Foresight — F.S.
Turning point — T.P
Station point — STA. PT.
Elevation — ELEV.

Learn the language of the trade. Memorize these terms and abbreviations. They will be helpful in interpreting field notes.

READING THE ROD

Figure 15-8 shows a Philadelphia rod. It is seven feet long but extends to thirteen feet. It is graduated according to rigid specifications. Notice how the even foot and the .5 graduation is emphasized by a spur-extended graduation. Study how the sample reading is taken in figure 15-8.

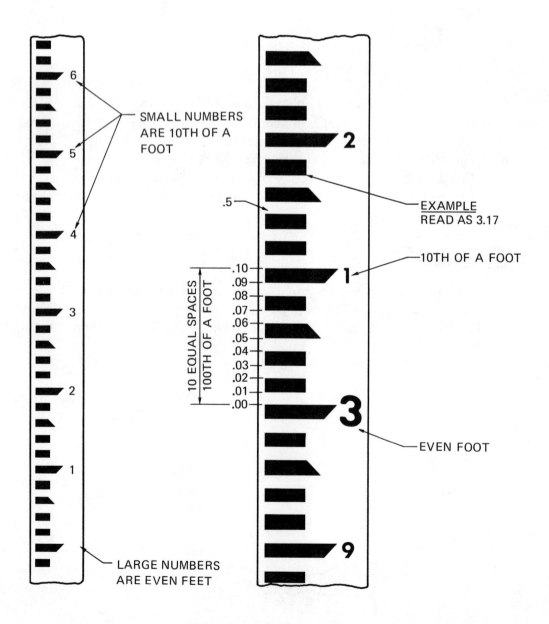

Fig. 15-8 Reading a rod

Holding a Rod Plumb

When leveling, the rod must be held *plumb,* or vertically straight, in order to obtain a correct reading. Study figure 15-9.

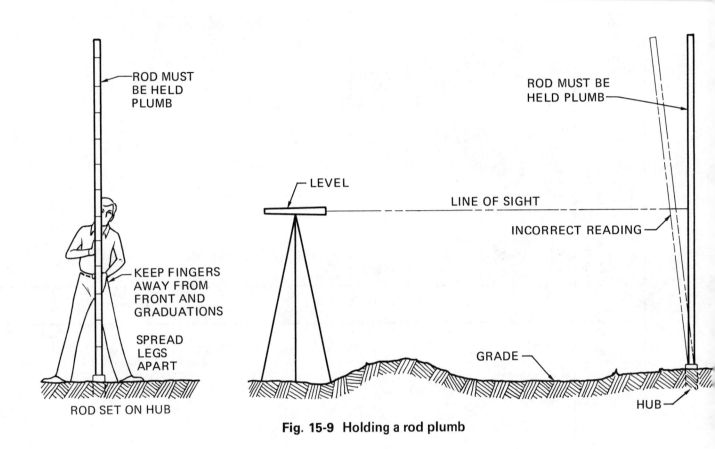

Fig. 15-9 Holding a rod plumb

Field Notes

Figure 15-10 is a sample page from the log that a survey recorder keeps. It is used to record data that is calculated in the field.

STA.	B.S. (+) BACKSIGHT	H.I.	F.S. (−) FORESIGHT	ELEV.	DATE	SURVEY PARTY	WEATHER
B.M.1	7.11 =	728.16		721.05	U.S.G.S. BM ETC.		
T.P.1	8.83	735.75	1.24 =	726.92	CURB		
T.P.2	11.72	746.36	1.11	734.64	SPIKE IN A POLE		
B.M.2	4.32	740.47	10.21	736.15	CONCRETE MONUMENT IN STREET CORNER		
T.P.3	3.06	733.57	9.96	730.51			
T.P.4	2.74	727.40	8.91	724.66			
T.P.5	0.81	716.59	11.62	715.78			
B.M.3			12.42	704.17			
ΣB.S.=	38.59	ΣFS=	55.47				
			38.59				
		DIFF=	16.88	CK			

(ELEVATION OF H.I. SHOULD ALWAYS BE RECORDED)

THIS PAGE SHOULD BE RESERVED FOR REMARKS AND BM DESCRIPTION.

Fig. 15-10 Field note page sample

FINDING UNKNOWN ELEVATIONS

To find an unknown elevation, start from the known elevation at the bench mark and set up the level as illustrated in figure 15-11. Take a reading to find the height of instrument (H.I.). Add it to the known elevation found at the bench mark. Set the rod on the unknown elevation, take a reading, and subtract from the height of the instrument. This is the *unknown elevation.*

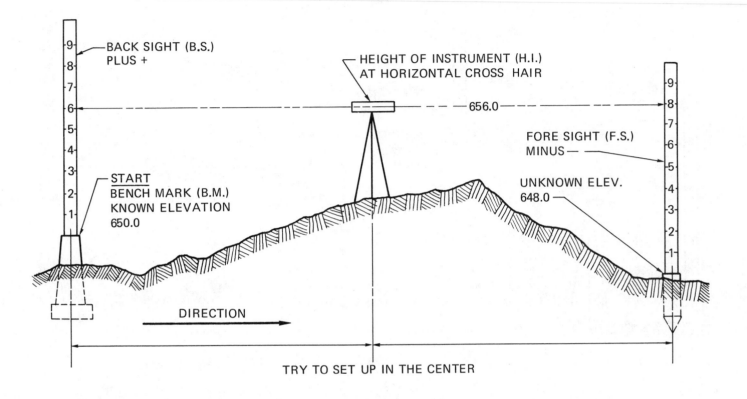

Fig. 15-11 Finding the unknown elevation

Figure 15-12 shows how to record this information in the log. Be sure you understand each entry and what information goes into each column.

STA.	(+) BACKSIGHT	H.I.	(–) FORESIGHT	ELEV.
B. M.				650.0
	6	656.0	8	648.0

Fig. 15-12 Sample of field notes

TURNING POINTS

Turning points are used for sighting over long distances or sights that cannot be seen. A turning point (T.P.) is nothing more than a temporary bench mark (T.B.M.). Take one reading as a foresight (–), reset the level, and use the same point as a backsight (+), figure 15-13.

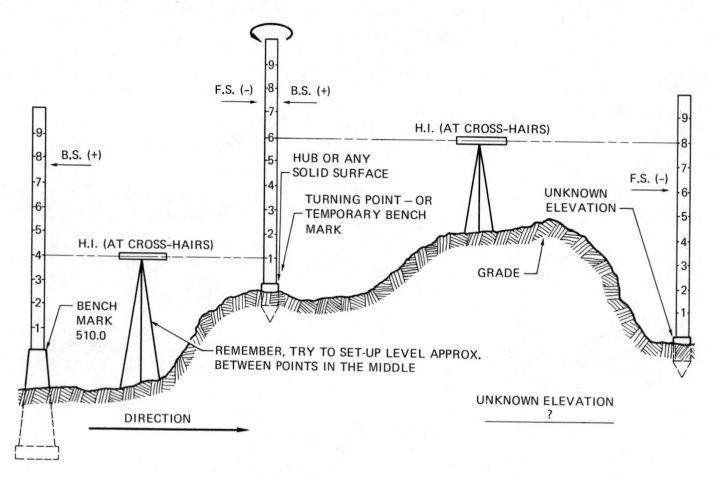

Fig. 15-13

These measurements are recorded in figure 15-14.

STA.	(+) BACKSIGHT	H.I.	(–) FORESIGHT	ELEV.
B.M.	–	–	–	510.0'
	4	514.0	1	513.0'
T.P. 1	6	519.0	8	511.0'

Fig. 15-14 Sample of field notes

Many times several turning points must be made, figure 15-15. A turning point can be a hub set in the ground, an edge of a sidewalk, a large stone in the field, a nail set in a tree, a side of a ledge, etc., all of which are clearly marked with chalk or paint. Many T.B.M.s are seen along new construction sites.

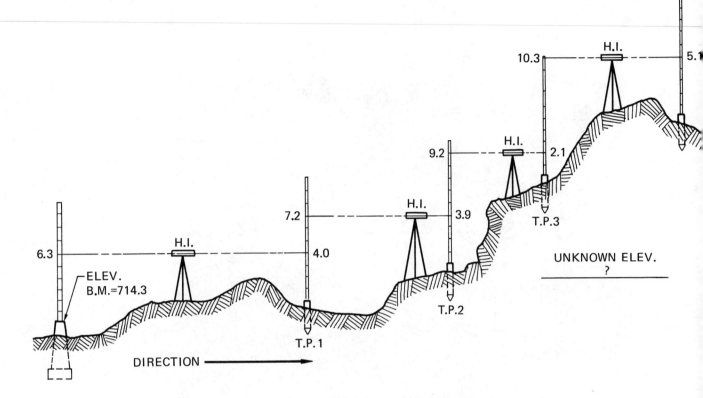

Fig. 15-15 Measuring, using several turning points

AERIAL PHOTOGRAPHY

Aerial photography is used to assist the cartographer in mapping large land areas. A series of pictures are taken from an airplane flying a straight course over the tract to be mapped. Each picture overlaps the one preceding it so that they may be aligned to make up the finished map, called a *photomosaic.* The photomosaic is actually a picture taken of all the photos combined on one surface, figure 15-16.

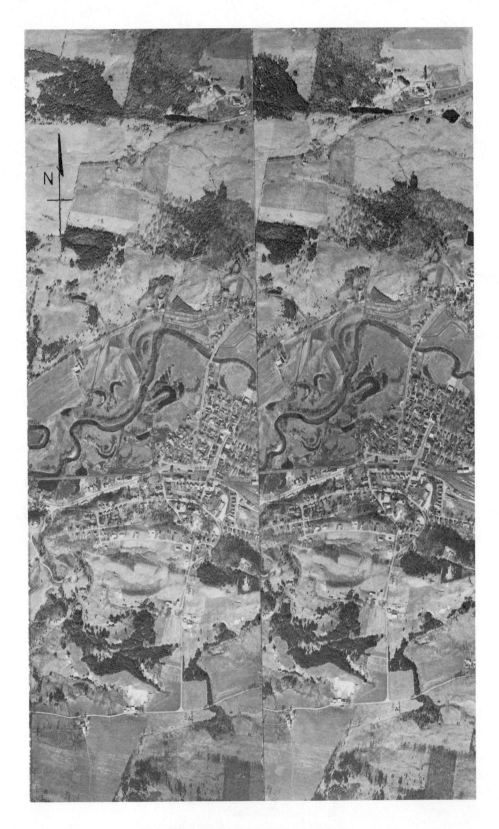

Fig. 15-16 Aerial photograph

Carefully study the aerial photograph. Note all the high and low elevations. Aerial photos are revised every twenty years.

An airplane flies over an area and takes a series of pictures. Each of these pictures overlap about 60 percent, figure 15-17.

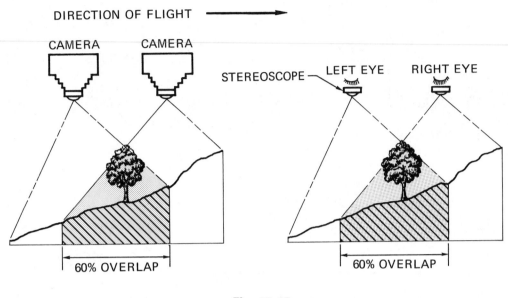

Fig. 15-17

Each photo viewed alone appears flat; but if the two photos are viewed through a stereoscope, they give a full, three-dimensional view as would be seen by actually flying over the area. The *stereoscope* is a devise that enables a cartographer to get a three-dimensional effect when looking at a pair of stereo aerial photographs, figures 15-16.

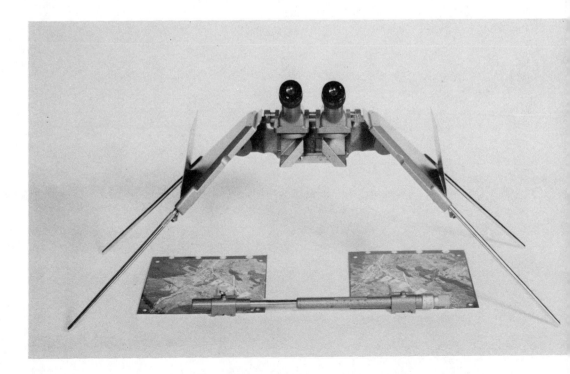

Fig. 15-18 A stereoscope is used to look at a stereo pair of aerial photographs in order to obtain a three-dimensional view of the area

CONTOUR MAPS

CONTOUR MAPS

Before a topographic map can be drawn, the contour of the land must be determined. A *contour map* shows the elevation of the land surfaces and the depth of water features. Once the contours are drawn, other natural and man-made features are added to complete the topographic map.

CONTOUR LINES

Elevations on a topographic map start at "0," which is *sea level* between high and low tides. Sea level is the *datum line* so every point on earth is measured above or below sea level.

A *contour line* is an imaginary line on the ground connecting all points that are the same elevation above or below sea level. They show the shape of the ground at each elevation. When contour lines are close together, the ground slopes very steeply. When they are spread out, the ground slopes moderately.

There are various kinds of contour lines, figure 16-1. They vary in line thickness. The elevation of the contour is numbered in a broken-out space on the line.

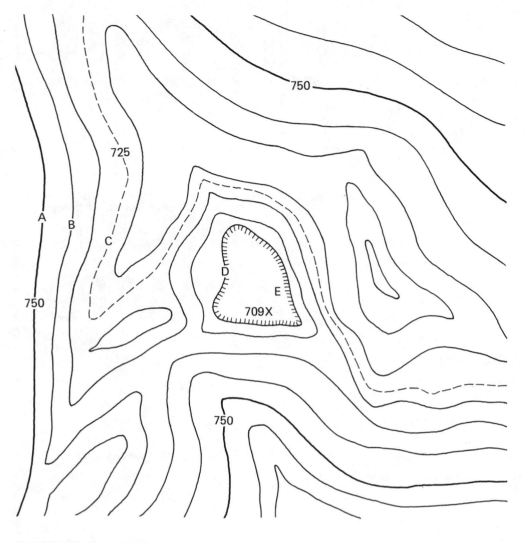

A INDEX—
  Every 5th line, numbered
B INTERMEDIATE—
  Between index contours
C SUPPLEMENTAL—
  Represents half interval
D DEPRESSIONS—
  Much lower elevation
E SPOT ELEVATION—
  Locates an exact elevation
  at a particular site
NOTE LINE THICKNESS

Fig. 16-1 Contour lines

CONTROL SURVEYS

Control surveys are required to present map features in correct relationship to each other and to the earth's surface. Vertical control provides the correct location for the contour lines. Permanent control points, often called *bench marks,* are metal markers 3 3/4 inches in diameter, figure 16-2, set in cement and anchored three to six feet into the ground. They are shown on maps by appropriate symbols.

Control points indicate the elevation of the point marked and the date the measurement was taken.

Fig. 16-2 Control point

PROFILE VIEW

A *profile view* is a vertical plane through a contour map that shows the vertical outline of the surface. Figure 16-3 shows a contour map of an area with a cutting-plane line (A-A) passing through it. Notice points A, J, and S. Each point is projected down the same way to form the profile or section view. The grid at the left side indicates the elevation in the feet above sea level.

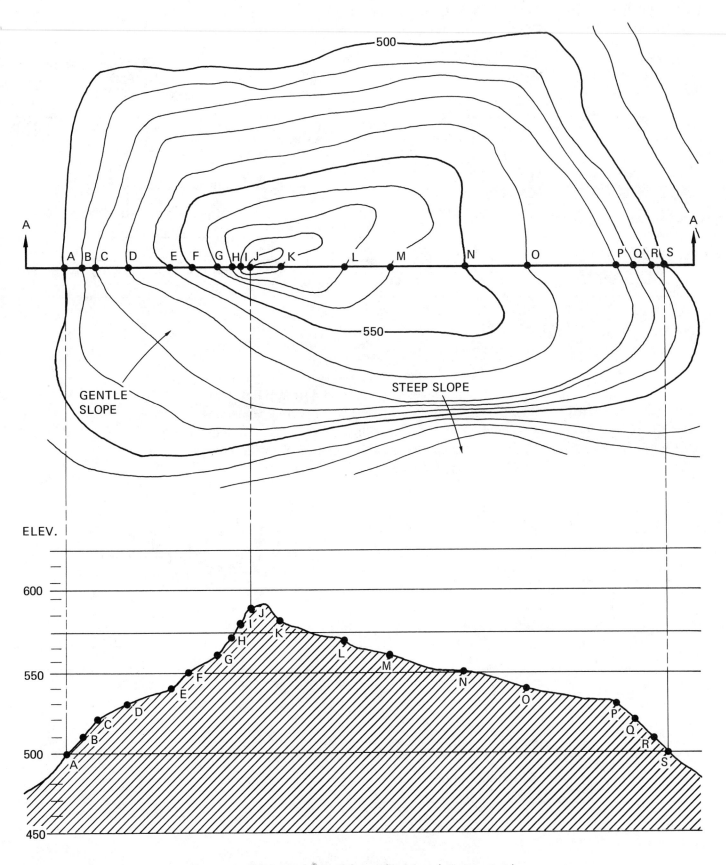

Fig. 16-3 Contour map with profile view (section A-A)

CONTOUR LAYOUT

A contour map drawn from field notes is not 100 percent correct. Sometimes a drafter must visit the site in order to complete a drawing or check the finished product. An experienced drafter, however, can come very close the the actual land shape by a method that, in theory, is correct.

In figure 16-4, point A is 615 feet, point B is 623 feet, and point C is 612 feet above sea level. It is, therefore, a good assumption that the ground slope is constant from A to B and from B to C. If a line is drawn from A to B to C (dashed), one has a fairly accurate actual ground illustration.

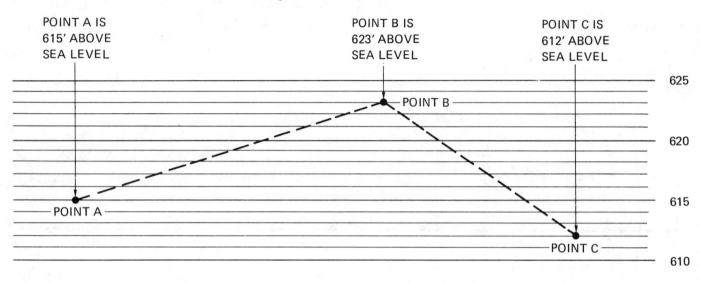

Fig. 16-4

A profile view of figure 16-4 looks like figure 16-5. Notice that from A to B there are, in theory, even spaces from 615 feet to 623 feet, and from B to C there are even spaces from 623 feet to 612 feet. A visit to the site would reveal any large dips or hollows that should be added to the illustration. The land could actually have a contour like that indicated by the thin line in the profile view, but it is assumed straight and drawn as indicated by the thick line.

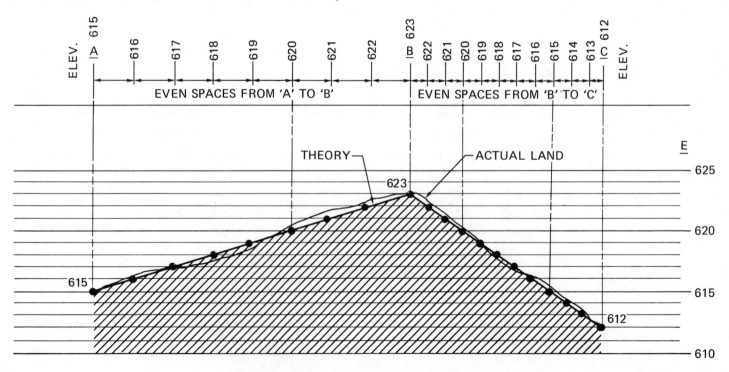

Fig. 16-5 Profile view of figure 16-4

EQUAL-SPACING DIVIDERS

Equal-spacing dividers are simple to use, figure 16-6. It is a very delicate and expensive tool, however, so care must be taken while working with it. As the name implies, the equal-spacing divider divides a given distance into a given number of equal parts.

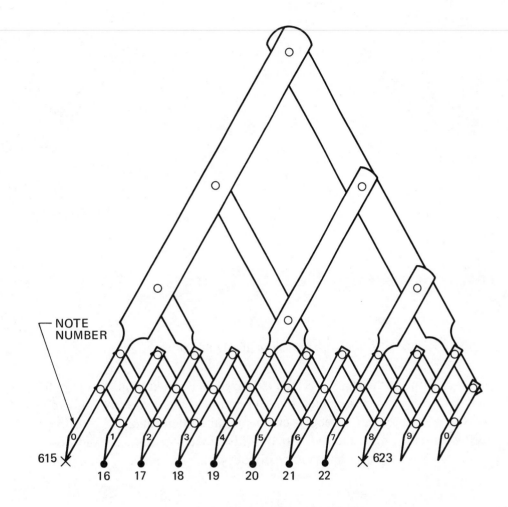

Fig. 16-6 Equal-spacing divider

Notice the numbers 0, 1, 2, 3, 4, 5, 6, 7, 8, 9, 0 at the tip of each point, figure 16-6. Starting with tip #0 on 615 foot elevation, move the points in or out to place point #8 on 623 foot elevation (623 minus 615 = 8). Put a dot at the end of each point and number 16, 17, 18, 19, 20, 21, 22. #9 and #0 at the right end are not necessary. With a little practice one can equally space any area very quickly. Be sure to *number each point* so there is no chance of error.

Using Field Notes to Lay Out a Contour Map

Step 1. Study figure 16-7. This is the information a drafter has to start a layout of a contour map. These figures were made directly to the field by a survey crew. They indicate the exact elevation above sea level at those points, 100 feet apart, as illustrated.

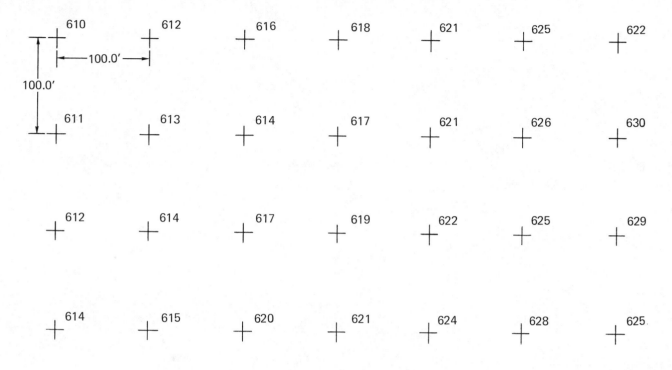

Fig. 16-7 Field notes

Step 2. Starting at the top left corner (610), go to the first point to the right (612), figure 16-B. It can be assumed that 611 feet is at the center as indicated. From 612 the next point is 616 feet. It can be assumed that there are four even spaces shown as 613, 614, and 615. Follow this procedure both up and down and from left to right, using equal-spacing dividers. Locate and label each point.

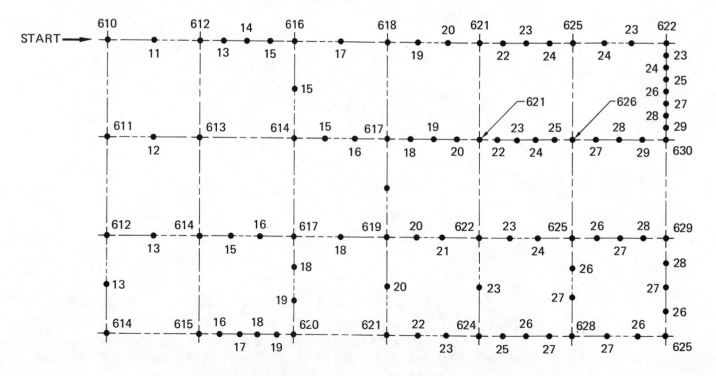

Fig. 16-8 Locating missing elevations

Step 3. Very carefully connect all lines of the same elevation, figure 16-9, with light, straight lines. Lines should not cross. Sometimes there is a question, as indicated by the (?) at elevation 625. The elevation seems to go in two directions. This problem can be solved by reasoning or by a visit to the site to determine what the ground level actually does. See how it was solved in figure 16-10.

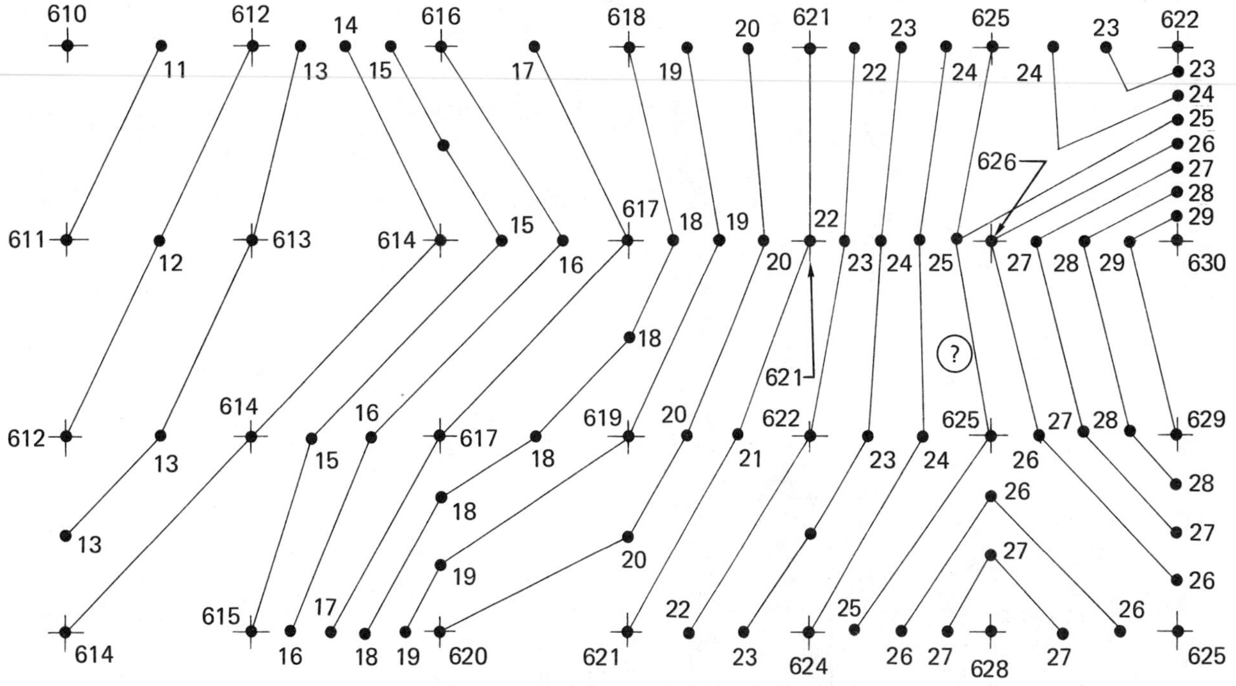

Fig. 16-9 Connecting elevation lines

Step 4. Select the index contour lines as they will be numbered and have a thicker line than the rest, figure 16-10. Because this process is approximate anyway, carefully freehand draw the index contours with a thick line. Draw the intermediate contours next. Round all sharp corners. Many times the contour lines are parallel to each other. If in doubt, make the lines parallel.

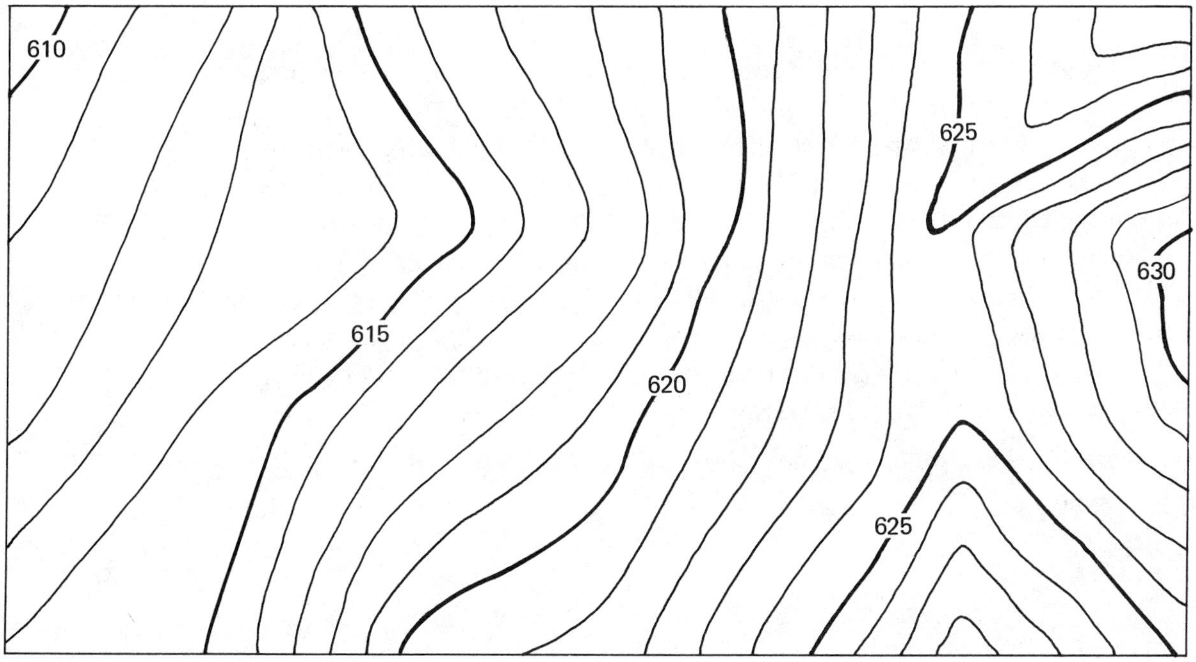

Fig. 16-10 Finished drawing

STATION POINT

Figure 16-11 is a sketch of a typical *station point* set in the field by a survey crew. A station point usually has three stakes. One thin, long post holds the *colored flag*. The color is usually coded to mean center of the road, edge of road, bottom of bank, etc.

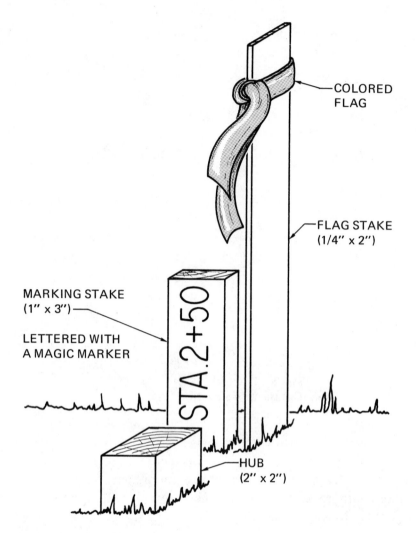

Fig. 16-11 Typical station point

Next to this post is a *marking stake.* A marking stake has the station number (STA) starting from the base or beginning point with 0+00. These numbers are in hundreds. The first number indicates hundreds from the starting point. 2+50 means 200 feet plus 50 feet, or 250 feet in all from the starting point. 5+37.5 would mean 537.5 feet from the base.

Next comes the *hub* which indicates line, distance, or elevation. It can give any combination of this information. Many times there is information on the back side of the marking stake, such as how much to *cut* or *fill.* "C" = cut and "F" = fill. C-10 means to cut down ten feet. F-4 means to fill in four feet from the top of the hub. Cut or fill is measured from the top of the hub.

See figure 16-12.

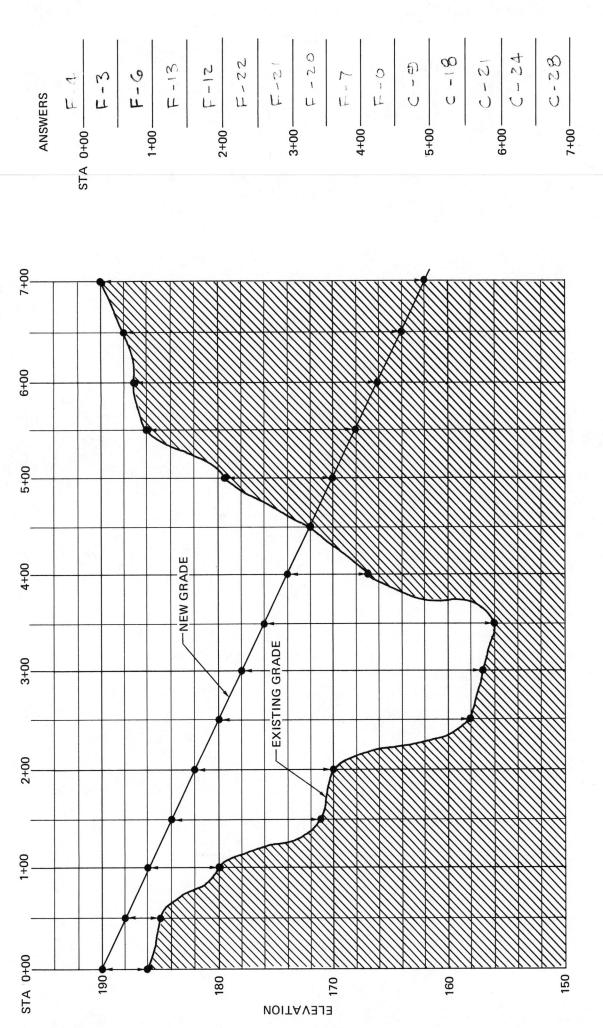

Fig. 16-12

SLOPES AND RATES OF GRADES

Slopes, or rates of grade, are called off in three different ways:

1. Slopes by angle, figure 16-13 is used in mechanical drafting.

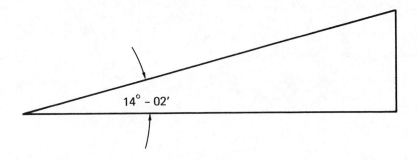

14° – 02′

Fig. 16-13 Slope by angle

2. Slopes by horizontal to vertical, figure 16-14 is used in architectural drafting.

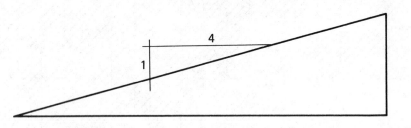

4

1

Fig. 16-14 Slopes by horizontal to vertical

3. Slope; by percentage, figure 16-15, is used in civil drafting. If in 100 feet the slope rose 25 feet, it would be called a 25% rise (+). Plus (+) indicates *rise,* while minus (–) indicates *fall.*

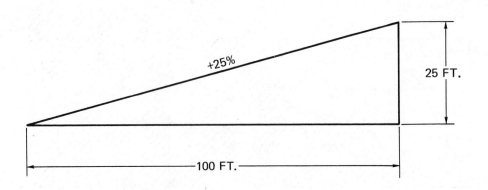

+25%

25 FT.

100 FT.

Fig. 16-15 Slopes by percentage

UNIT 17

BASIC DIMENSIONING

DIMENSIONING

Previous units have covered correct line weight, neatness, accuracy, and general constructions. To be of any value, however, it is most important that a drawing be dimensioned properly. This unit covers the rules of standard dimensioning.

Drafters should place themselves in the position of the person reading the drawing and dimension the drawing accordingly. If a drafter is in doubt whether a dimension is needed, it should be included. Other basic practices are:

- It should not be necessary to scale a drawing to determine a dimension.

- It should not be necessary to calculate to determine a dimension.

- It should not be necessary to assume anything to determine a dimension.

DIMENSIONING SYSTEMS

The two systems used to dimension a drawing are: aligned and unidirectional. In an *aligned system* all dimensions are read from the bottom and right side of the page, figure 17-1. All dimensions are in line (aligned) with the dimension line. This system is used in architectural drafting.

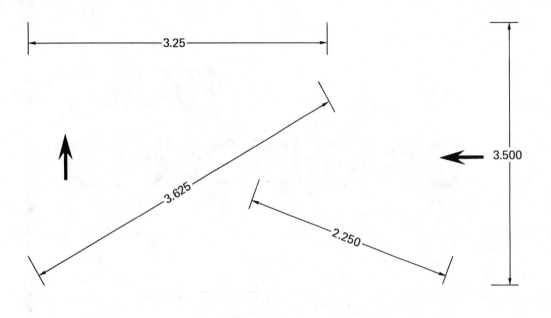

Fig. 17-1 Aligned dimensioning

In a *unidirectional system* all dimensions are read from the bottom of the page, figure 17-2. This system is used for mechanical drafting.

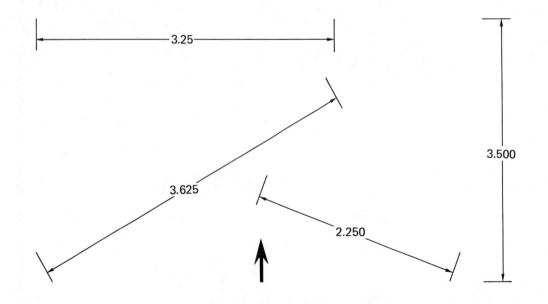

Fig. 17-2 Unidirectional dimensioning

ARROWHEADS

A good arrowhead proportion is about 1/8 inch (3) long and has a width equal to approximately 1/3 of the length. Practice making arrowheads using figures 17-3 and 17-4 as a guide.

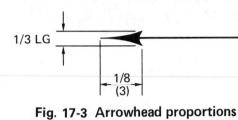
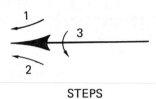

Fig. 17-3 Arrowhead proportions　　**Fig. 17-4 Steps in making an arrowhead**

RULES FOR DIMENSIONING

The general rule when dimensioning is to place the first dimension a minimum of 5/8 inch (15) away from the object, figure 17-5. All succeeding dimensions are spaced a minimum of 3/8 inch (9) apart. There is a visible gap between extension lines and the object that extends approximately 1/8 inch (3) past the last dimension line. This is important as it will enhance the quality of the drawing and its comprehension.

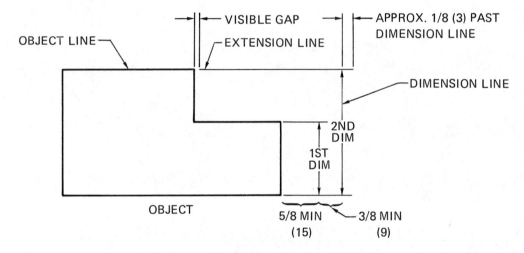

Fig. 17-5 Placement of dimensions

Dimension Lines

The general rule is to place the shortest dimension line closest to the object, figure 17-6 at right, so extension lines do not cross any more than necessary.

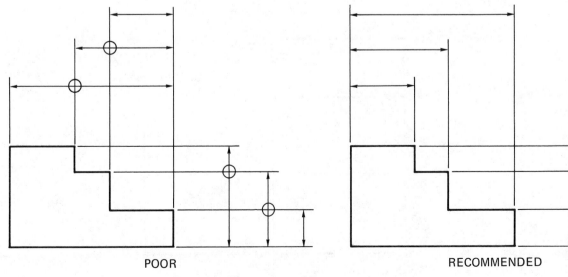

Fig. 17-6 Placement of lines

Leaders

The *leader* is an inclined straight line with a short, horizontal portion extending to the midpoint of the note or dimension, figure 17-7. They are drawn at an angle of 30 to 60 degrees. On a circle, the leader starts at the edge of the circle on a line that projects to the center.

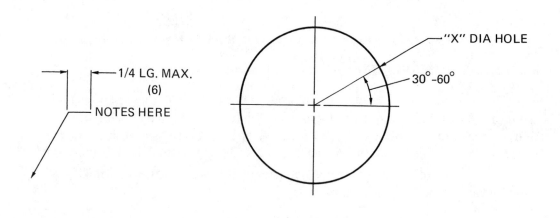

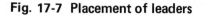

Fig. 17-7 Placement of leaders

Basic Shapes

When dimensioning, think about the size of the basic shape and how it will be machined. Most drawings have width (WD), height (HGT), and depth (DP). Start with these and try to place them between views, figure 17-8.

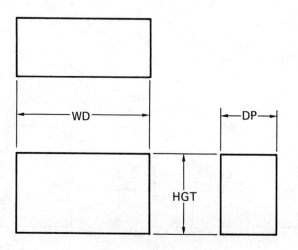

Fig. 17-8

Arrowheads

A general rule for arrowheads when dimensioning radii and diameters:

- Radii — arrowheads inside
- Diameters — arrowheads outside

Figure 17-9 shows how the arrowheads are placed on a drawing. Do not dimension to a hidden line or to the center line of a hidden circle.

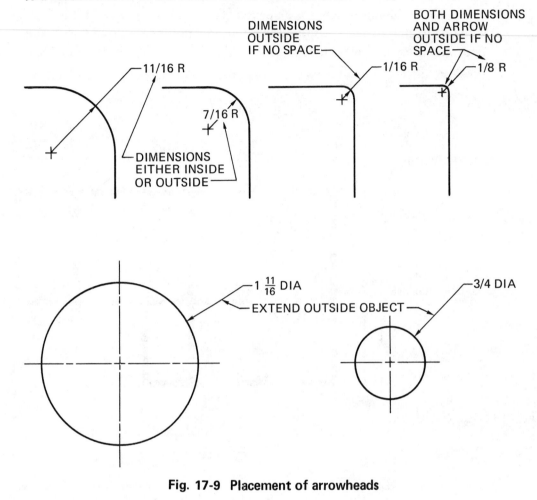

Fig. 17-9 Placement of arrowheads

Unnecessary Dimensions

Always omit unnecessary dimensions. The missing dimension in figure 17-10 does not need to be there. If it is shown it must be identified as a REF dimension.

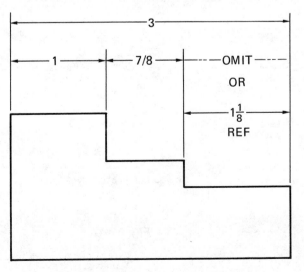

Fig. 17-10 Proper dimensioning

Rules Of Architectural Dimensioning

1.) The aligned system of dimensioning is used in architectural dimensioning, see figure 17-1, that is read from the bottom and right hand side of the paper.

2.) The first dimension line should be placed approximately 5/8″ outside the object; all subsequent dimension lines 3/8″ apart. Extension lines should *not* touch the object, see figure 17-5.

Often, three dimension lines are needed along each wall. The first dimension line from the object, window and door location; the second dimension line, wall offsets and the third dimension line, the over-all dimensions. See figure 17-11.

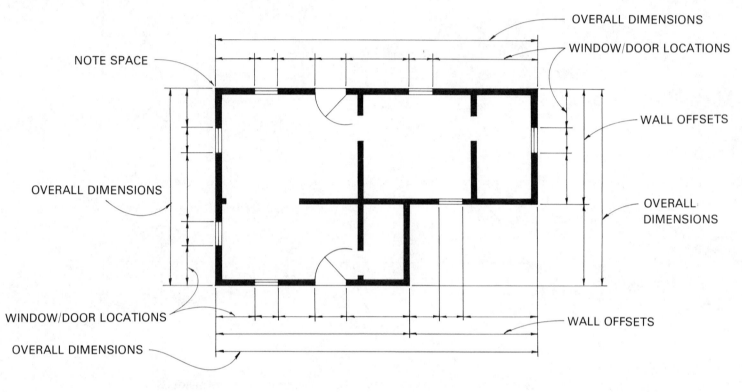

Fig. 17-11

3.) The arrow head is preferred in illustrating dimension lengths, see figures 17-3 and 4, but as architectural drafting does not have national standards, dots, triangles, diagonal lines, and even heavy lines are sometimes used. See figure 17-12.

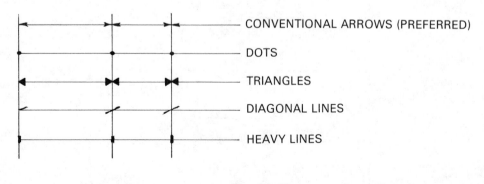

Fig. 17-12

4.) In architectural drafting, dimension lines are not broken; they are thin, continuous lines with the dimensions neatly printed above them. (Note, in mechanical drafting, the dimension is placed in the center of the dimension line, see figure 17-10). A good practice is to measure above the dimension line and draw two *light* guide lines 1/16" up and 1/18" apart, for the dimensions. See figure 17-13. Dimension figures should not touch the dimension line and dimensions should be 1/8" high.

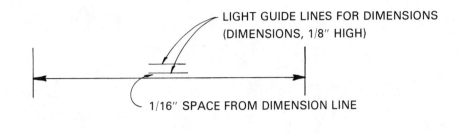

LIGHT GUIDE LINES FOR DIMENSIONS
(DIMENSIONS, 1/8" HIGH)

1/16" SPACE FROM DIMENSION LINE

Fig. 17-13

5.) All dimensions over twelve inches are called-off in feet and inches, to the nearest sixteenth of an inch. (Note in mechanical drafting, the cut-off is 72 inches, not twelve inches).

6.) The symbol for feet (') and inches (") with a dash (-) between figures must be used on all dimensions.
Example: 8"   1'-0"   20'-8"

7.) It is best to dimension to the sides of doors and windows, *not* to the center as the people constructing the building need to know the sides of doors and windows, not centers. Note this method illustrated on figure 17-11.

8.) Add enough dimensions so no one will have to add or subtract to figure out what a distance should be.

9.) It is best to give window and door sizes on a "schedule," see page 125, figure 9-1.

10.) House drawings are usually drawn to 1/4" = 1'-0". Larger buildings to 1/8" = 1'-0". All detail drawings are usually drawn to 3/4" = 1'-0" or 1 1/2" = 1'-0" and sometimes even 3" = 1'-0".

11.) Use neat legible letters and numbers at all times. It is a good idea to letter all dimensions in place, lightly, then check and re-check *before* darkening in.

12.) There are many methods used to dimension interior walls. Each drafting department has their own "standard" which should be followed. Illustrated below is only one method, that is, from outside wall to the center of interior walls, to the outside wall. This method is preferred as these interior dimensions should total up to the exterior overall dimension. See figure 17-14. Some drafting departments dimension all *inside* dimensions; others use dimensions for outside dimensions and place room sizes under the room title. Example: *Living Room* 12'-6" x 18'-0"

It is easy to adjust your method to whatever "standard" is used. The important thing is to be neat and consistent.

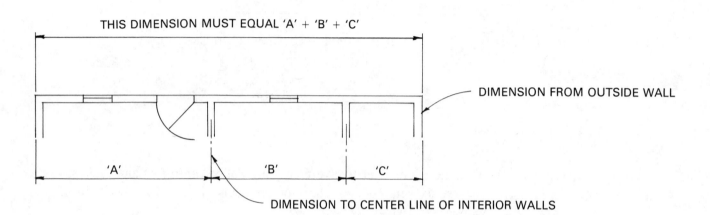

THIS DIMENSION MUST EQUAL 'A' + 'B' + 'C'

DIMENSION FROM OUTSIDE WALL

'A'   'B'   'C'

DIMENSION TO CENTER LINE OF INTERIOR WALLS

Fig. 17-14

UNIT 18

BASIC ISOMETRICS

ISOMETRIC

An *isometric drawing* is a form of pictorial drawing used to make three-view drawings easier to visualize. It is made with a 30°–60° triangle. An isometric is actually a three-dimensional drawing because height, width, and depth are all drawn on a single plane. Figure 18-1 illustrates the difference between an isometric and orthographic view. An *orthographic view* is formed by projecting perpendicular lines from an object onto a single plane.

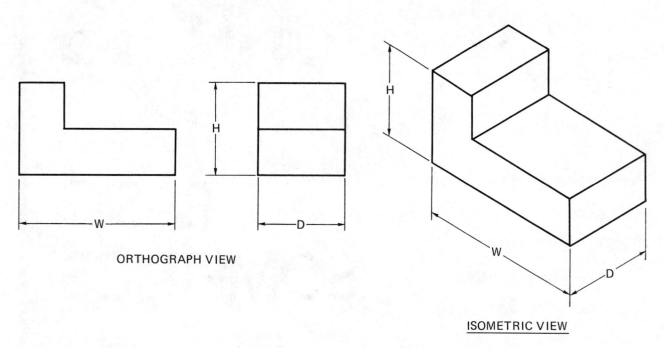

ORTHOGRAPH VIEW

ISOMETRIC VIEW

Fig. 18-1 Orthographic and isometric drawings of the same object

Isometric lines are drawn parallel to an isometric axis, figure 16-2. Horizontal and vertical measurements are taken directly from the orthographic view and transferred to the corresponding isometric lines. Measurements may be made on any isometric axis line or lines parallel to them. Hidden edges are not shown on isometric drawings.

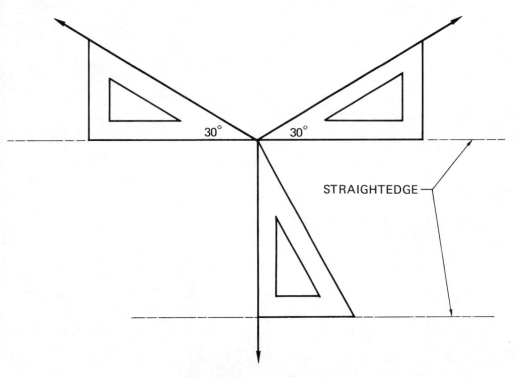

STRAIGHTEDGE

Fig. 18-2 Isometric axis

NON-ISOMETRIC LINES

A *non-isometric line* is one that is not parallel to any of the lines on an isometric axis. Angles, for instance, are non-isometric lines and cannot be found with a protractor. Non-isometric lines are found by locating their ends with points and then connecting these points.

Plotting Non-Isometric Lines

Steps 1 through 4 outline the procedure to follow to plot non-isometric lines.

Step 1. Number the ends of non-isometric lines.

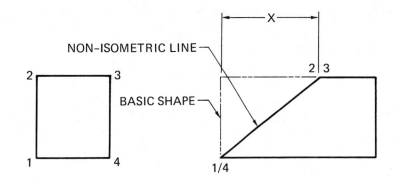

Step 2. Lightly draw the basic shape in isometric.

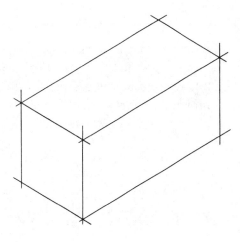

Step 3. Locate points or *ends of lines.* Note measurement "x."

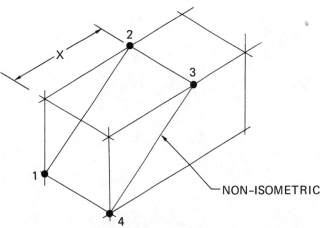

Step 4. Complete the drawing with all lines of object line thickness.

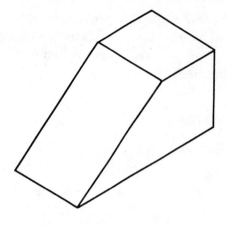

HIDDEN EDGES IN ISOMETRIC

Hidden edges are shown in an isometric drawing only if it is the only drawing available for measurement and detail. Isometrics, however, are most often shown along with a three-view drawing for clarification. In such cases, hidden edge lines are not used.

ISOMETRIC CONSTRUCTION

Box Method

Figure 18-3 shows one method of isometric construction when drawing an object made up of non-isometric lines. In this case a box is made using the basic shape and size of the figure. Known points are plotted on the isometric lines and joined to form the completed isometric drawing.

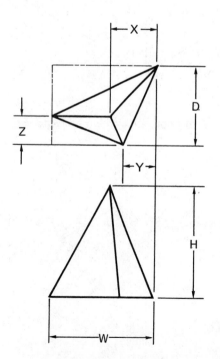

Fig. 18-3 Two-view drawing of a pyramid

Step 1. Lightly draw the basic shape using measurements taken directly from the two-view drawing.

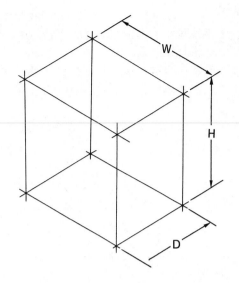

Step 2. Locate all points. Project at 30 degrees where necessary to locate positions which are not on the box lines.

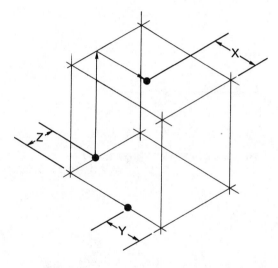

Step 3. Using the two-view drawing as a guide, complete the drawing by connecting all plotted points.

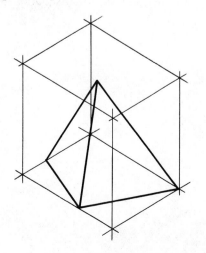

ISOMETRIC CONSTRUCTION

Skeleton Method

The skeleton method of isometric drawing is very similar to the box method. The main difference between the two is that only the base of the basic shape is drawn when using the skeleton method, and heights are located by drawing vertical lines from the points located on the base. The top of the pyramid shown in figure 18-4 is located H distance above the point at which X and Z intersect.

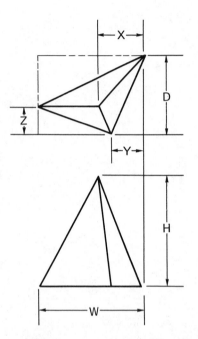

Fig. 18-4 Two-view drawing of a pyramid

Step 1. Lightly draw the base using measurements taken directly from the two-view drawing.

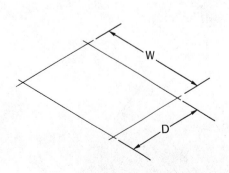

Step 2. Locate all points on the base and project them at 30 degrees to find height position. Draw a vertical line where lines X and Z cross. Locate the height (H) on this line.

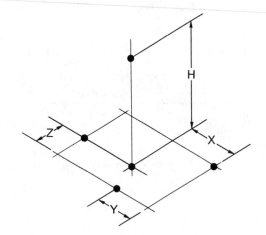

Step 3. Using the two-view drawing as a guide, complete the drawing by connecting all plotted points.

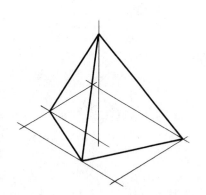

CURVES IN ISOMETRIC

Lines which make up curves in isometric drawings are non-isometric lines and are made by plotting points, figure 18-5.

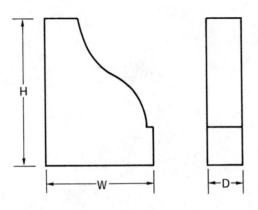

Fig. 18-5 Two-view drawing

Step 1. Draw several vertical or horizontal lines on the surface of the view. Number the ends of these lines.

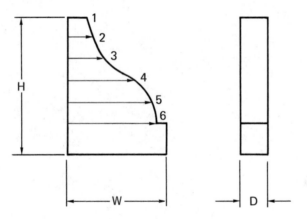

Step 2. Lightly draw the basic shape using the box construction method. Draw lines 1 through 6 at 30-degree spaces as in step 1. Transfer line lengths 1 through 6. Lay out the curve with a French curve.

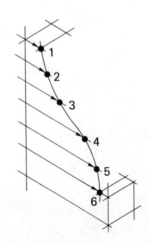

Step 3. Project lines 1 through 6 at 30-degree to the right and measure the thickness on each line. Draw the opposite curve with a French curve.

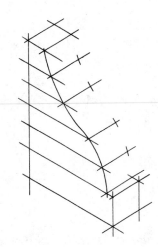

Step 4. Darken all lines using correct line weight.

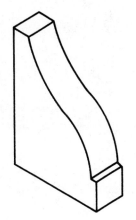

ELLIPSE TEMPLATE

Drawing an ellipse with a compass takes much longer than drawing it with the aid of a template. For this reason *ellipse templates* are used, figures 18-6, 18-7, and 18-8.

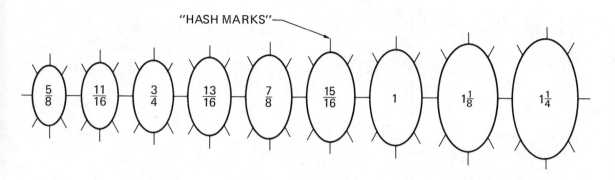

Fig. 18-6 Various diameters drawn with an ellipse template

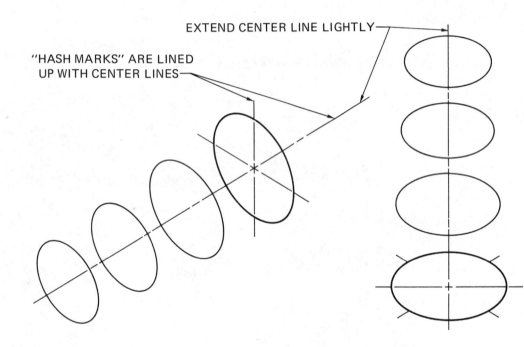

Fig. 18-7 Use of hash marks to align template with center lines. Illustrated are isometric circles at 35° 16′

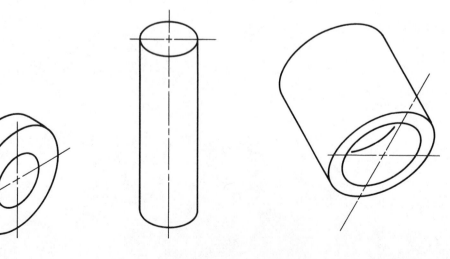

Fig. 18-8 Examples of objects made with ellipse templates

ISOMETRIC CIRCLES

There are two methods used to make circles in isometric. Method 1 is faster to use than method 2 but not as accurate.

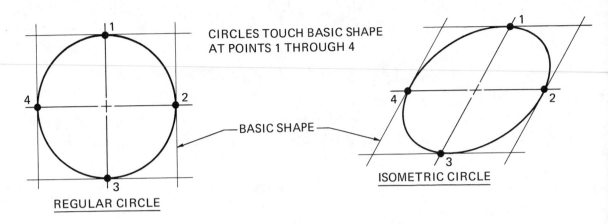

REGULAR CIRCLE

CIRCLES TOUCH BASIC SHAPE AT POINTS 1 THROUGH 4

BASIC SHAPE

ISOMETRIC CIRCLE

Fig. 18-9 Regular and isometric circles

Method 1

Step 1. Draw a horizontal center line. Through the center, draw an isometric vertical center line using a 60-degree angle. Set the compass at the radius required and swing the arcs to cut center lines.

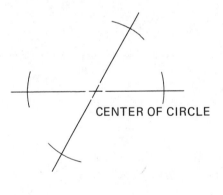

CENTER OF CIRCLE

Step 2. Draw the basic shape and locate points 1 through 4. Draw perpendicular lines to the basic shape from the key points.

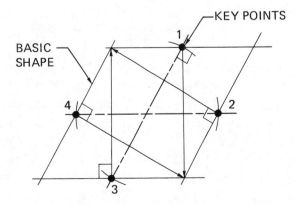

KEY POINTS

BASIC SHAPE

Step 3. Center points for radii 1-2 and 3-4 are located where perpendicular lines cross at points a and b. Swing arcs 1-2 and 3-4.

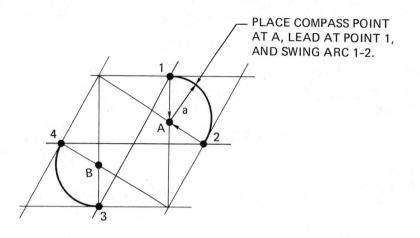

PLACE COMPASS POINT
AT A, LEAD AT POINT 1,
AND SWING ARC 1-2.

Step 4. Center points for radii 2–3 and 1–4 are found at outside corners c and d. Swing arcs 2–3 and 1–4. Each radius forms 1/4 of an isometric circle. Arcs, therefore, are drawn from one center line to the next center line. Darken all arcs using correct line weight.

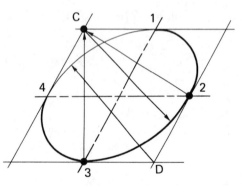

ISOMETRIC RADII

Isometric radii are drawn using the same procedure as method 1 for drawing isometric circles except that only that part of the isometric basic shape needed is used.

In figure 18-10, point A is used as the center for arc 1-2. The inside arc shows the thickness and is drawn for point A'. Point A' is formed by drawing a 30-degree line from point A that measures the width of the stock given. The radius for the new arc will be exactly the same as arc 1-2. The same procedure is used to locate point C'. Point B, the center for radius 2-3, is found using the procedure detailed in method 1 for drawing isometric circles.

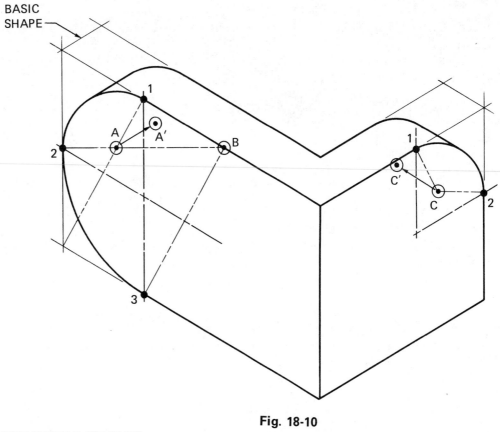

BASIC
SHAPE

Fig. 18-10

ISOMETRIC CIRCLES

Method 2

The procedure for making isometric circles using method 2 is slower than method 1, page 259, because it is done by plotting points, then connecting those points with French curves. It is, however, more accurate than method 1, figure 18-11.

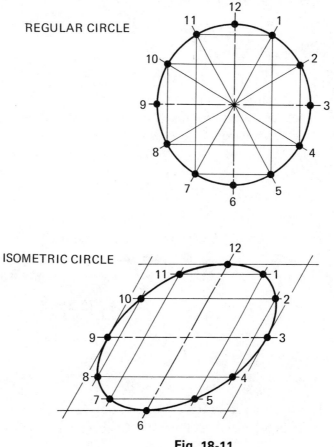

REGULAR CIRCLE

ISOMETRIC CIRCLE

Fig. 18-11

Step 1. On scrap paper, draw a full-size circle using the diameter of the given object. Divide the circle into twelve equal parts with a 30°–60° triangle. Number all parts.

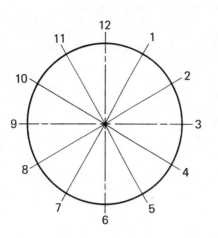

Step 2. Where the lines cross the circle draw rectangles.

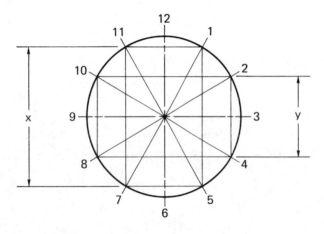

Step 3. Begin the finished drawing by locating the center lines of the isometric circle. With dividers, locate points 3, 6, 9, and 12 on the isometric center lines. Complete the basic shape.

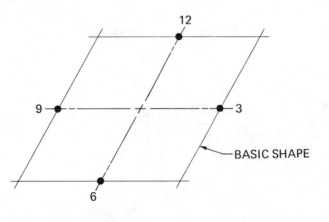

Step 4. From the sketch made in steps 1 and 2, transfer measurements on and about isometric center lines. Number all points. Connect with French curves. Darken drawing to correct line weight.

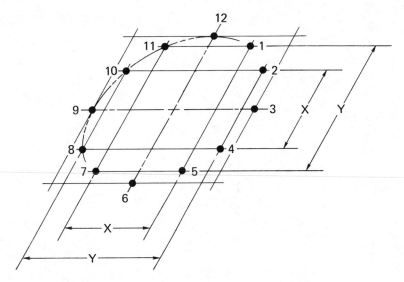

ISOMETRIC ELLIPSE

An ellipse can be drawn in isometric in much the same way as isometric circles by using method 2.

A truncated cylinder is illustrated in figure 18-12. The word *truncated* means cut off. The basic principle of this method is to consider the various points in the basic shape as having height. If all heights were drawn from the points in the basic shape, and all heights were located on these straws, the points forming the ellipse would be located. These points would be connected with French curves to form the ellipse.

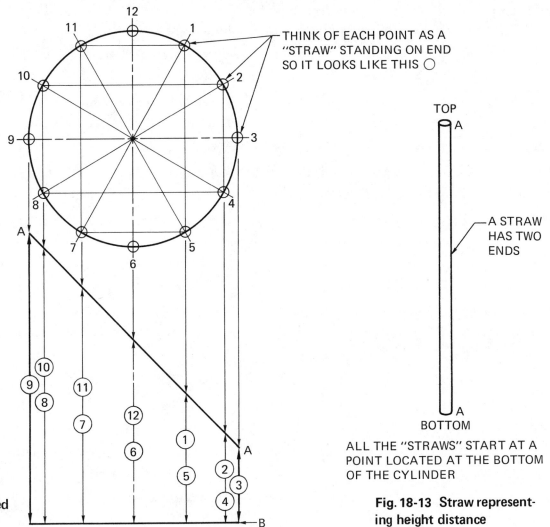

THINK OF EACH POINT AS A "STRAW" STANDING ON END SO IT LOOKS LIKE THIS ◯

TOP

A STRAW HAS TWO ENDS

BOTTOM

ALL THE "STRAWS" START AT A POINT LOCATED AT THE BOTTOM OF THE CYLINDER

Fig. 18-12 Truncated cylinder

Fig. 18-13 Straw representing height distance

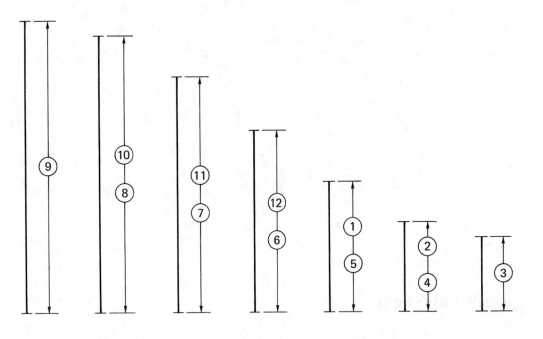

Fig. 18-14 Examples of line lengths taken from figure 18-12

How to Draw an Ellipse

Step 1.   Draw basic shape of cylinder shown in figure 18-12.

Step 2.   Draw an isometric circle within basic shape of cylinder base, using method 2.

Step 3.   Add points 1 through 12.

Step 4.   Project straws 30 degrees from each point. On these straws, transfer lengths of lines from the given view shown in figure 18-12.

Step 5.   Connect the ends of these lines with French curves.

Step 6.   Thicken lines.

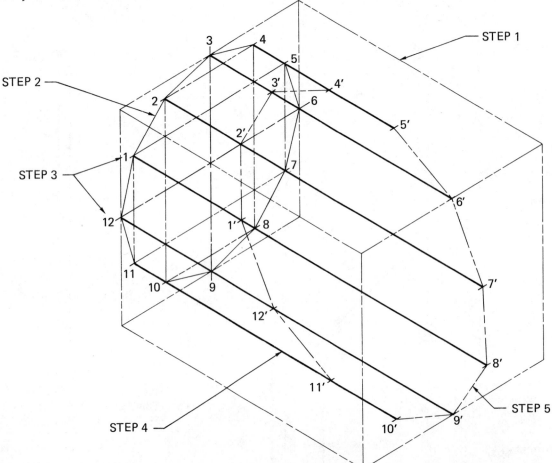

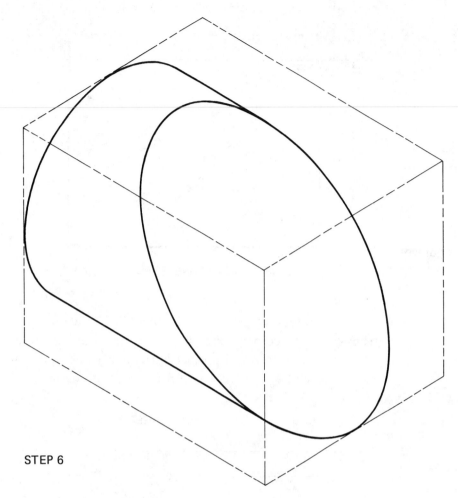

STEP 6

SPACING

Proper centering of the object in the work area, as well as the position of the work area, is important to accomplish a well-balanced drawing. Many times an illustration is laid out on one sheet of paper and then traced and finished on another sheet. Figure 18-5 illustrates the same object centered within two areas of equal size.

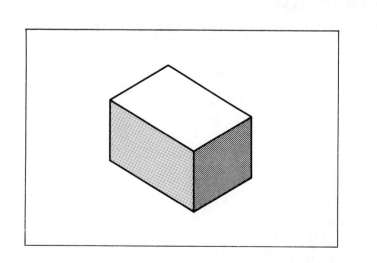

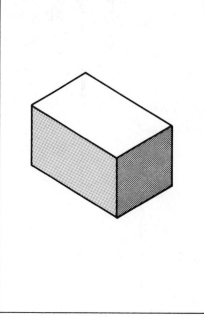

Fig. 18-15

GOLDEN RECTANGLE

A *golden rectangle* is a rectangle drawn to a predetermined shape. This form is derived from Euclidian geometry. Rectangular shapes should be either a golden rectangle or one made from one of the options shown in figure 18-16.

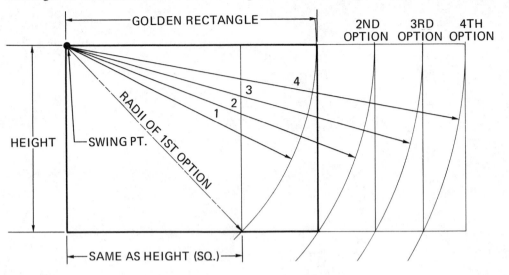

Fig. 18-16 Euclid's golden rectangle

Enlarging

One method of enlarging an original is shown in figure 18-17. Draw a line from corner to corner, extending it outwards as illustrated. Select the size of enlargement desired and project horizontally and vertically from the diagonal line. This method can be used for any size or shape.

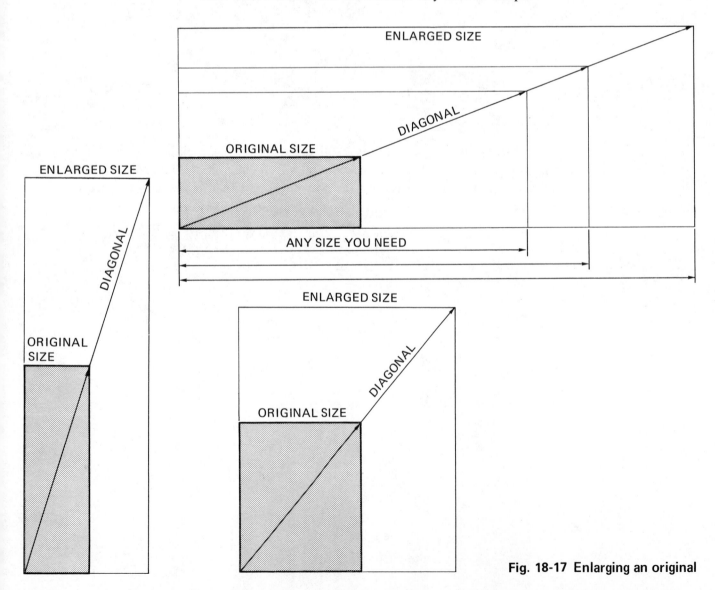

Fig. 18-17 Enlarging an original

Reducing

Originals can be reduced to any smaller size by using the same method as that used to enlarge a rectangle, figure 18-18.

Most technical illustrations are drawn and then reduced in size for printing. This retains the fine detail which can only be included on larger drawings.

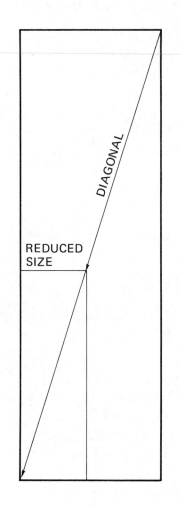

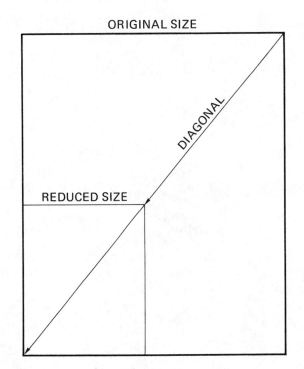

Fig. 18-18 Method used to reduce an original

SHADING

The main purpose of a pictorial drawing is to illustrate the object as close to what it actually looks like as possible. Shading gives the illusion of distance and depth, creating a three-dimensional effect on a flat sheet of paper.

Only three sides of an object are normally shown in a pictorial drawing. The horizontal surface is usually shaded the lightest in value, the frontal plane is a medium value overall, and the profile plane is shaded the darkest, figure 18-19. An edge is formed where contrasting values meet.

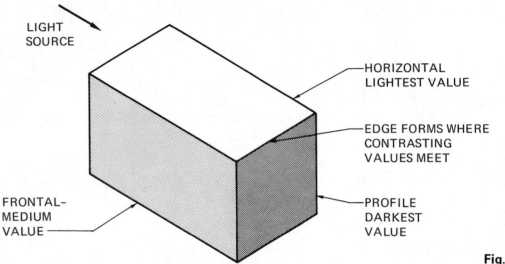

Fig. 18-19 Shading

Line Shading

Line shading varies the light intensity of the paper surface by placing thin lines closer together.

First, think of where the light is coming from. It is usually from over the left shoulder and from above. Thus, where the light shines is the lightest. It gets progressively darker as movement away from the light and into the shadows takes place, figure 18-20.

In line shading, simply draw the lines closer together for a darker effect and space them out further as the light source is approached, figure 18-21.

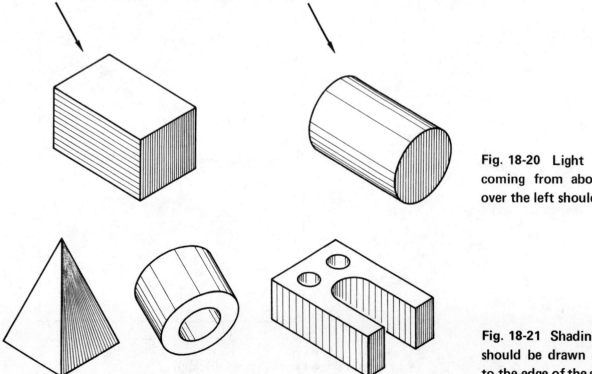

Fig. 18-20 Light source coming from above and over the left shoulder

Fig. 18-21 Shading lines should be drawn parallel to the edge of the surface

Stippling

Stippling is a method of shading that uses a series of dots placed close together to represent dark areas and spaced apart to represent light areas. The same basic instructions for line shading apply to stippling. Stippling produces pleasing and realistic illustrations, figures 18-22 and 18-23.

There are *shading films* available on the market which can eliminate the repetitious job of stippling. In order to use these films most effectively, other methods of shading must first be mastered.

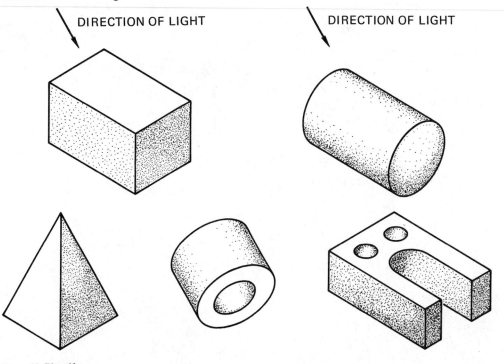

Fig. 18-22 The light source is shown originating above and from the left

Fig. 18-23 Examples of objects which have been shaded using the stippling method

Pencil Shading

Pencil shading uses the same theory as line shading and stippling A 2H or softer pencil is used to pencil shade.

Loose *graphite* is often used to improve the appearance of drawings shaded with pencils. The graphite is placed on the drawing and smudged with the index finger or a tightly rolled piece of paper. All changes should be gradual from white to very black. An eraser and erasing shield is used to erase smudges that go outside of the drawing area and to highlight any important light areas. Practice this method on scrap paper, figure 18-24.

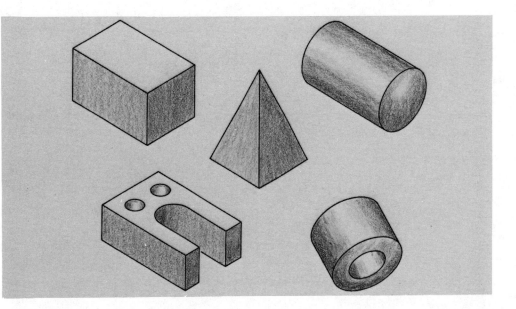

Fig. 18-24 Examples of objects which have been shaded with pencil and graphite

Adding Shadows

Sometimes a shadow is required in order to further emphasize the object. Figure 18-25 illustrates a suggested method of adding shadows to finished objects.

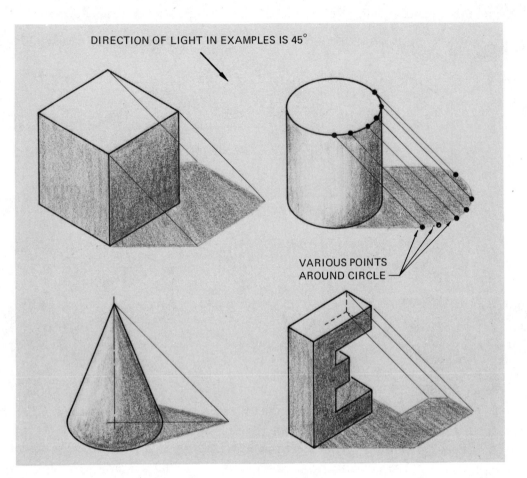

DIRECTION OF LIGHT IN EXAMPLES IS 45°

VARIOUS POINTS AROUND CIRCLE

Fig. 18-25 Adding shadows

PERSPECTIVE DRAWING

ISOMETRIC PERSPECTIVE

Figures 19-1, 19-2, 19-3 are examples of a *three-view drawing,* an *isometric drawing,* and a *perspective drawing* of the same object. The three-view drawing is used by the craftsman to make the object. The isometric and perspective drawings are types of pictorial representations to make interpreting the three-view drawing easier.

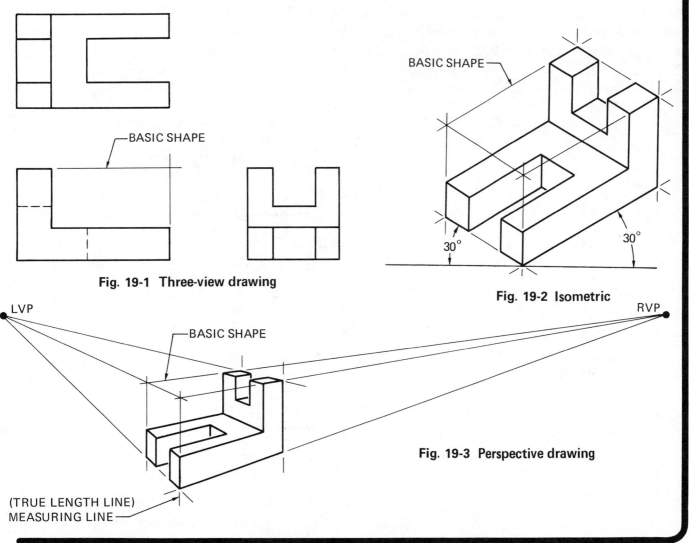

Fig. 19-1 Three-view drawing

Fig. 19-2 Isometric

Fig. 19-3 Perspective drawing

As previously explained, isometric drawings are made around an *isometric axis*, Figure 19-4. All true measurements are laid out on these axis lines consisting of 30-degree angular lines projected to the left and right of center, and a vertical line projected upwards from center. The finished isometric gives a satisfactory pictorial drawing but is somewhat distorted.

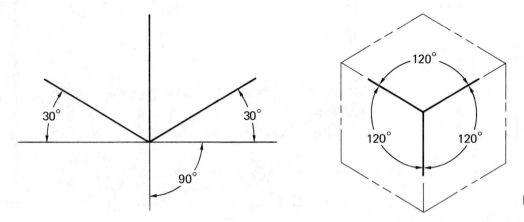

Fig. 19-4 An isometric axis

Perspective drawings are drawn with all true measurements on the true length line, see figure 19-3. Heights are drawn from that line to the vanishing points. This type drawing produces *pictorial drawings* which appear like actual photographs.

ONE-POINT PERSPECTIVE

One-point perspective is the simplest perspective to draw. Take a standard front view of an object and extend all other lines to one vanishing point (VP). Other variations are possible, figure 19-5. Boxes A and B show the bottom as well as one side because they are *above* eye level. Boxes C and D show one side but neither the top nor bottom because they are located *on* eye level. Boxes E and F show one side and the top because they are located *below* eye level.

Care should be used in selecting one point perspective views as they can be so close to pictorial views (A, B, E, F) that a pictorial view might actually be a

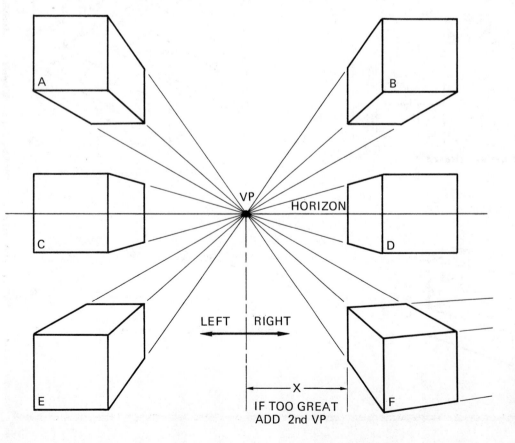

Fig. 19-5 Various layouts using one-point perspective

better choice and a great deal easier to draw. The main difference will be that receding lines will be parallel in pictorial views rather than converge. Also, if the object is placed too far to one side of the vanishing point (X), distortion occurs and a second vanishing point should be used.

Fig. 19-6 Objects drawn using one-point perspective

TWO-POINT PERSPECTIVE

Two-point perspective is similar to one-point perspective except that edges are projected to two points instead of one. Study the drawings which result by placing the object above, on, and below the horizon line, or eye level, in figure 19-7. The bottom of the object is visible when it is placed above the horizon line. Neither the top nor bottom of the object can be seen when the object's center is placed on the horizon line. The top is visible when the object is blaced beneath eye level.

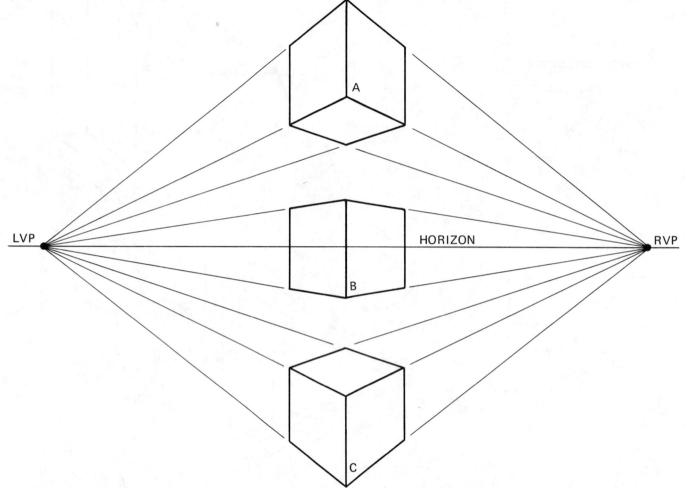

Fig. 19-7 An object drawn in two-point perspective on, above, and beneath eye level

Sketch as many objects as possible using this method. Two-point perspective is used more frequently than other methods and will be used to complete assignments in this unit.

Illustrated in figures 19-8 and 19-9 are two uses of two-point drawings. Figure 19-8 is an outside view of a building using two-point perspective. Notice how the

Fig. 19-8 Outside view in two-point perspective

windows get closer together and smaller as they go back in space, giving the impression of distance.   The same is true of the inside view of a room using two-point perspective in figure 19-9.

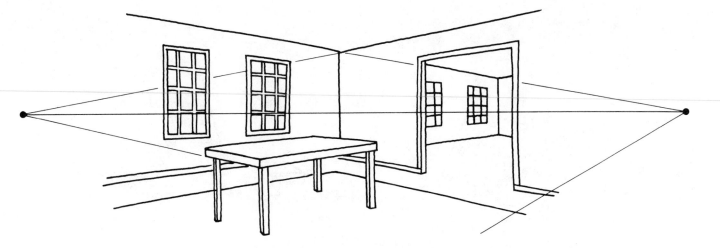

Fig. 19-9 Inside view in two-point perspective

THREE-POINT PERSPECTIVE

Three-point perspective is more difficult to draw than the other methods covered and, for this reason, is not often used. There are no parallel edges in a three-point drawing as all edges converge to one of the three vanishing points. Figure 19-10 shows an object drawn beneath the horizon. As in one- and two-point perspectives, objects using the three-point method can be placed on, above, or below the horizon line depending on the view desired.

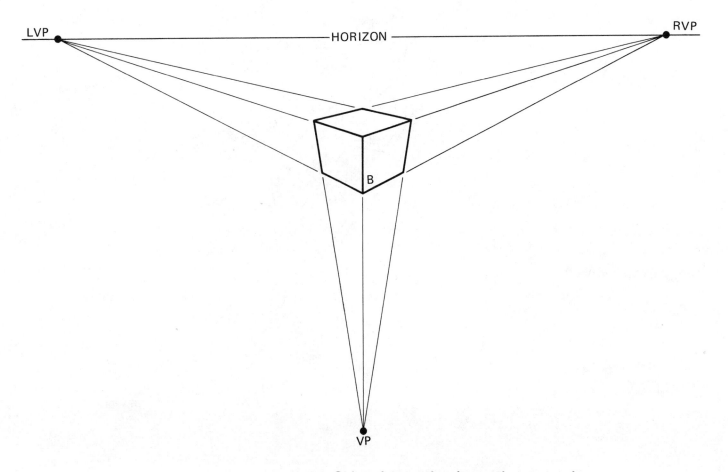

Fig. 19-10 Object drawn using three-point perspective

Three-point perspective is used only in special cases. Practice three-point perspective sketches by viewing the same objects from different positions, figure 19-11.

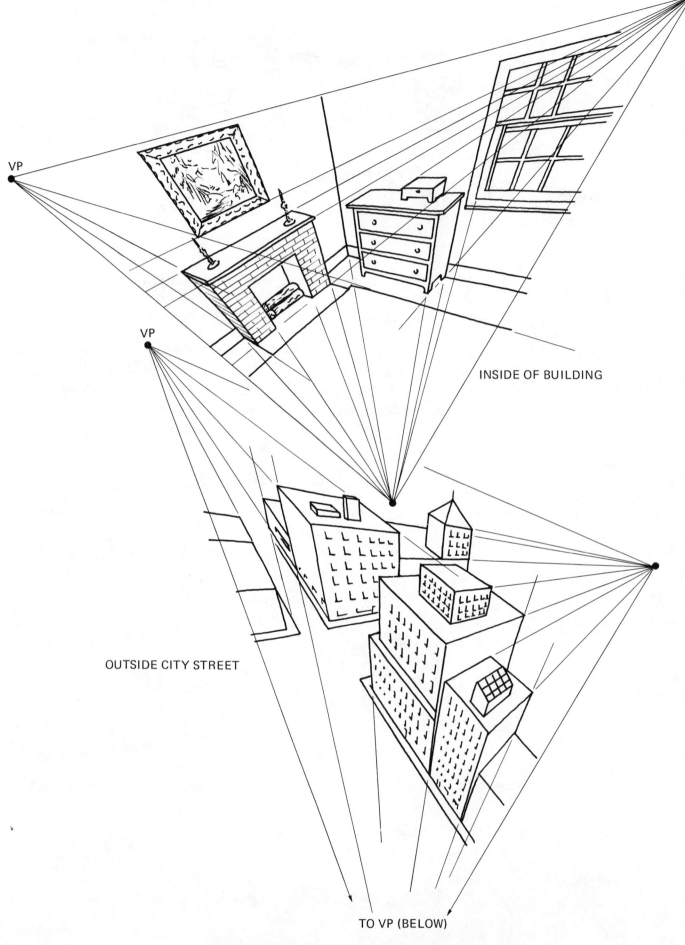

VP

VP

VP

INSIDE OF BUILDING

OUTSIDE CITY STREET

VP

TO VP (BELOW)

Fig. 19-11 Example of three-point perspective

PERSPECTIVE DRAWING TERMS

Figure 19-12 illustrates the terms used in perspective drawing. Refer to the illustration as the terms are defined.

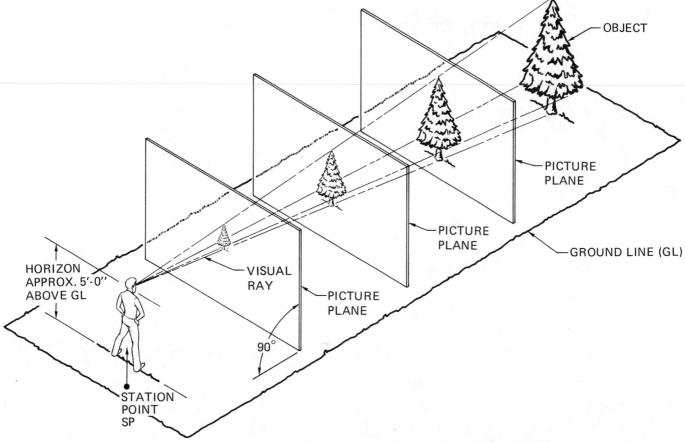

Fig. 19-12   Perspective drawing: definition of terms

The projecting lines for a perspective drawing converge at the eye of the observer and are called *visual rays*. The *picture plane* (PP) is the surface upon which the drawing is made. It is a vertical plane 90 degrees from the horizon plane. Think of it as a piece of glass located between the observer and the object. The *horizon plane* passes through the eye of the observer. The *vanishing points* (VP) are located on the horizon plane. These vanishing points are where all lines converge. Drawings can have more than one vanishing point. The *station point* (SP) represents the position where the observer is standing while viewing the object. The *ground line* (GL) represents the plane upon which the observer is standing. Assuming the observer to be of normal height, the horizon line is located approximately 5'-0" (eye level) above the ground line. The *measuring line* is a vertical line upon which actual heights are made and from which actual heights are drawn to the vanishing points.

Think of the picture plane (PP) line as a piece of glass set 90 degrees from the ground line (GL). Notice where the observer is standing (SP) and that the horizon line is approximately five feet above the ground line. As you move the picture plane line closer to the object, the object gets larger. The visual rays extend from the observer's eyes to the object.

DRAWING A ONE-POINT PERSPECTIVE

When drawing a one-point perspective, lay out the top view so the proper depth of the object can be located on the lines going to the vanishing points. This avoids guesswork and will result in a more professional looking drawing.

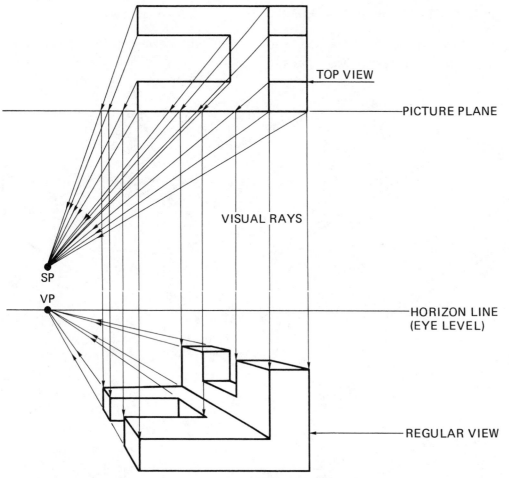

TOP VIEW

PICTURE PLANE

VISUAL RAYS

SP
VP

HORIZON LINE
(EYE LEVEL)

REGULAR VIEW

Fig. 19-13 Method of laying out a one-point perspective

The bottom edge of the top view is placed on the picture plane line, figure 19-13. A point is arbitrarily placed on the paper beneath the picture plane line to represent the station point. This point may be on, to the right, or to the left of the center. It represents where the person viewing the object is standing. The distance this point is away from the picture plane represents the distance the person is away from the object.

A point representing the vanishing point is placed directly beneath the station point any convenient distance apart. A line drawn horizontally through this point represents eye level (horizon line).

Next, the front view of the three-view drawing is drawn directly beneath the top view by projecting lines downward, figure 19-14. The front view may be placed on, above, or below the horizon line depending upon the finished view desired. All edges of the front view are projected to the vanishing point. All edges of the top view not touching the picture plane are drawn to the station point. At the point these projected lines cross the picture plane, they are projected downward to establish the correct depth.

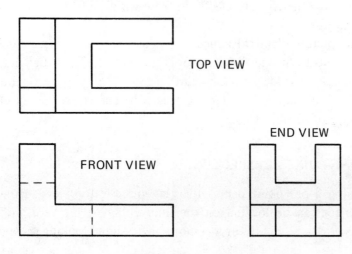

TOP VIEW

FRONT VIEW

END VIEW

Fig. 19-14 Working drawing of the object being drawn in figure 19-13

One-Point Perspectives in Architecture

Figure 19-15 shows one use of one-point perspective in architecture.

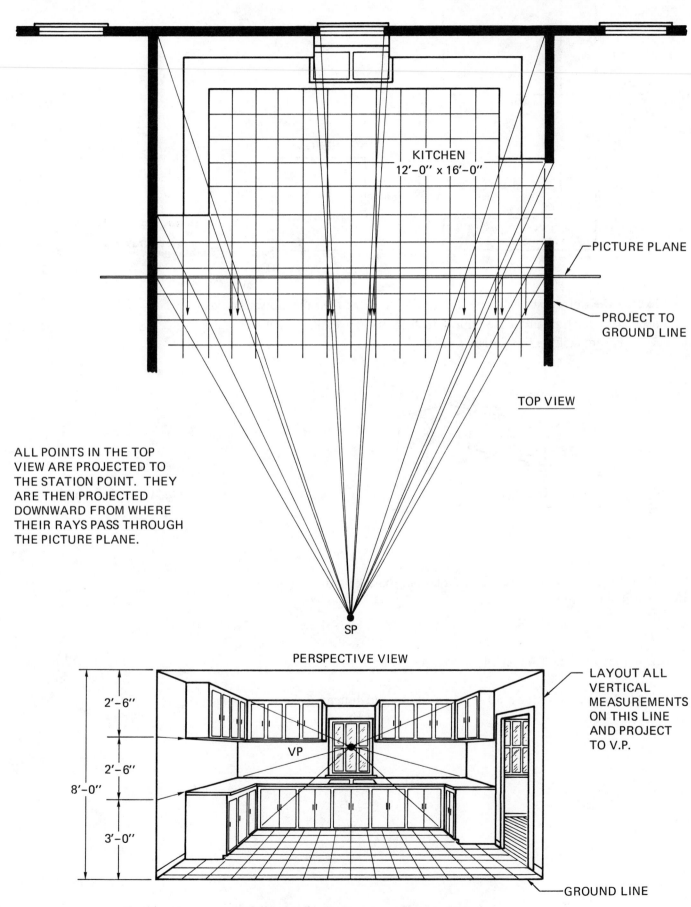

KITCHEN
12'-0'' x 16'-0''

PICTURE PLANE

PROJECT TO
GROUND LINE

TOP VIEW

ALL POINTS IN THE TOP
VIEW ARE PROJECTED TO
THE STATION POINT. THEY
ARE THEN PROJECTED
DOWNWARD FROM WHERE
THEIR RAYS PASS THROUGH
THE PICTURE PLANE.

SP

PERSPECTIVE VIEW

LAYOUT ALL
VERTICAL
MEASUREMENTS
ON THIS LINE
AND PROJECT
TO V.P.

2'-6''

VP

2'-6''

8'-0''

3'-0''

GROUND LINE

Fig. 19-15 One-point perspective of kitchen

DRAWING A TWO-POINT PERSPECTIVE

To begin drawing a two-point perspective, start with the normal, three-view drawing, figure 19-16. Decide which position best illustrates the object.

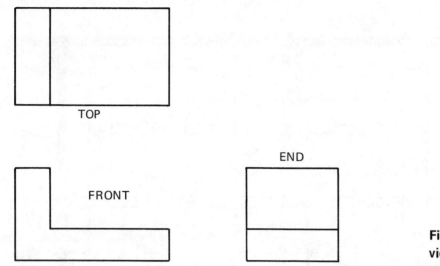

TOP

FRONT

END

Fig. 19-16 Three-view drawing

Sketch the object's basic shape, figure 19-17. Turn the object into the position needed to illustrate all of the important features. Several rough sketches may be needed before making this decision.

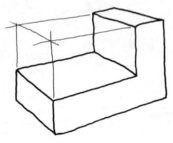

Fig. 19-17 Sketch of object

Select the best sketch and use that layout to make a true two-point perspective as outlined in the following steps.

Step 1

1. Draw a light line horizontally across the paper. This represents the picture plane.
2. Draw the top view at a 30-degree angle to and touching the picture plane, figure 19-18.

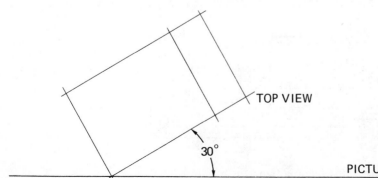

TOP VIEW

30°

PICTURE PLANE

Fig. 19-18 Step 1

Step 2

1. Project a line 90 degrees from the point at which the picture plane and top view touch, figure 19-19.

2. Place a point on the picture plane as far to the right of the paper as possible. Draw line a through this point parallel to the right side of the top view.

3. Station point b is located where line a crosses the line drawn in step 1.

4. Through station point b, draw a line parallel to the left side of the top view.

5. Project lines c and d from the top view to the station point (b). Measure the angle formed by these lines. The angle should be less than 30 degrees. If it is more than 30 degrees either the points on the picture plane or the top view must be moved out. In either case, the entire process must be repeated.

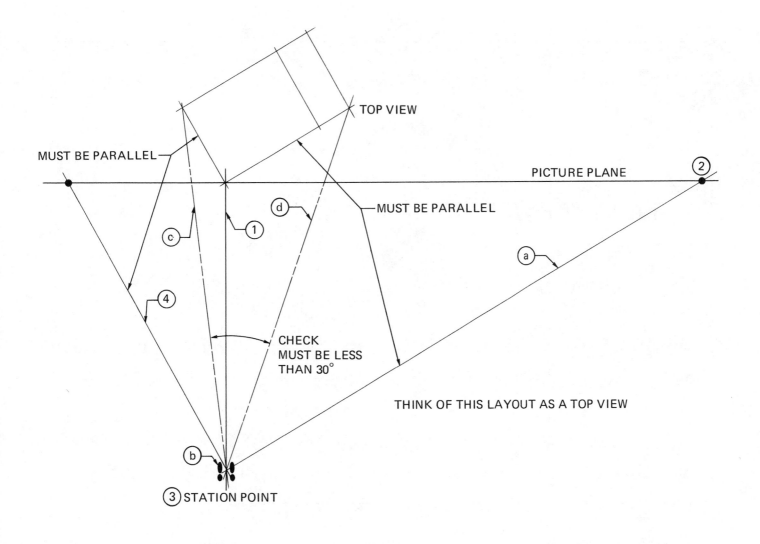

Fig. 19-19 Step 2

Step 3

1. Project lines from each point of the top view downward to the station point. These lines are the visual rays, figure 19-20.
2. Draw the horizon plane representing eye level at some convenient distance below the station point.
3. Project lines downward from points 'A' and 'B' on the picture plane until they intercept the horizon plane. The points at which they intercept become the left vanishing point (LVP) and right vanishing point (RVP).

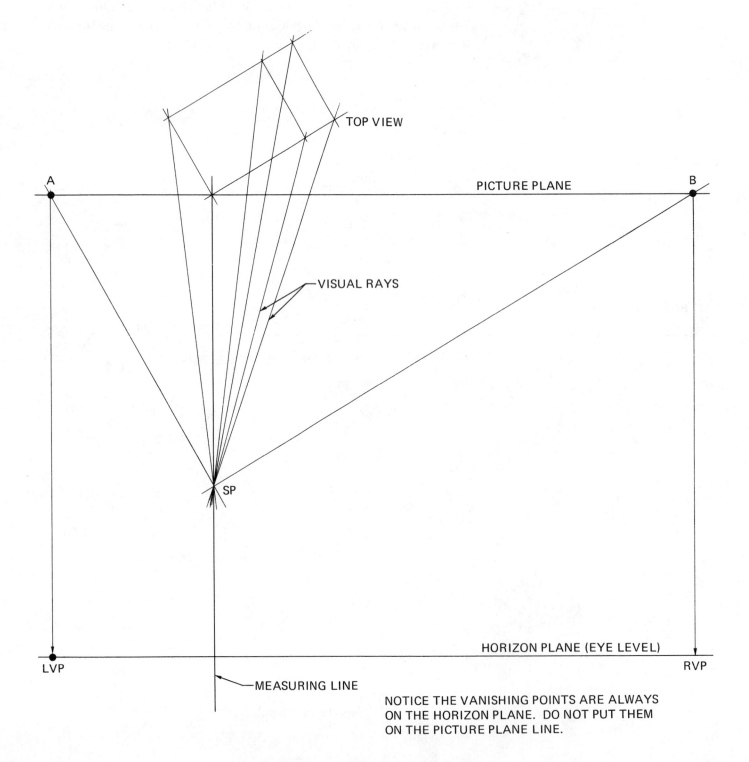

Fig. 19-20 Step 3

Step 4

1. Draw the front view of the object in the position illustrated, placing its base at the ground line. Project true height over to the measuring line, figure 19-21.
2. Project lines downward from the points where the outside visual rays pass through the picture plane.
3. Construct the basic shape of the object by projecting to the vanishing points, as shown.

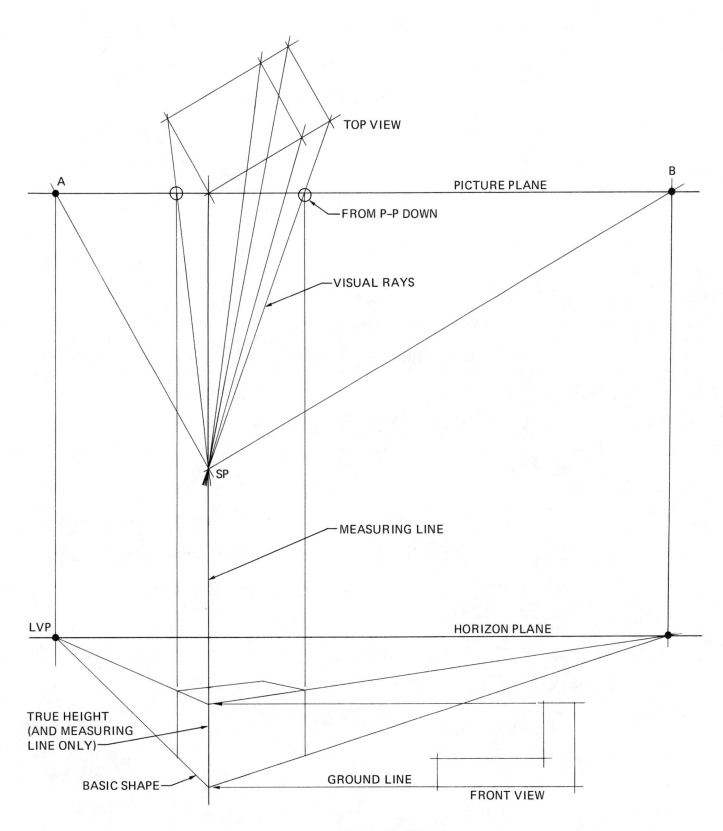

Fig. 19-21 Step 4

Step 5

1. Project downward all other points from the picture plane and complete the true perspective view inside the basic shape, figure 19-22.

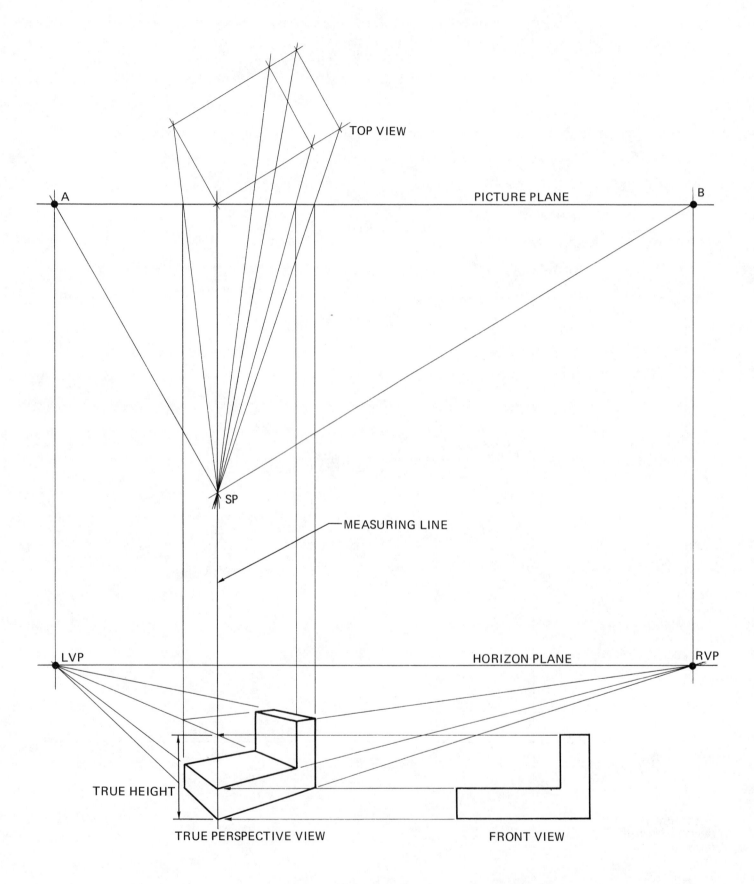

Fig. 19-22 Step 5

A standard three-view drawing is illustrated in figure 19-23, followed by perspective sketches showing the object in several different positions, figure 19-24.

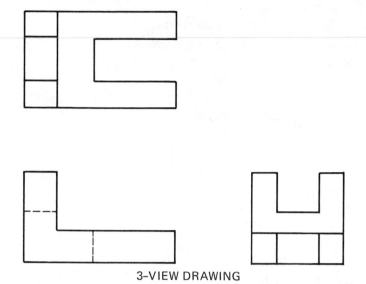

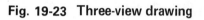

3-VIEW DRAWING

Fig. 19-23 Three-view drawing

(a)
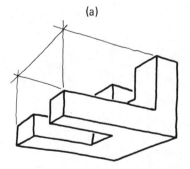

(b)
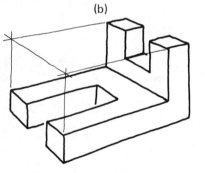

(c)
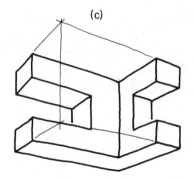

(d)
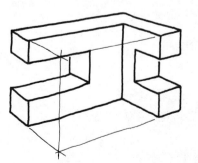

(e)
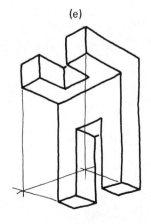

(f)
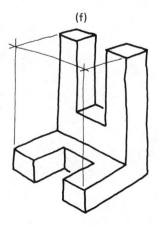

Fig. 19-24 Perspective sketches

SAMPLE PERSPECTIVE LAYOUTS

The elevation selected and the placement of that elevation in relationship to the horizon plane is most important. Study the two examples shown in figure 19-25.

House A is drawn above the horizon plane and appears as if it were located on a hill. House B is drawn below the horizon plane and appears as if it were located in a valley. Neither position is normally used to show a house in perspective. They are used occasionally, however, for special assignments.

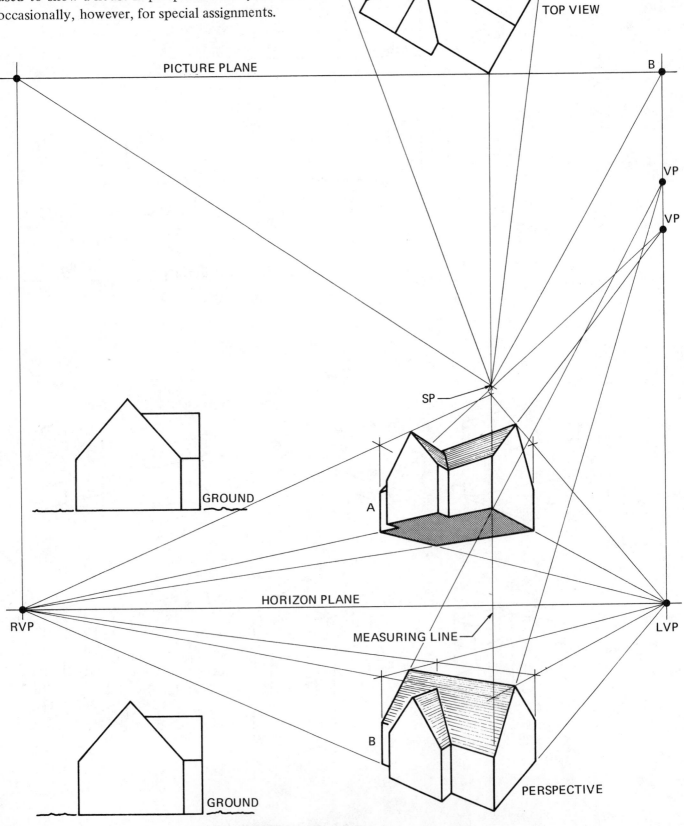

Fig. 19-25 Examples of perspective layouts

A house perspective is usually difficult to draw because the vanishing points are out so far. It may be easier to reduce the floor plan and one elevation to 1/8" = 1'0", draw the perspective at that scale, then enlarge only the perspective to a convenient size.

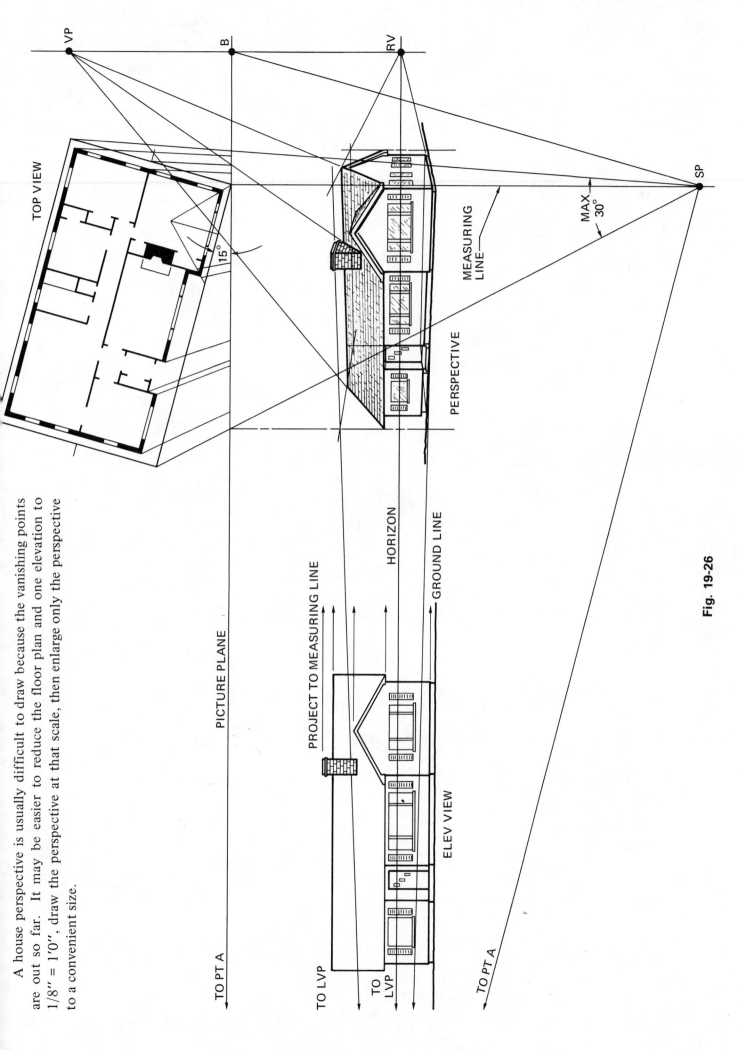

VP

B

RV

SP

TOP VIEW

15°

MEASURING LINE

PERSPECTIVE

MAX 30°

PICTURE PLANE

TO PT A

PROJECT TO MEASURING LINE

HORIZON

GROUND LINE

TO LVP

TO LVP

ELEV VIEW

TO PT A

Fig. 19-26

UNIT 20

MECHANICAL LETTERING

MECHANICAL LETTERING

Mechanical lettering can be done with a template and scriber, a lettering typewriter, or by using pressure-sensitive letters. Figure 20-1 illustrates one method of mechanical lettering.

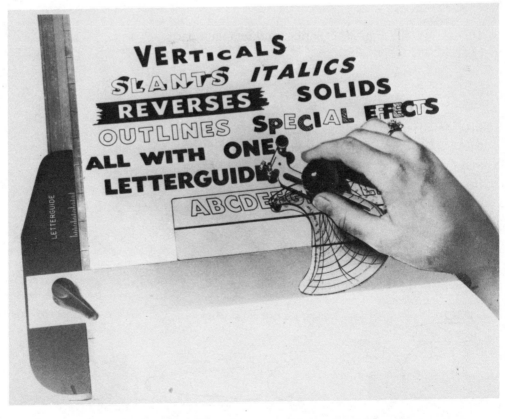

Fig. 20-1 Mechanical lettering with template and scriber

SCRIBER TEMPLATES

Scriber templates consist of laminated strips with engraved grooves to form letters. A *tracer pin* moving in the grooves guides the scriber pen or pencil in forming the letters, figure 20-2.

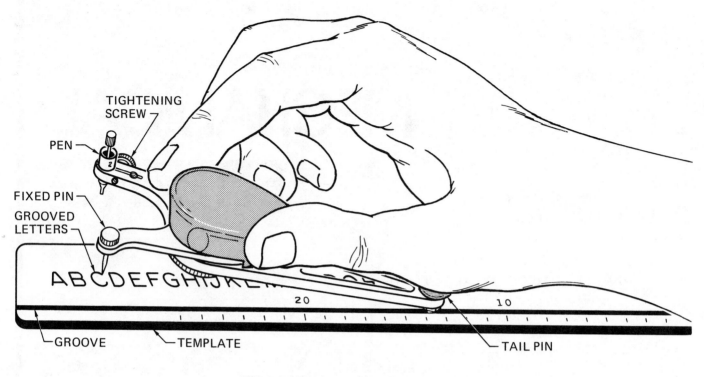
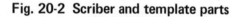

USE A VERY LIGHT DELICATE TOUCH.

Fig. 20-2 Scriber and template parts

Guides for different sizes and kinds of letters are available for any of the lettering devices. Different point sizes are made for special pens so that fine lines can be used for small letters and wider lines for larger letters. Scribers may be adjusted to get vertical or slanted letters of several sizes from a single guide by simply unlocking the screw under the scriber and extending the *arms*, figures 20-3 and 20-4.

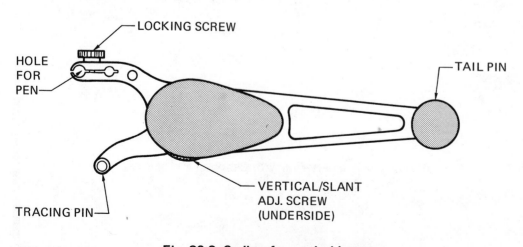

Fig. 20-3 Scriber for vertical letters

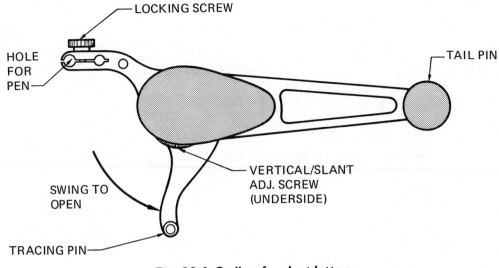

Fig. 20-4 Scriber for slant letters

One of the principal advantages of lettering guides is in maintaining uniform lettering, especially where there are a number of drafters. Another important use is for lettering titles, note headings, and numbers on drawings and reports.

Letters used to identify templates are:

U = UPPERCASE
L = LOWERCASE
N = NUMBERS

Thus a template 8-ULN means it is 8/16 inches high (1/2″) and has uppercase and lowercase letters and numbers.

Tracing Pin

Better, more expensive scribers use a double tracing pin. The blunt end is used for single-stroke lettering templates or very large templates which have wide grooves. The sharp end is used for very small lettering templates, double-stroke letters, or script-type lettering using a fine groove. Most tracing pins have a sharp point, but some do not, figure 20-5. Always screw the cap back on after turning the tracing pin. Be careful with the points as they will break if dropped and can cause a painful injury if mishandled.

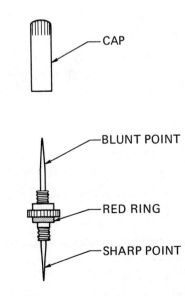

Fig. 20-5 Tracing pin (fixed pin)

INK

Always use fresh ink in the pens. In warm weather the ink will plug the pen if it is not changed weekly. Always clean the ink out of the pens if they will not be used for three or four days.

LETTERING SET

One *Leroy® lettering set* is designed for the beginning illustrator. The set contains the basic components needed to do controlled lettering, figure 20-6.

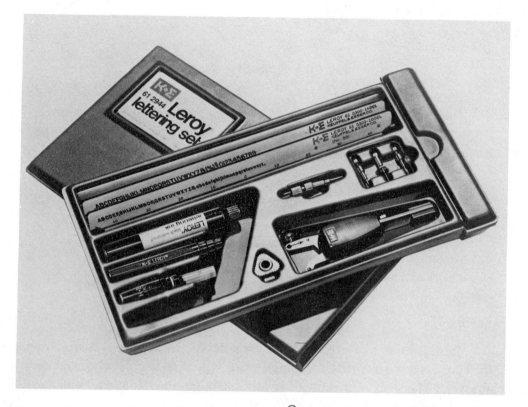

Fig. 20-6 A Leroy® lettering set

STANDARD TEMPLATE

Learning to form mechanical letters requires a great deal of practice. Figure 20-7 shows a template having three sets of uppercase and lowercase letters. Practice forming each size letter and number until they can be made rapidly and neatly. Use a very light, delicate touch so as not to damage the template, scriber, or pen.

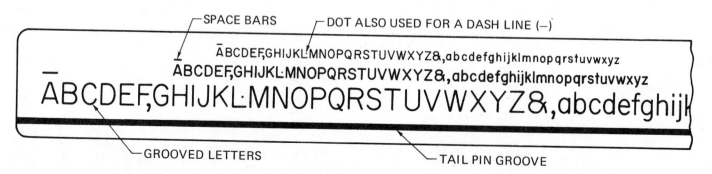

Fig. 20-7 Template

SIZE OF LETTERS

The size or height of the letter is called out by the number used to identify each set. Sizes are in thousandths of an inch. A #100 is 0.100 inch high or slightly less than an eighth of an inch, while a #240 is 0.240 inch high, or slightly less than a quarter of an inch.

There is another system of template sizes which use simple numbers. These numbers are placed over 16 to give the height of the letter. The number 3, for instance, would be 3/16 inch in height.

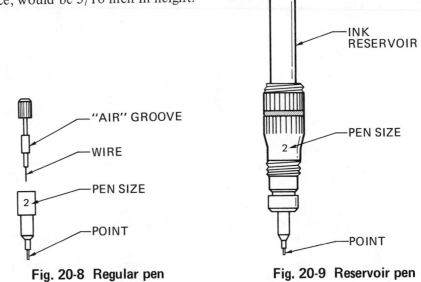

Fig. 20-8 Regular pen   Fig. 20-9 Reservoir pen

PENS

There are two types of pens, the regular pen and the reservoir pen. The regular pen must be cleaned after each use. The reservoir pen should be cleaned when it gets "sluggish" or before being stored for long periods of time, figures 20-8, 20-9, and 20-10.

Fig. 20-10 Technical pens. Note points. Top: pen is used for lines only. Bottom: pen is used for lines and in lettering scribers.

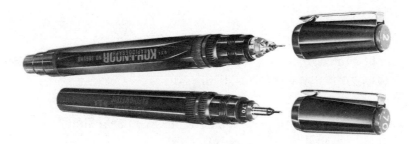

Figure 20-11 shows the recommended pen sizes for given letter heights.

Height of letter	Recommended Pen Size
.080	0 0 0
.100	0 0
.120	0
.140	1
.175	2
.200	3
.240	3
.290	4
.350	4
.425	5
.500	6

Fig. 20-11

Point Sizes

There are fourteen (14) point sizes ranging from #000, which is very thin and very delicate, through #14, which is very thick, figure 20-12. Extreme care must be used in replacing the fine wire into the body of the pen.

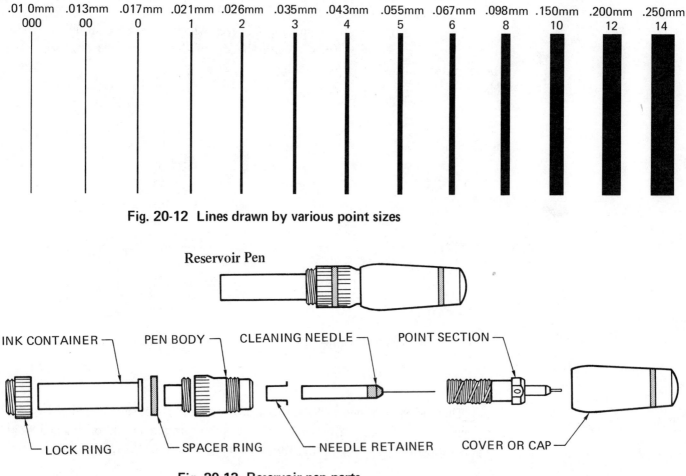

| .010mm | .013mm | .017mm | .021mm | .026mm | .035mm | .043mm | .055mm | .067mm | .098mm | .150mm | .200mm | .250mm |
| 000 | 00 | 0 | 1 | 2 | 3 | 4 | 5 | 6 | 8 | 10 | 12 | 14 |

Fig. 20-12 Lines drawn by various point sizes

Reservoir Pen

INK CONTAINER ‚ PEN BODY ‚ CLEANING NEEDLE ‚ POINT SECTION ‚

LOCK RING   SPACER RING   NEEDLE RETAINER   COVER OR CAP ‚

Fig. 20-13 Reservoir pen parts

Reservoir Pen

Cleaning. Pens can be ruined by improper cleaning. Study steps one through five and follow them closely when cleaning pens, figure 20-13.

1. Remove cap and ink container.
2. Soak the body of the pen in hot water. The ink container should also be soaked if ink has dried in it.
3. After soaking, remove the pen body from the water. Hold the knurled part of the body with the top downward. Unscrew and remove point section. Remove the end of the cleaning wire weight. Do not bend the cleaning wire or it will break.
4. Immerse all body parts in a good pen cleaning fluid or hot water mixed half with ammonia.
5. Dry and clean.

Filling. To fill the pen, follow steps one through five:

1. Unscrew and remove knurled lock ring.
2. Remove ink container. Leave spacer ring in place.
3. Fill ink container with lettering ink. Do not fill more than 3/4 inch from top.
4. Hold filled container upright and insert pen body into container.
5. Replace knurled lock ring.

Use. Remove the cap from the pen body. To start the flow of ink, force the point downward and shake rapidly against a cloth. The pen is ready for use when ink appears on the cloth. Filled pens should be capped and kept in a vertical position with their tips upward when not in use.

JUSTIFYING COLUMNS

Printed text in newpapers and magazines are arranged in columns of equal width. Each line of type starts at the left-hand margin and ends at the right-hand margin. All of the lines are equal in length. The process of obtaining printed columns with lines of equal length is called *justification.*

BUTTERFLY-TYPE SCRIBER

Basic Parts

The *butterfly-type scriber* shown in figure 20-14 is a delicate, precision tool that will do its job without requiring any adjustments, repairs, or maintenance.

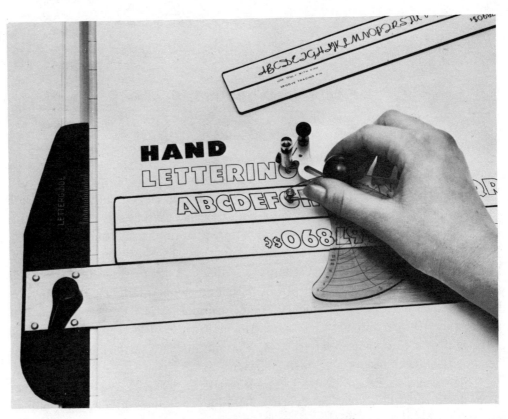

Fig. 20-14 A butterfly-type scriber

The vinyl base of the scriber bears the setting chart used in adjusting the pen arm for enlargements, reductions, verticals, and slants to be produced by tracing the engraved letters of a letter guide template.

The pen arm of the scriber holds the pen accessories for the various jobs to be performed. The pen and the arm have a thumb tightening screw device for securing the pen being used, and an adjustable pressure post screw with locking nut for controlling the amount of pressure and/or depth the pen or knife is set at, figure 20-15. The pressure post rides on the surface of the work when in use and is used only in conjunction with the swivel knife. The "bull's-eye" setting marker at the opposite end of the pen arm offers a concise, accurate means of setting the scriber for the various percentages and angles desired.

The tracing pin is the hardened tool steel point used in tracing the template letter. The tail pin serves as the pivot point for the triangular action of the scriber. This pin travels in the center groove of the template.

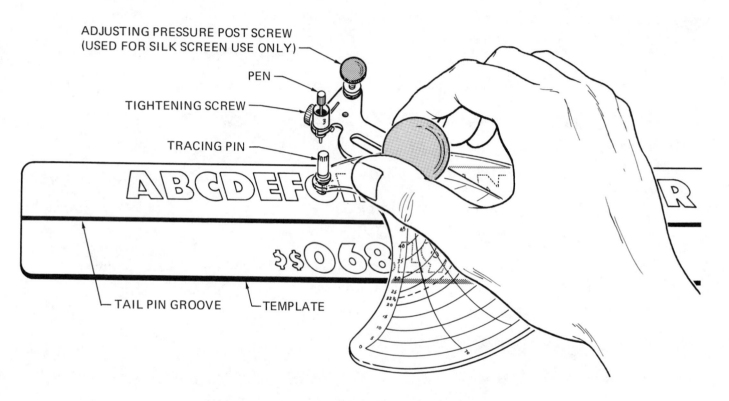

ADJUSTING PRESSURE POST SCREW
(USED FOR SILK SCREEN USE ONLY)

PEN

TIGHTENING SCREW

TRACING PIN

TAIL PIN GROOVE   TEMPLATE

Fig. 20-15 Using a butterfly-type scriber

Operation

This precision lettering tool is the key to producing clean, sharp, controlled lettering. The setting chart, using the bull's-eye at the end of the pen arm for a marker, begins at the outer edge with a starting line marked "vertical." In this position the scriber produces a vertical letter of normal size from the template being used. To enlarge this letter, set the bull's-eye at a position above the 100 percent intersection. At 120 percent, the scriber will produce a letter 20 percent greater in height than at 100 percent. A reduction can be produced by setting the bull's-eye at a position below the 100 percent intersection. Variations in height range from 100 percent up to 140 percent and down to 60 percent. The extreme settings produce condensed letters while the intermediate settings produce either headings, subheadings, or large or small letters.

Slants in all sizes are easily produced by setting the bull's-eye on a line other than the vertical line. Normal slants or italics are produced in all height adjustments by setting the bull's-eye on either the 15-degree or 22 1/2-degree line, and at the desired percentage of height of the letter on the template. Variations may be produced in slants ranging from 0 degrees to 50 degrees forward.

Tracing the engraved template letter requires a very light and delicate touch. This results in more accurately traced letters and less wear on the equipment. Each lettering application will require its own specific pen and will place at the fingertips of the drafter the very best in standard typeface and hand-lettered alphabets for fast, easy rendering.

LARGE LETTER SERIES LETTER GUIDES

Scriber settings differ for all letter guide templates bearing letters larger than number 12. For these large letter series letter guides, start with the bull's-eye set on the dotted line marked 22 1/2 degrees for all vertical letters. The intersection of this 22 1/2-degree line with the 100 percent line marks the setting for the normal size vertical letter from the template being used. All size 16, 20, 26, and 32 letter guides produce slants and reductions. Enlargements and some back-slants are possible with all sizes except 32. Two-inch lettering is the maximum size possible.

Fig. 20-16 Sample letters using a Letter Guide Collegiate-A Template

LETTER SPACING

Fast and optically correct spacing requires practice. After starting the heading by tracing the first letter, place the tracing pin of the scriber in the left-hand side of the next letter, slide the template and scriber into the proper optically spaced position, and proceed to trace. Perfect optical spacing can be obtained, even when lettering such letter combinations as AV, LA, YA, etc., by first planning the heading as normal, close, or wide space. Headings can be letter spaced to fit any required word length.

BALL-POINT PEN

A ball-point pen is an excellent tool for producing fast, sharp, concise lettering. The sealed-in ink supply is adequate for tracing upwards of 1000 letters.

CENTERING

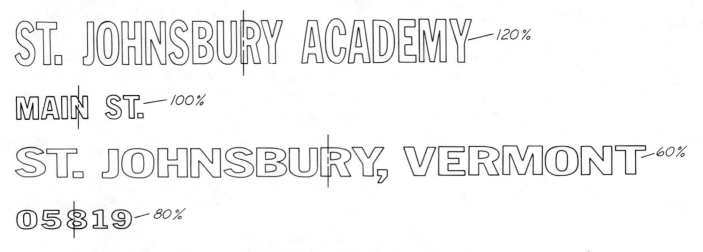

Fig. 20-17 Sample letters with heights (step 1) and centers (step 2) indicated

Step 3. Cut the lettering into strips of paper, figure 20-18.

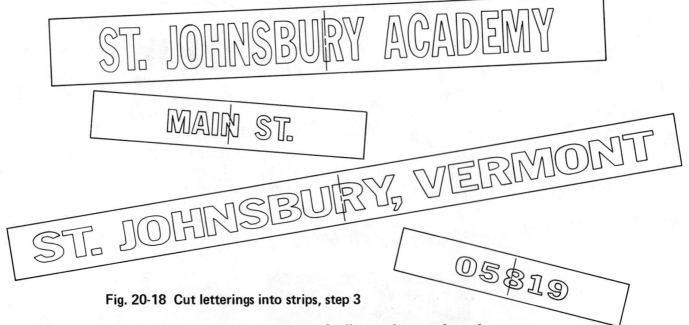

Fig. 20-18 Cut letterings into strips, step 3

Step 4. Lightly draw a center line on a piece of vellum to locate where the printing is to be placed. Draw light horizontal lines to locate the bottom of the lettering, figure 21-19.

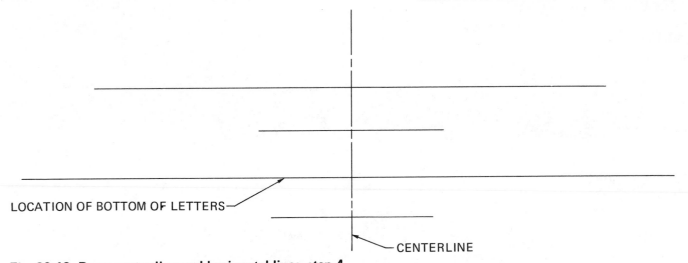

LOCATION OF BOTTOM OF LETTERS

CENTERLINE

Fig. 20-19 Draw center line and horizontal lines, step 4

Step 5. Tape the cut strips under the vellum, lining up the center line on the paper with the center line on the strips. Line up the bottom of the words with the horizontal lines drawn in step 4. Fasten as illustrated, figure 20-20, using a minimum amount of tape.

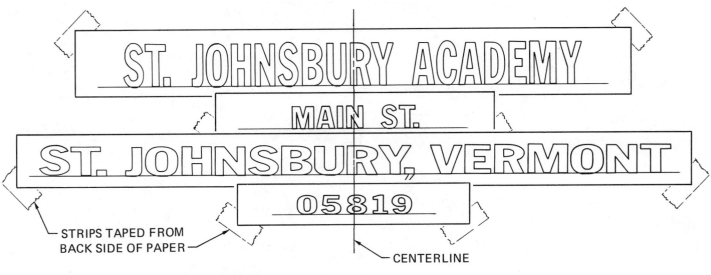

STRIPS TAPED FROM
BACK SIDE OF PAPER

CENTERLINE

Fig. 20-20 Fasten strip under vellum, step 5

Step 6. Study the layout. If it appears centered and has no errors, reprint (trace) the words. Fill in lettering neatly. Recheck again. Note that when lettering on a card or using a border, always leave a little more space at the bottom of the lettering than at the top, figure 20-21.

ST. JOHNSBURY ACADEMY
MAIN ST.
ST. JOHNSBURY, VERMONT
05819

Fig. 20-21 Letter centering completed

UNIT 21

THE ENGINEERING DEPARTMENT

DRAFTING DEPARTMENT PRACTICES

All engineering departments operate differently as each varies in size, personnel, function, and scope. New personnel should fully understand the structure of the organization. Engineering organizations must work as efficiently as possible to provide an orderly flow of drawings. To accomplish this, a uniform procedure or standard is followed by all of its members.

An architectural organization provides drawings for new buildings, improvement of old buildings, plans for additions and or alterations, and many other products. This unit explains some of the basic procedures, paper work, and steps necessary to insure the best efficiency. The following items are included:

- Architectural organization
- How to check a drawing
- Personal technical file
- Employer-employee agreement
- Job descriptions

ORGANIZATION

Figure 21-1 illustrates a small engineering organization employing 26 people, divided into three organizational elements: detailers, clerks, and typists. In larger organizations comprising one or more departments, depending on the work load, drafters are moved from department to department. The higher the position, the more responsibility and the higher the pay.

CHECKING

Though the drafter is responsible for the accuracy of his work, some companies employ a *checker* to double check all drawings. Some of the things a checker looks for include:

- How is the drawing's general appearance? (legibility, neatness, etc.)
- Does it follow all drawing and company standards?
- Are dimensions and instructions clear and understandable?
- Is the drawing easy to understand?
- Are all dimensions included? A contractor must not have to calculate to find a size or location, assume anything, or have any question whatsoever as to what is required.
- Are there unnecessary dimensions?
- Is the drawing prepared so the building may be constructed the most economical way?
- Is the title block complete? Does it include the title, number of the part, drafter's name, any other required information?

Because of the high cost of errors, it is important that the drafter check and double check work before releasing the drawing. An engineering drawing must be 100 percent correct.

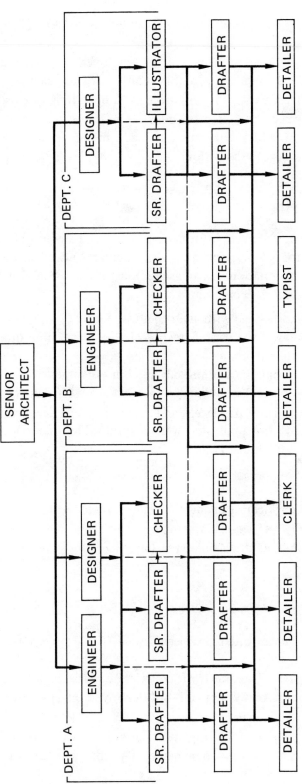

Fig. 21-1   Organization chart

EMPLOYER-EMPLOYEE AGREEMENT

Usually companies that work at designing or creating new devices or processes will have all employees sign an *employer/employee agreement.* Simply stated:

1. You must promise not to reveal any company secrets.
2. If you invent something or discover some new process or method, it belongs to the company.
3. You will not attempt to infringe on any company ideas, processes, or inventions.

This agreement is usually in effect while you are employed and extended for a given time after you leave the company, often six months to two years.

As a rule, you do not get extra compensation for a new design or process, but most companies recognize your efforts and in time adjust your salary or position. In many instances a bonus payment is made in the form of bonds, company stocks, or other forms of recognition.

PERSONAL TECHNICAL FILE

It is important to locate technical information quickly. Usually a company manufacturing a certain product or performing a particular kind of engineering will use certain technical information. A conscientious drafter should develop and update a *personal technical file* containing:

- All company products associated with assignments
- Notes, copies, or clippings from various technical magazines, literature, etc. associated with the company product
- Information on standard materials commonly used in assignments
- Miscellaneous information that would make your job more efficient
- Records of various supervisors, pay levels, and dates of special assignments.
- Various pages of units in this book that were helpful. This material should be neatly organized in a loose leaf binder.

CHANGES

The paper work on an engineering change order must include the engineering change request number, why the change was made, who requested the change, what the dimensions were *before* the change, the impact of the change

Change Procedure

After an engineering change order has been issued, the drafter or detailer makes the change.

If the change is extensive: The drawing is completely redrawn and given the same drawing number. The obsolete original is not destroyed but marked "obsolete" and filed.

If the change is fairly simple: The original is carefully erased (so as not to damage the original) where the change is to be made. The change is then carefully added.

If the change is very minor: In the event the change is very minor, such as a small dimension change, the dimension alone is changed and a *wavy line* may be drawn under that dimension indicating it is "out-of-scale." Time is money in an engineering department so all changes must be made in the best and most efficient way.

NUMBERING SYSTEMS

All companies have a system of identifying and recording drawings. There is no standard system used by all companies. The most common kind is a letter (A, B, C, D) denoting sheet size, followed by the actual drawing number issued and recorded by a record clerk.

CAREERS IN DRAFTING

The student who develops excellent skills in a particular area of drafting can find many opportunities for employment. Although these positions may be at a junior detailer level, the student could expect to advance to more important positions as knowledge and experience is gained. Each promotion will bring more responsibility and a higher salary. There is no limit to how far the student can advance in drafting as long as the student qualifies for the next step. This requires hard work and study.

The occupational chart in figure 21-2 shows some of the different jobs available in the various fields of drafting.

The next few pages outline various *job descriptions.* Study each one. Notice how a beginning drafter must go through various steps in the drafting field in order to advance in the profession.

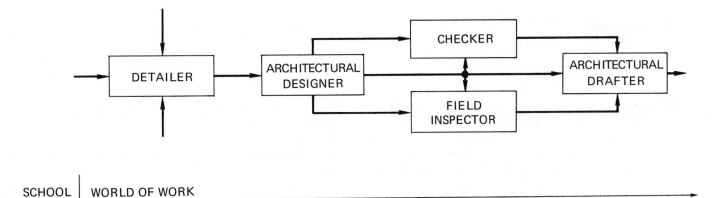

Fig. 21-2 Occupational chart, drafting

TITLE: Junior Detailer

DEPARTMENT: Engineering

REPORTS TO: Chief Drafter (or supervisor)

SUPERVISES: No one

TYPICAL DUTIES:

See detailer. Junior detailer's duties are similar to those of detailer, but limited to less complicated types of drawings requiring less experience.

SPECIFICATIONS:

Education: High school graduate

Experience: None

Job Preparation: This is a beginning job or a promotion from tracer. May be promoted to detailer.

DISTINGUISHING
CHARACTERISTICS:

May be promoted to detailer when able to perform the duties of that classification in a competent manner with a minimum of supervision.

TITLE: Detailer

DEPARTMENT: Engineering

REPORTS TO: Chief Drafter

SUPERVISES: No one

TYPICAL DUTIES:

1. Detailing: Makes detail parts drawings from layouts, minor assembly drawings, setting plans, piping and wiring diagrams, and catalog or repair manual charts and illustrations. Works from sketches, layouts, notes, or current drawings. Makes drawings to scale indicating dimensions, material specifications, and other standard information required to make drawings clear.

2. Changes: Makes changes on current drawings on the basis of change orders received. May prepare change order releases, bills of material, and assist with other clerical work in the engineering department.

SPECIFICATIONS:

Education: High school graduate. Courses in drafting desirable.

Experience: Previous experience as tracer or start directly in this job if adequately trained in drafting skills.

Job Progression: May have been promoted from tracer or started directly in this job if adequately trained in drafting skills. May be promoted to drafter, when qualified.

DISTINGUISHING
CHARACTERISTICS:

Must be able to produce parts and minor assembly drawings which are sufficiently clear, complete, and accurate for use in shop manufacturing operations.

TITLE: Detailer-Drafter

DEPARTMENT: Engineering

REPORTS TO: Chief Drafter

SUPERVISES: No one

TYPICAL DUTIES:

1. Detailing and drafting: Prepares clean and accurate detail and some assembly drawings of some complexity from sketches, notes, current drawings, and verbal instructions. Draws to scale. Establishes dimensions, material specifications, and other information necessary for manufacture. Establishes some mathematical calculations.

2. Changes: Makes some drawing and design changes on the basis of change orders. Makes plan releases, bills of materials, etc.

SPECIFICATIONS:

Education: High school graduate. Courses in drafting desirable.

Experience: Equivalent of two years detailing experience.

Job Progression: An employee in the detailer classification making satisfactory progress may be promoted to this classification after reaching the top rate for detailer. May be promoted sooner, if qualified. An employee adequately trained in detailing may be placed directly in this classification.

DISTINGUISHING
CHARACTERISTICS:

Must be able to prepare accurate finished drawings of parts and assemblies showing dimensions; some mathematical calculations.

TITLE: Drafter

DEPARTMENT: Engineering

REPORTS TO: Chief Drafter

SUPERVISES: No one

TYPICAL DUTIES:

1. Drafting: Prepares clear, complete, and accurate detail and assembly drawings of average complexity from rough sketches, notes, or verbal instructions. Establishes dimensions, machining tolerances, materials, and other information necessary for manufacture. Makes all necessary mathematical calculations.

2. Change Orders: Makes drawing and design changes on the basis of engineering change orders. Writes change orders, lists, and releases.

3. Checking: May do some checking for accuracy of drawings prepared by detailers or tracers.

SPECIFICATIONS:

Education: High school graduate. Courses in drafting desirable.

Experience: Previous experience as a detailer required. May be promoted when qualified and work is available.

Job Progression: Promoted from detailer. May be promoted to layout drafter.

DISTINGUISHING
CHARACTERISTICS:

Must be able to prepare complete and accurate finished drawings of average difficulty showing all dimensions, tolerances, etc., after making all necessary mathematical calculations.

TITLE: Senior Drafter

DEPARTMENT: Engineering

REPORTS TO: Chief Drafter

SUPERVISES: Leads, directs, trains, and checks the work of less experienced drafters.

TYPICAL DUTIES:

1. Drafting: Makes layout drawings of new, revised, special, or salvage parts and assemblies from specifications, drawings, sketches, or general design data. Establishes dimensions. May make complex detail drawings. Makes sketches and original designs from verbal instructions.

2. Analysis: Analyzes layout parts for strength, weight, wear, ease of manufacturing and assembly.

3. Checking: Checks the work of drafters, detailers, and tracers for accuracy and practicality of manufacture.

4. Consultations: Works with the manufacturing and process departments on methods of manufacturing applicable to the products being designed. Checks patterns and sample castings, observes and assists with test operations, and revises drawings according to valid suggestions from other departments.

SPECIFICATIONS:

Education: High school graduate. Appropriate courses in mathematics and drafting.

Experience: No time limit. Must be a thoroughly experienced and versatile drafter, able to do top quality work of the highest complexity without assistance.

Job Progression: Promoted from drafter. May be promoted to checker or design drafter.

DISTINGUISHING
CHARACTERISTICS:

Only drafters who are able to do first class work on the most complex assignments are placed in this classification.

TITLE: Design Drafter

DEPARTMENT: Engineering

REPORTS TO: Chief Engineer

SUPERVISES: Directs, trains, and checks the work of drafters of various grades.

TYPICAL DUTIES:

1. Designing: Designs equipment or components. Makes preliminary investigations, calculations, studies, sketches, and basic working layouts for modifications of current designs or for new products.

2. Calculations: Performs necessary calculations on strength of materials, springs, gears, capacity, working fits, etc.

3. Follow Up: Follows designs through periods of detailing. Checks assemblies and tests. Keeps supervisor advised on difficulties encountered. Consults with personnel in tool design, processing, cost, pattern shop, foundry, etc., on matters of design, manufacture, materials, and cost.

SPECIFICATIONS:

Education: Equivalent of two years college engineering.

Experience: Minimum of five to eight years in drafting, design, and related work.

DISTINGUISHING
CHARACTERISTICS:

Design drafters have a specialized knowledge of a particular product line. They may be as expert as the engineers in this restricted field, but their training is less comprehensive and diversified.

WHERE TO LOOK FOR A JOB

Jobs can be found almost anywhere if a drafter's skills are good. It is often said that the best jobs are not advertised, which means a drafter must devise ways to find them.

Personal Contacts. Make a list of everyone who might know of a job opening or contact. Talk with relatives about their friends and business associates who might serve as references. Do not overlook teachers, clergy, or doctors. Guidance counselors have contacts, booklets, and lists which may be helpful in a job search.

Yellow Pages. Use the Yellow Pages of the phone book to make a list of companies, large and small, who hire drafters. When the list is complete, apply directly to the company or organization. Do not expect an immediate interview. In most cases, an application blank must first be completed.

Trade Associations. A drafter should also investigate *trade associations*. These are organizations of people, companies, and groups in one particular field. Some have their own placement services and most publish their own magazines or newsletters which carry classified advertising about employment opportunities.

Newspapers. Read the newspapers every day. Read every section — the arts, finance, news stories. News items contain valuable information, such as the opening of a new company. Write down the name and address and call them.

Newspaper ads are the most obvious place to look for jobs. Is that opening the right one, or does it just sound good? Sometimes advertising writers make a position sound interesting when it is actually very routine. Do not reply to ads that are not appropriate. Consider such things as the time it takes to travel to the job, how much knowledge and experience the job requires, etc. Follow the ad's instructions exactly. If instructed to "reply in your own handwriting," do so. The job probably requires legible handwriting. Keep a record of queries and replies. Make a carbon of any letter sent out. Clip the ad and staple it to the carbon copy.

Employment Agency. Consider an employment agency. A good one does all the tedious detail work. An agency representative has many more contacts than the average person seeking a job. A great many companies deal only with agencies when hiring new people because they do not have enough time or personnel to screen applicants themselves. An agency can actually carry out a complete job hunt for an applicant. This service is free until a job is secured. At that time a fee, equal to a certain percentage of the monthly wage, is paid to the agency. *Find out what the fee will be before working with an agency.*

After an interview with a company, report back to the agency. The agency may know how the interview was received and what are the chances of getting that particular job. Remember, although a fee may seem large, it is tax deductible. Do not refuse interviews for jobs that do not pay the fee. Take all interviews of interest. Interview experience is invaluable. If a job is offered, however, do not take it unless it is really worth the price of the agency fee.

If job hunting is done with care, more than one job offer may have to be considered. Do not just grab the first one that comes along. Any big decision, like how to spend half a lifetime, requires time to think. Most companies realize this. Even if the right job seems to come along, it is a good policy to ask for time (a few days is reasonable) to think it over.

It is impossible to predict for certain how well a particular job will turn out. If a drafter is conscientious in the search, success is attainable.

WRITING A RESUME

A *resume* is a brief, one-page outline or summary of an applicant's qualifications. A resume should stimulate interest in order to get an interview with a prospective employer. The initial impression from the resume is very important. Take the time to do a thorough self-examination of your attributes before writing it. Be sure to omit any trivial information.

There are many different ways of writing a resume. The important thing to remember is that a resume should be neat, easy to read, and attractively arranged on the page. Figure 21-3 shows an example of a resume.

A resume should contain the following information, though not necessarily in this order:

- Name, address, and telephone number
- Occupational objective
- Work experience
- Education
- Personal data (optional)
- References

Every resume begins with the applicant's full name and address, including zip code, and telephone number.

A resume should include an occupational objective that states exactly what kind of job the applicant is looking for. This should be interesting enough to motivate a prospective employer to read the rest of the resume.

Work experience should include the names and addresses of employers, job title, job description, dates of employment, and supervisor's name. List jobs in reverse chronological order, starting with the most recent job and working backwards. Try to highlight strong points and important accomplishments.

Educational information includes the name and address of all institutions attended, special training, whether or not the applicant graduated, and the degree or course of study. If it is pertinent to the job or highlights an impressive quality, mention such things as class standing, honors, extracurricular activities, etc. Dates of graduation and attendance need not be listed.

Resume of

JAMES A. BROWN
107 Elmwood Drive
Palma, CA 04402

CAREER OBJECTIVE

To enter the drafting field as a detailer in order to gain basic experience and qualify, by performance, to become a drafter.

EDUCATION

Hamilton High School; 17 Oak Street; Palma, CA 04402

Graduated:	June 1982
Major:	Vocational drafting
Class Standing:	15th in a class of 87
Honors:	Architectural Drafting Award, Spring 1982
Activities:	VICA, 1-4; Baseball 3-4

Dixon County Community College; Adult Education Program; Beacon, CA 05904

Summer 1982
Course: Landscaping (ten week course)

WORK EXPERIENCE

June, 1980 to present	Eagle Supermarket; 1550 West Drive; Beacon, CA 05904
	Supervisor: Mr. Albert Smith
	Position: Clerk (part-time). Stocked shelves and displays, cashier, deliveries
Summer, 1981	Palma Summer Theatre; 200 Sunset Road, Palma, CA 04402
	Director: Mrs. Lillian Garver
	Position: I worked on the stage crew constructing sets for the theatre's five summer stock productions.

PERSONAL DATA

Birth date:	April 14, 1963
Marital Status:	Single
Social Security:	#005-44-0045
Health:	Good

REFERENCES

Mr. Robert Eckerle, Set Designer; Palma Summer Theatre; 200 Sunset Road; Palma, CA 04402
The Rev. Roger Fredericks; First Lutheran Church; 12 Church Street; Palma, CA 04402
Miss Jennifer May, Drafting Teacher; Hamilton High School; 17 Oak Street; Palma, CA 04402

Fig. 21-3 Sample resume

If it is to the applicant's advantage, personal data may be included on the resume. However, the applicant does not have to provide information regarding age, marital status, sex, number of dependents, race, creed, physical limitations, etc. The applicant may wish to do so if it will increase the chance of securing a job. Outside activities and hobbies, for instance, may indicate areas of competence that will impress an employer.

References should also be included on the resume. If there is not enough room, simply state that "references are available upon request" at the bottom of the resume. These references should include two people who can attest to the applicant's occupational skills and willingness to do a good job. A third reference should be able to vouch for the applicant's character.

Do not include the date on a resume. This is written on the cover letter. Do not include salary requirements. This is discussed during the personal interview. Do not forget that the resume forms an employer's first opinion of an applicant. A resume that rambles and is confusing will find its way into the wastebasket. Be sure the resume is neat, clearly typed, and includes all necessary information.

THE COVER LETTER

A *cover letter* accompanies a resume. It is a short, concise letter designed to arouse a prospective employer's interest in the candidate. It should convince the employer to read the resume and set up an interview. Figure 21-4 shows a sample cover letter.

The opening paragraph of a cover letter states the purpose of the letter — that the applicant feels he or she is the best possible choice for the job. The first paragraph also mentions how the applicant found out about the job or whether this is a letter of inquiry about any available positions.

The middle paragraph(s) explains why the candidate feels he or she is the right person for the job. This is a good place to stress qualities that may not be immediately apparent by reading the resume, such as an applicant's ability to work with others or to handle responsibility. Remember the cover letter does not simply repeat what is in the resume, it explains and expands the data. After reading the cover letter, the employer will *want* to read the resume to learn more about the applicant.

The closing paragraph usually asks for an interview. Applicants should state that they are available for an interview at the company's convenience and how they can be reached (telephone number, etc.).

107 Elmwood Drive
Palma, CA 04402
September 23, 1982

Mr. Edwin A. Larson, Personnel Director
North-Central Home Manufacturing, Inc.
395 Colvin Avenue
Los Angeles, CA 90014

Dear Mr. Larson:

I feel my high school training in drafting qualifies me for the position of detailer advertised in the Los Angeles Tribune on September 22, 1982.

As indicated on the enclosed resume, I recently graduated from Hamilton High School where I participated in a comprehensive two-year drafting program. This included an intensive one year drawing course in basic drafting skills. The second year concentrated on architectural, technical illustration, civil, and mechanical drafting. I received the highest average in architectural drafting. My drawings of a contemporary residence were displayed at the Palma First National Bank during Student Appreciation Week, June 12–17, 1982.

To supplement my high school studies, I took a summer course in landscaping to learn how plants can improve exterior house design. In addition, by working with the stage crew at Palma Summer Theatre, I gained practical experience in construction. I enjoyed working with others towards a common goal in both of these ventures.

I am available for an interview at your convenience and can be reached at 555-2000 every weekday morning. At that time, I can bring a few of the drawings I made in the architectural drafting course.

Sincerely,

James A. Brown

James A. Brown

Fig. 21-4 Sample cover letter

THE INTERVIEW

If the cover letter and resume show that the applicant has the qualifications for the job, a company representative will most likely invite the applicant to a personal interview. During the interview, the prospective employer will seek information about the applicant that is not available on the application or resume. In return, the applicant asks about salary, future progression, benefits, etc. The interview, therefore, benefits both the employer and the applicant.

An interview usually lasts twenty or thirty minutes. Its main purpose is to give the applicant a chance to tell why he or she is the right person for the job. Some questions which may be asked during the interview include:

- Why do you want to be a drafter?

- What qualifies you to be a drafter?

- Why did you pick this company?

- Which position interests you most?

- What other jobs have you had?

- Can you take and follow instructions?

- What do you expect to be doing in ten years?

- What pay scale do you expect to start at?

- What have you done that shows initiative?

- Do you have any special abilities?

Confidence impresses an employer. An applicant should give a relaxed and self-controlled appearance. It helps to dress neatly and to arrive 15 minutes early. Greet the interviewer with a firm handshake and maintain eye contact throughout the interview. Know as much about the company as possible before the interview and decide which questions to ask during the interview. Be sincere, poised, and in control. Applicants should also bring a few drawing samples to illustrate their level of competence.

During the interview, the interviewer will often fill out an evaluation form similar to the one in figure 21-5.

Upon returning home from an interview, the applicant should write a short letter thanking the interviewer for the meeting. This letter stresses that the interview was informative and that the applicant still feels he or she is right for the job and company. An example of a follow-up letter appears in figure 21-6.

NAME _James A. Brown_   PHONE _716-3257_

POSITION APPLIED FOR _Detailer_

DRESS			**5**
Careless	Neat	Very neat	
1 2	3 4	(5) 6	

APPEARANCE–HEALTH			**5**
Sickly	Good health	Excellent health	
1 2	3 4	(5) 6	

IS APPLICANT AT EASE			**4**
Embarrassed	Not at ease	At ease	
1 2	3 (4) 5	6	

VOICE			**5**
Unpleasant	Pleasant	Very pleasant	
1 2	3 4	(5) 6	

TRAINING FOR JOB (EDUCATION - EXPERIENCE)			**3**
Lacks training	Good training/fair experience	Excellent	
1 2	(3) 4 5	6	

ATTITUDE			**5**
Over-bearing	Reasonable	Excellent	
1 2	3 4	(5) 6	

PERSONALITY			**5**
Unstable	Satisfactory	Outstanding	
1 2	3 4	(5) 6	

	TOTAL RATING	
REMARKS _Direct from H.S._		**32**

Good education / No work exper.

Fig. 21-5   Sample evaluation form

107 Elmwood Drive
Palma, CA 04402
September 30, 1982

Mr. Edwin A. Larson, Personnel Director
North-Central Home Manufacturing, Inc.
395 Colvin Avenue
Los Angeles, CA 90014

Dear Mr. Larson:

I certainly enjoyed our interview on Wednesday and appreciate the time you spent telling me about North-Central Home Manufacturing and the position of detailer.

Judging from your description of the position, I feel I can meet the company's rigid specifications. The potential for learning and advancement within the company convinces me even further that I would like to work at North-Central.

Thank you for this opportunity to discuss my qualifications.

Sincerely,

James A. Brown

James A. Brown

Fig. 21-6 Sample follow-up thank you letter

EMPLOYMENT APPLICATION

For proper consideration answer all questions completely & accurately - Print in black ink

Type of work applied for

Last name	First	Middle	Social Security Number

Home address (no. street & State

Phone number

U.S. Citizen	☐ Yes ☐ No	Are you between the ages of 18 and 65? ☐ Yes ☐ No

Do you have any emotional or physical limitations that will prevent you from performing the job you are applying for? ☐ Yes ☐ No

Have you ever been convicted of a crime? If yes, explain.

School	Location	Did You Graduate?	Major	Degree
H.S.				
TECH				
COLLEGE				
OTHER				

List any special training

List all full time, part-time jobs held

Name/Address	Type of work	Date	Reason for leaving

References (3)

Name	Address	Occupation

Signature _____

Fig. 21-7 Sample application form

THE APPLICATION FORM

At some point before the interview, all applicants must fill out an *application form,* figure 21-7. These are usually from two to four pages long. Read all instructions before filling in an application. Some forms must be lettered in black ink or typed.

Lightly fill out the application first. Check all answers, particularly dates, names, addresses, telephone numbers, and spelling. If a question does not apply, place a dash through it so the interviewer knows it was read but does not apply. Once everything has been checked, complete the application in ink or as directed. Be neat. Remember, that as a drafter, legible lettering is an important skill.

INVENTION AGREEMENT

Anyone who works in a job that is creative, such as drafters and engineers, must sign an agreement form giving the company the right to any new invention designed while working for the company. The form usually puts in writing that the employee will not reveal any of the company's discoveries or projects.

The invention agreement is in effect for six months to two years after an employee leaves the company, depending upon the company. This is so employees will not invent something, quit, and patent it themselves.

A company does not usually give extra pay for an invention. This is what an employee is paid to do. However, a company usually recognizes talent and will reward an employee with promotions, stocks, bonds, or possibly a raise.

Signing an employer/employee invention agreement is a normal request in any company. Read the contract before signing it. However, if an applicant does not sign the agreement, he or she will probably not be offered the job.

A PROFESSIONAL ATTITUDE

Being a skilled and efficient drafter is only part of the job. Drafters must always conduct themselves in a professional manner as well. This professional attitude is not easy to define, but here are some of the characteristics associated with true professionalism.

Professionals:

- Do not require close supervision or direction. They plan their own activities and work independently.

- Regard their supervisors as fellow professional workers and, in return, are treated the same way.

- Adjust their working hours to meet the necessities and responsibilities of the job, even when this requires working overtime.

- Take full responsibility for the results of their efforts and actions. They seek advice and counsel but do not attempt to transfer responsibility for their own mistakes to others.

- Continually seek self-improvement and take advantage of every opportunity to learn.

- Contribute to the skill and knowledge of their profession by developing new ideas, plans, and materials which are gladly shared with fellow workers.

- Respect the confidence of others. The welfare of others often requires that information concerning them remain confidential.

- Are loyal to fellow workers and to those they serve.

- Avoid rumor and hearsay. Professionals secure information only from those authorized to release it.

- Meet their professional obligations. The professional completes all agreements, whether legal or moral obligations.

- Do not advance themselves at the expense of others. Professionals strive for promotion only through their own performance.

- Are proud of their profession. They always reflect this pride and satisfaction with their work to those outside their profession.

APPENDIX A

INCH/METRIC — EQUIVALENTS					
	Decimal Equivalent			**Decimal Equivalent**	
Fraction	**Customary (in.)**	**Metric (mm)**	**Fraction**	**Customary (in.)**	**Metric (mm)**
1/64 —.015625		0.3969	33/64 —.515625		13.0969
1/32 —————.03125		0.7938	17/32 —————.53125		13.4938
3/64 —.046875		1.1906	35/64 —.546875		13.8906
1/16 —————————.0625		1.5875	9/16 —————————.5625		14.2875
5/64 —.078125		1.9844	37/64 —.578125		14.6844
3/32 —————.09375		2.3813	19/32 —————.59375		15.0813
7/64 —.109375		2.7781	39/64 —.609375		15.4781
1/8 —————————————.1250		3.1750	5/8 —————————————.6250		15.8750
9/64 —.140625		3.5719	41/64 —.640625		16.2719
5/32 —————.15625		3.9688	21/32 —————.65625		16.6688
11/64 —.171875		4.3656	43/64 —.671875		17.0656
3/16 —————————.1875		4.7625	11/16 —————————.6875		17.4625
13/64 —.203125		5.1594	45/64 —.703125		17.8594
7/32 —————.21875		5.5563	23/32 —————.71875		18.2563
15/64 —.234375		5.9531	47/64 —.734375		18.6531
1/4 —————————————.250		6.3500	3/4 —————————————.750		19.0500
17/64 —.265625		6.7469	49/64 —.765625		19.4469
9/32 —————.28125		7.1438	25/32 —————.78125		19.8438
19/64 —.296875		7.5406	51/64 —.796875		20.2406
5/16 —————————.3125		7.9375	13/16 —————————.8125		20.6375
21/64 —.328125		8.3384	53/64 —.828125		21.0344
11/32 —————.34375		8.7313	27/32 —————.84375		21.4313
23/64 —.359375		9.1281	55/64 —.859375		21.8281
3/8 —————————————.3750		9.5250	7/8 —————————————.8750		22.2250
25/64 —.390625		9.9219	57/64 —.890625		22.6219
13/32 —————.40625		10.3188	29/32 —————.90625		23.0188
27/64 —.421875		10.7156	59/64 —.921875		23.4156
7/16 —————————.4375		11.1125	15/16 —————————.9375		23.8125
29/64 —.453125		11.5094	61/64 —.953125		24.2094
15/32 —————.46875		11.9063	31/32 —————.96875		24.6063
31/64 —.484375		12.3031	63/64 —.984375		25.0031
1/2 —————————————.500		12.7000	1 —————————————1.000		25.4000

APPENDIX B

CIRCUMFERENCES AND AREAS (0.2 to 9.8; 10 to 99)*

Diameter	Circum.	Area	Diameter	Circum.	Area	Diameter	Circum.	Area
0.2	0.628	0.0314	11	34.55	95.03	56	175.9	2,463
0.4	1.26	0.1256	12	37.69	113	57	179.1	2,551.8
0.6	1.88	0.2827	13	40.84	132.7	58	182.2	2,642.1
0.8	2.51	0.5026	14	43.98	153.9	59	185.4	2,734
1	3.14	0.7854	15	47.12	176.7	60	188.5	2,827.4
1.2	3.77	1.131	16	50.26	201	61	191.6	2,922.5
1.4	4.39	1.539	17	53.4	226.9	62	194.8	3,019.1
1.6	5.02	2.011	18	56.54	254.4	63	197.9	3,117.3
1.8	5.65	2.545	19	59.69	283.5	64	201.1	3,217
2	6.28	3.142	20	62.83	314.1	65	204.2	3,318.3
2.2	6.91	3.801	21	65.97	346.3	66	207.3	3,421.2
2.4	7.53	4.524	22	69.11	380.1	67	210.5	3,525.7
2.6	8.16	5.309	23	72.25	415.4	68	213.6	3,631.7
2.8	8.79	6.158	24	75.39	452.3	69	216.8	3,739.3
3	9.42	7.069	25	78.54	490.8	70	219.9	3,848.5
3.2	10.05	7.548	26	81.68	530.9	71	223.1	3,959.2
3.4	10.68	8.553	27	84.82	572.5	72	226.2	4,071.5
3.6	11.3	10.18	28	87.96	615.7	73	229.3	4,185.4
3.8	11.93	11.34	29	91.1	660.5	74	232.5	4,300.8
4	12.57	12.57	30	94.24	706.8	75	235.6	4,417.9
4.2	13.19	13.85	31	97.39	754.8	76	238.8	4,536.5
4.4	13.82	15.21	32	100.5	804.2	77	241.9	4,656.6
4.6	14.45	16.62	33	103.7	855.3	78	245	4,778.4
4.8	15.08	18.1	34	106.8	907.9	79	248.2	4,901.7
5	15.7	19.63	35	110	962.1	80	251.3	5,026.6
5.2	16.33	21.24	36	113.1	1,017.9	81	254.5	5,153
5.4	16.96	22.9	37	116.2	1,075.2	82	257.6	5,281
5.6	17.59	24.63	38	119.4	1,134.1	83	260.8	5,410.6
5.8	18.22	26.42	39	122.5	1,194.6	84	263.9	5,541.8
6	18.84	28.27	40	125.7	1,256.6	85	267.0	5,674.5
6.2	19.47	30.19	41	128.8	1,320.3	86	270.2	5,808.8
6.4	20.1	32.17	42	131.9	1,385.4	87	273.3	5,944.7
6.6	20.73	34.21	43	135.1	1,452.2	88	276.5	6,082.1
6.8	21.36	36.32	44	138.2	1,520.5	89	279.6	6,221.2
7	21.99	38.48	45	141.4	1,590.4	90	282.7	6,361.7
7.2	22.61	40.72	46	144.5	1,661.9	91	285.9	6,503.9
7.4	23.24	43.01	47	147.7	1,734.9	92	289.0	6,647.6
7.6	23.87	45.36	48	150.8	1,809.6	93	292.2	6,792.9
7.8	24.5	47.78	49	153.9	1,885.7	94	295.2	6,939.8
8	25.13	50.27	50	157.1	1,963.5	95	298.5	7,088.2
8.2	25.76	52.81	51	160.2	2,042.8	96	301.6	7,238.2
8.4	26.38	55.42	52	163.4	2,123.7	97	304.7	7,389.8
8.6	27.01	58.09	53	166.5	2,206.2	98	307.9	7,543.0
8.8	27.64	60.82	54	169.6	2,290.2	99	311.9	7,697.7
9	28.27	63.62	55	172.8	2,375.8			
9.2	28.9	66.48						
9.4	29.53	69.4						
9.6	30.15	72.38						
9.8	30.78	75.43						
10	31.41	78.54						

*The formulas for circumference and area of circles are the same regardless of the system of measurement, so these values are accurate for both inches and millimetres.

APPENDIX C

	U.S. STANDARD GAUGES OF SHEET METAL				
GAUGE	THICKNESS		WT. PER SQ. FT.		GAUGE
10	.1406″	3.571 MM	5.625 LBS	2.551 Kg.	10
11	.1250″	3.175 MM	5.000 LBS	2.267 Kg.	11
12	.1094″	2.778 MM	4.375 LBS	1.984 Kg.	12
13	.0938″	2.383 MM	3.750 LBS	1.700 Kg.	13
14	.0781″	1.983 MM	3.125 LBS	1.417 Kg.	14
15	.0703″	1.786 MM	2.813 LBS	1.276 Kg.	15
16	.0625″	1.588 MM	2.510 LBS	1.134 Kg.	16
17	.0563″	1.430 MM	2.250 LBS	1.021 Kg.	17
18	.0500″	1.270 MM	2.000 LBS	0.907 Kg.	18
19	.0438″	1.111 MM	1.750 LBS	0.794 Kg.	19
20	.0375″	0.953 MM	1.500 LBS	0.680 Kg.	20
21	.0344″	0.877 MM	1.375 LBS	0.624 Kg.	21
22	.0313″	0.795 MM	1.250 LBS	0.567 Kg.	22
23	.0280″	0.714 MM	1.125 LBS	0.510 Kg.	23
24	.0250″	0.635 MM	1.000 LBS	0.454 Kg.	24
25	.0219″	0.556 MM	0.875 LBS	0.397 Kg.	25
26	.0188″	0.478 MM	0.750 LBS	0.340 Kg.	26
27	.0172″	0.437 MM	0.687 LBS	0.312 Kg.	27
28	.0156″	0.396 MM	0.625 LBS	0.283 Kg.	28
29	.0141″	0.358 MM	0.563 LBS	0.255 Kg.	29
30	.0120″	0.318 MM	0.500 LBS	0.227 Kg.	30

APPENDIX D

GENERAL OUTLETS

Ceiling   Wall

○ —○   Outlet Drop cord

Ⓢ —Ⓢ   Pull Switch

Ⓙ —Ⓙ   Junction Box

CONVENIENCE OUTLETS

Duplex outlet

Weatherproof

Range outlet

Special purpose

SWITCH OUTLETS

S   Single pole switch S_3 Three way switch

S_2 Double pole switch   Scb   Circuit breaker

Lighting panel

Power panel

Ⓣ   Power transformer

Push button

Telephone

ABBREVIATIONS USED ON WORKING DRAWINGS

AWG	American Wire Gauge		GL	Glass
B	Bathroom		HB	Hose Bibb
BR	Bedroom		C	Hundred
BD	Board		INS	Insulation
BM	Board Measure		INT	Interior
BTU	British Thermal Unit		KD	Kiln Dried
BLDG	Building		K	Kitchen
CLG	Ceiling		LAV	Lavatory
C to C	Center to Center		LR	Living Room
CL or ₵	Centerline		MLDG	Molding
CLO	Closet		OC	On Center
COL	Column		REF	Refrigerator
CONC	Concrete		R	Riser
CFM	Cubic feet per minute		RM	Room
CU YD	Cubic Yard		SPEC	Specification
DR	Dining Room		STD	Standard
ENT	Entrance		M	Thousand
EXT	Exterior		T & G	Tongue and Groove
FIN	Finish		UNFIN	Unfinished
FL	Floor		WC	Water Closet
FTG	Footing		WH	Water Heater
FDN	Foundation		WP	Waterproof
GA	Gauge		WD	Wood

APPENDIX E

PLAN AND SECTION INDICATIONS

EARTH, ETC.

EARTH

BOCK

STONE FILL

CONCRETE

STRUCTURAL CONCRETE

LT. WEIGHT CONCRETE

BLOCK

BRICK

COMMON

FACE

FIRE BRICK ON COMMON

WOOD

FINISH

ROUGH

STUD WALL AND PARTITION

METAL

STEEL, IRON

SHEET METAL AND ALL METALS AT SMALL SCALE

STRUCTURAL STEEL

REINFORCING BARS

INSULATION

LOOSE FILL OR BATTS

BOARDS, OR QUILTS

STONE

CUT STONE

RUBBLE

CAST STONE (CONCRETE)

SLATE, BLUESTONE, SOAPSTONE

GLASS

SHEET AND PLATE

STRUCTURAL

ELEVATION INDICATIONS

GLASS

ASHLAR STONE

RUBBLE STONE

SQUARED STONE

RUNNING BOND MASONRY

CONCRETE PLASTER

SHINGLES SIDING

BRICK

CERAMIC TILE

STACK BOND MASONRY

PLUMBING SYMBOLS

FLOOR DRAIN

SHOWER DRAIN

HOT WATER TANK

SINGLE SINK 18 X 24

DOUBLE SINK 21 X 32

LAVATORY

TOILET

BUILT IN TUB

BUILT-IN LAVATORY

329

APPENDIX F

TOPOGRAPHIC MAP SYMBOLS

VARIATIONS WILL BE FOUND ON OLDER MAPS

Primary highway, hard surface . . . .

Secondary highway, hard surface . . . .

Light-duty road, hard or improved surface . . . .

Unimproved road . . . .

Road under construction, alinement known . . . .

Proposed road . . . .

Dual highway, dividing strip 25 feet or less . . . .

Dual highway, dividing strip exceeding 25 feet . . . .

Trail . . . .

Railroad: single track and multiple track . . . .

Railroads in juxtaposition . . . .

Narrow gage: single track and multiple track . . . .

Railroad in street and carline . . . .

Bridge: road and railroad . . . .

Drawbridge: road and railroad . . . .

Footbridge . . . .

Tunnel: road and railroad . . . .

Overpass and underpass . . . .

Small masonry or concrete dam . . . .

Dam with lock . . . .

Dam with road . . . .

Canal with lock . . . .

Buildings (dwelling, place of employment, etc.) . . . .

School, church, and cemetery . . . .

Buildings (barn, warehouse, etc.) . . . .

Power transmission line with located metal tower . . . .

Telephone line, pipeline, etc. (labeled as to type) . . . .

Wells other than water (labeled as to type) . . . . oOil . . . . . oGas

Tanks: oil, water, etc. (labeled only if water) . . . . ● ● ● ⊘Water

Located or landmark object; windmill . . . . o

Open pit, mine, or quarry; prospect . . . . ✕ x

Shaft and tunnel entrance . . . . ▪ . . . . Υ

Horizontal and vertical control station:

    Tablet, spirit level elevation . . . . BM△5653

    Other recoverable mark, spirit level elevation . . . . △5455

Horizontal control station: tablet, vertical angle elevation VABM△95I9

    Any recoverable mark, vertical angle or checked elevation △3775

Vertical control station: tablet, spirit level elevation . . . . . BM✕957

    Other recoverable mark, spirit level elevation . . . . ✕954

Spot elevation . . . . ✕7369 ✕7369

Water elevation 670 670

Boundaries: National . . . .

    State . . . .

    County, parish, municipio . . . .

    Civil township, precinct, town, barrio . . . .

    Incorporated city, village, town, hamlet . . . .

    Reservation, National or State . . . .

    Small park, cemetery, airport, etc. . . . .

    Land grant . . . .

Township or range line, United States land survey . . . . . .

Township or range line, approximate location . . . .

Section line, United States land survey . . . .

Section line, approximate location . . . .

Township line, not United States land survey . . . .

Section line, not United States land survey . . . .

Found corner: section and closing . . . .

Boundary monument: land grant and other . . . . ▫ . . . . ▫

Fence or field line . . . .

Index contour . . . . | Intermediate contour . .

Supplementary contour | Depression contours . .

Fill . . . . | Cut . . . .

Levee . . . . | Levee with road . . . . .

Mine dump . . . . | Wash . . . .

Tailings . . . . | Tailings pond . . . .

Shifting sand or dunes | Intricate surface . . . . .

Sand area . . . . | Gravel beach . . . .

Perennial streams . . . . | Intermittent streams . .

Elevated aqueduct . . . . | Aqueduct tunnel . . . . .

Water well and spring . . | Glacier . . . .

Small rapids . . . . | Small falls . . . .

Large rapids . . . . | Large falls . . . .

Intermittent lake . . . . . | Dry lake bed . . . .

Foreshore flat . . . . | Rock or coral reef . . . .

Sounding, depth curve . | Piling or dolphin . . . . .

Exposed wreck . . . . | Sunken wreck . . . .

Rock, bare or awash; dangerous to navigation . . . .

Marsh (swamp) . . . . | Submerged marsh . . . .

Wooded marsh . . . . | Mangrove . . . .

Woods or brushwood . . | Orchard . . . .

Vineyard . . . . | Scrub . . . .

Land subject to
controlled inundation | Urban area . . . .

INDEX